Gates County North Carolina

Minutes

of the

Court *of* Pleas

and

Quarter Sessions
- 1794-1799 -

(Volume #2)

Complied by:
Raymond Parker Fouts

Southern Historical Press, Inc.
Greenville, South Carolina

This volume was reproduced
from a personal copy located in
the Publishers private library

Please direct all correspondence and book orders to:
SOUTHERN HISTORICAL PRESS, Inc.
PO Box 1267
Greenville, SC   29602-1267

Copyright 1984 by: Raymond Parker Fouts
Copyright Transferred 2023 to:
              Southern Historical Press, Inc.
ISBN #978-1-63914-182-1
Printed in the United States of America

PREFACE

These records were transcribed from microfilm reel C.041.30001, 1779-1803, obtained from the North Carolina State Archives, Raleigh, North Carolina.

Gates County was formed in 1779, from Chowan, Hertford and Perquimans Counties. The Court Minutes from 1779 through 1793 have been abstracted by Marilyn Poe Laird and Vivian Poe Jackson, published by Poe Publishers, 15414 Drexel Avenue, Dolton, Illinois 60419.

The following pages were missing on the microfilm and photostatic copies of the originals were obtained by the kind assistance of Col. Ransom McBride, Editor of The North Carolina Genealogical Society Journal: p. 260, August 1795; pp. 277 & 278, February 1796; pp. 90 & 91, May and August 1798; pp. 128 & 129, May and August 1799. Page 259 was omitted in the original page numbering.

The volume containing the years 1794-1796 is numbered only on even-numbered pages. Each page has been assigned a number, within parentheses. The name and location indexing refer to these assigned numbers. The page number of the original record is to the right of the assigned number. Original record page number 232, assigned number 57, was inadvertently omitted by the typist.

The following letters are look-alikes: a & o, a & u, e & i, r & s, ue & eu, L & S. The indicates a crossed-out word. It is noted at the beginning of each entry that has been entirely crossed-out. When legible, the names in these entries are indexed. ---- indicates crossed-out and illegible. Georg emphasizes verbatim spelling. Geor__ indicates missing letters. Customary usage for a particular writer, e.g., audite, buisness, etc., is underlined only in the first instance found. Abbreviations were written Adm^r, Junr, Novr. and have been typed Admr, Junr, Novr..

Three names have been noted that share the peculiarity of having been written with another name, enclosed in parentheses, following. The apparent purpose would be to distinguish between two men with the same name. They are John PARKER (Gatling), Demsey JONES (Odom), and John PARKER (Babtist). Gatling, Odom and Babtist appear to have been middle names and all three are indexed under the capitalized surnames.

TABLE OF CONTENTS

1794	1-24
1795	24-46
1796	46-68
1797	68-90
1798	90-112
1799	112-134
Index	135-150
Location Index	151

MINUTES OF COUNTY COURT OF PLEAS AND QUARTER SESSIONS

GATES COUNTY, NORTH CAROLINA

1794-1799

VOLUME I

Vol.: Not numbered   Years: Feb. 1790-Feb. 1796   Pages: 1-286

(1) 176 State of North Carolina   17 Feby 1794
At a Court of Pleas and Quarter Sessions begun and held for the County of Gates at the Court House on the third Monday in February in the XVIIIth year of American Independence and in the year of our Lord one thousand seven hundred & Ninety four.

    Present
    Thomas HUNTER)
    James GREGORY) Esquires Justices
    Jethro SUMNER)

Account of Sales of the Estate of Amos TROTMAN decd sold the 30th November 1793 was exhibited into Court by Amos TROTMAN Exor &c

Moses HOBBS Guardn. to Wm HOBBS & Jesse HOBBS orpan of Guy HOBBS decd exhibited his account with said orphans wherein there appeared to be a Bale due to Wm HOBBS the sum of £41.2.10 & to Jesse HOBBS the sum of £31.2.3

Grand Jury impannelled & Sworn for Feby Term 1794 is as follows vizt. John B WALTON Foreman William PIERCE Demsey LANGSTON Moses HILL, Jonathan LASSITER Wm WARREN jr Jonathan WILLIAMS Charles EURE, Francis SPEIGHT Joseph TAYLOR, William HUNTER, Lewis WALTERS Jas B SUMN__ Demsey TROTMAN, John Parker GATLING

Ordered that John TAYLOR orphan of Jonas TAYLOR about nine years of age be bound as an apprentice to Elijah SPIVEY to learn the Business of A Cooper.

(2)   John WEATHERLEY Junr came into Court and mooved for Administration on the Estate of John WEATHERLEY decd which was considered of and granted Ordered that he give Bond and Security in the sum of one thousand five hundred pounds at same time Jesse SAUNDERS & Henry LEE came into Court and offered themselves as Securitys &c who were approved of

Deed of Sale James PHELPS jr to James PHELPS senr. proved by the oath of Humphry HUDGINS &c.

Bill of Sale James RANSOM to Philip ROGERS proved by the oath of William GOODMAN &c

Deed of Sale Josiah PARKER to James PARKER ackd &c

Isaac COSTEN & James COSTEN Guardians to the Orphans of Demsey COSTEN decd exhibited their account with said Orphans the sum of Three hundred & twenty Eight pounds, 17/2½ as also to Thomas COSTEN Twenty five pounds as a legacy from his Unkle James COSTEN decd

Bill of Sale Hardy EASON to George EASON proved by the oath of James BAKER &c

David KELLY Guardian to Seth & Senith SPIVEY exhibited his accot with sd Orphans wherein there appears to be a Ball due Seth ₤34..17..9 3/4 & to Senith ₤34.17.9 3/4.

The Last Will & Testament of John GORDON decd was exhibited into Court by Jacob GORDON & Benjn GORDON Exors therein appointed and was proved by the oaths of Charles POWELL & Eliza WALTON two of the Subscribing Witnesses thereto and on motion was ordered to be Recorded at the same time the said Executors came into Court and qualified themselves for that office &c.

Joseph RIDDICK Exr of Thos. TROTMAN decd exhibited his account with Thos TROTMAN Orpn of the decd. wherein there appears to be a Balance due the Orphan the sum of 8..10 11

(3) 178 Deed of Sale Henry COPELAND & Uxr to John ODOM ackd. and private examination taken by William GOODMAN Esqr. who reported that she relinqushed her right of dower.

Deed of Sale of Land Henry COPELAND & Uxr. to Benjamin BARNES ackd and private examination taken by Wm GOODMAN Esqr. who reported that she relinquished her right dower.

Deed of Sale of Land Henry COPELAND & Uxr. to Isaac LANGSTON Ackd and was privately examined by William GOODMAN Esqr who reported that she relinquished her right of Dower &c

Deed of Sale of Land Henry COPELAND & Uxr. to Isaac LANGSTON Ackd. and was privately examined by Wm GOODMAN Esquire who reported that she relinquished her right of dower &c

Deed of Sale of Land Henry COPELAND & Uxr. to John ODOM ackd. by Henry COPELAND and private examination of Sally COPELAND taken by Wm GOODMAN Esqr. who reported that she relinquished her right of dower &c

Deed of Sale of Land Henry COPELAND & Uxr. to John ODOM ackd by Henry COPELAND and private examined by Wm GOODMAN Esquire who reported that she relinquished her right of dower

Deed of Sale of Land Demsey TROTMAN to William HUNTER Ackd &c

Accot of Sales of the Estate of Dorcas VANN decd was exhibited into Court by Isaac LANGSTON on oath &c

The Last Will and Testament of Elisha PARKER decd. was exhibited into Court by Esther PARKER Executrix therein appointed and was proved by the oath of Danl PARKER & Pa HEGERTY two of the subscribing Witnesses thereto and on motion was ordered to be recorded at the same time the said Extrix came into Court and quallified herself for that office &c

(4) Deed of Sale of Land Thos NORRIS & Uxr to Mills LANDING proved by the oath of James LANDIN &c

Feb. 1794

Inventory of the Goods and Chattels rights & Credits which were of the Estate of Elisha PARKER decd was exhibited into Court by Esther PARKER Administratrix &c

Ordered that Charles BUTTERTON orphan of James BUTTERTON abt Seventeen years of age 1 Feby 1794 be bound as an Apprentice to Micajah PHELPS to Learn the Business of a Cooper

Ordered that Benjamin BEASLEY orphan of Benjamin BEASLEY decd be bound an Apprentice to David CROSS to learn the Business of a Planter the said Orphan about twelve years of age.

William DOUGHTY Guardian to Benjamin BAKER orphan of Samuel BAKER decd. exhibited his accot with said Orphan wherein there appears to be a Bale due the said Orpn &c

Winnefred TAYLOR Guardian to the Orphans of William TAYLOR decd exhibited his accot with said Orphans wherein there appears to be a Ball due the said Orphan the sum of ₤17..19..3

Joseph TAYLOR Guardian to Sally SPIVEY orphan of Thomas SPIVEY decd exhibited his account with said Orphan wherein there appears to be a Ball due the said orphan the sum of ₤44.12.10½

William WALTERS Guardian to Bray BAKER Orphan of Saml BAKER decd. exhibited his accot with said Orphan wherein there appears to be a Bale due said. (End of entry.)

Ordered that Robert MILLER Orphan of John MILLER about fourteen years of age be bound as an Apprentice to John DUKE to Learn the Business of a Blacksmith &c.

Ordered that Reuben MILLER orphan of John MILLER about Twelve years of age be bound to William CARTER to Learn the Business of a Wheelright &c

(5) 180 Ordered that James BEASLEY orphan of Benjamin BEASLEY about the age of 10 years be bound as an Appe to Abel CROSS to learn the Busr?iness of a Farmer &c.

Ordered that Benjamin BARNES be appointed overseer of the Road in the room and stead of Cyprian CROSS resigned

Ordered that Jno WEATHERLEY Admr of John WEATHERLEY decd sell as much of the Personal Estate of the decd as will pay his just Debts &c

Susanna BAKER Guardian to Peggy BAKER orphan of Saml BAKER decd. exhibited her account with said Orphan wherein there appeared to be a Balance due the said Orphan the sum of ₤24.17..7½

Account of Sales of the Estate of Thomas PILAND decd. was exhibited into Court by James PILAND Admr on oath &c

William VOLINTINE Guardian to Docton BAGLEY, Henry BAGLEY & Trotman BAGLEY orphans of Jacob BAGLEY decd & to Miles HILL orphan of Kedar HILL decd. exhibited his accot with said orphans on oath &c

Ordered that William BAKER, John BAKER, William GOODMAN & Henry GOODMAN or any three of them Audite State and settle the accounts of Willis RIDDICK Admr of James RIDDICK decd and that they also make a Division of the said Estate &c

Lease for a Sain place William H BAKER Admr of B B BAKER to Kedar PARKER & Absolom WILLIAMS proved by the oath of John WEATHERLEY &c

Elisha HARE Guardian to Mourning NORFLEET orphan of Jacob NORFLEET exhibited his accot with said Orphan &c on oath.

(6) Deed of Sale of Land John BAKER to George WILLIAMS Ackd.

William HINTON Guardian to Robert HILL & Whitmill HILL orphans of Kedar HILL decd exhibited his account with said Orphan on oath &c

James RAWLS Guardian to the Orps of William BOOTH decd exhibited his accot with said Orphans on oath &c

Eliza KITRELL Guardian to Charity KITTRELL exhibited her Accot with said Orphan on oath &c

James BAKER Guardian to Thomas TROTMAN orphan of Thomas TROTMAN decd exhibited his accot. with said orphan on oath &c

Jos RIDDICK Moses HILL & Simon STALLINGS three of the Gentn who were appointed to audite State and settle the accots of Amos TROTMAN Executor of Amos TROTMAN decd. made report of their proceedings &c

James GATLING Guardian to John ROGERS & William ROGERS orphans of Stephen ROGERS decd exhibited his account with said Orphans on oath &c

Inventory of the Estate of Edwin SUMNER decd was exhibited into Court by Jethro SUMNER Esqr on oath &c

The Last Will and Testament of Michel LASSITER was exhibed into Court by Jethro LASSITER Admr and was proved by the oath of Keziah BLANSHARD DAVIS one of the Subscribing Witnesses thereto and was Ordered to be Recorded at the same time the said Exr. came into Court and quallified himself for that office &c

(7) 182 Deed of Sale of Land Demsey JONES to Elisha Hance BOND proved by the oath of Richard BOND &c

Deed of Sale of Land James GOODMAN to Richard BARNES Ackd &c

Bill of Sale for a Negro Boy PETER, James NORFLEET to Abraham NORFLEET proved by the oath of John COWPER &c

James GOODMAN Guardian to Priscilla ROGERS orphan of Stephen ROGERS decd. exhibited his accot with said Orphan on oath &c

Demsey TROTMAN Guardian to Sarah SCOTT Joseph SCOTT & Christian SCOTT orphans of Sarah SCOTT decd exhibited his account with said Orphans on oath &c

Demsey JONES Guardian to Selah BOND orphan of Demsey BOND decd exhibited his accot with said Orphan on oath &c

Moses HOBBS Guardian to William HOBBS & Jesse HOBBS orphans of Guy HOBBS decd exhibited his accot with said Orpns on oath &c

Amos TROTMAN Exr of the Estate of Amos TROTMAN decd exhibited into Court by an accot of the Sales of part of the Estate of the decd. &c

Cyprian CROSS Guardian to Partheny BOYCE & Jonathan BOYCE Orphans of Jonathan BOYCE decd exhibited his accot with said Orphans on oath &c

William BERRYMAN Guardian to James FREEMAN Orphan of Richard FREEMAN decd exhibited his accot with said orphan on oath &c

(8)   Jonathan WILLIAMS Guardian to Blake BAKER orphan of Samuel BAKER decd exhibited his accot with said orphan on oath &c

Demsey WILLIAMS Guardian to Saml BAKER orphan of Samuel BAKER decd exhibited his accot with said Orphan on oath &c

George EASON Guardian to Samuel HOBBS orphan of John HOBBS decd exhibited his accot with said Orpn on oath &c

Abraham HURDLE Guardian to Jacob SUMNER Son of Abraham SUMNER exhibited his accot with said Child on oath &c

Elizabeth KITTRELL Guardian to William KITTRELL Elizabeth KITTRELL & George KITTRELL orphans of Moses KITTRELL decd exhibited his account with said Orphans on oath &c

Deed of Sale William BAKER to William MATTHEWS Ackd.

An entry made by Abel CROSS & Cavited by Wm KING ordered that the Sheriff Summons a Jury and go on the premises &c

Ordered that Simon STALLINGS Moses HILL William VOLINTINE and James WALTON or any three of them Audite State & Settle the accots of Jos RIDDICK Exor of Rachel TROTMAN with said Estate &c

Ordered that Simon STALLINGS Moses HILL William VOLINTINE and James WALTON or any three of them Audite State and settle the accots of Jos RIDDICK Admr of Mary ROUNTREE decd &c

Ordered that Simon STALLINGS Moses HILL Wm VOLINTINE & James WALTON or any three of them make a division of the Estate of

(9) 184 Mary ROUNTREE decd agreeable to Law and in case a Division cannot be made without a Sale of the property or a part thereof then and in that case the Admr to sell such part of said Estate agreeable to Law as to make it conveniunt to make a division &c

Mary SPIVEY Guardian to Frederick BLANSHARD Wm BLANSHARD & Mary BLANSHARD orphans of Absolom BLANSHARD decd exhibited her accots with said Orphans on oath &c

Wm GOODMAN Francis SPEIGHT & Lawrence BAKER three of the Gentn who were appointed to Audite State & Settle the accots of Abel CROSS with the Orphans of Henry KING decd exhibited his accot made report of their proceedings thereon &c

Deed of Sale Moses BOYCE to Sion BOYCE proved by the oath of Patrick HEGARTY &c

William FREEMAN appointed Guardian to Charles ROUNTREE & John ROUNTREE orphans of

John ROUNTREE decd Ordered that he give Bonds & Security in the of Five hundred & fifty pounds each at same time James OUTLAW & Seth ROUNTREE came into Court & offered themselves as Securitys &c

Jethro SUMNER Wm WALTERS & William DOUGHTIE three of the Gentn who were appointed to audite State & Settle the accounts of Jeremiah BENTON orphan of Samuel BENTON decd and that they also make a Division of the Estate of the decd &c

Seth ROUNTREE came into Court and exhibited his accot as Guardian wth Penay ROUNTREE Orphan of Thomas ROUNTREE decd. on oath &c

(10) Ordered that James ROBBINS Son of Sarah ROBBINS about the age Ten years in August next be bound as an Apprentice to William LEWIS to learn the Buisiness of a House Carpenter & Joiner

Ordered that John ROBBINS Son of Nanny ROBBINS about Eleven years of Age on the 10th of Augt last be bound as an Apprentice to William LEWIS to learn the Buisiness of a House Carpenter & Joiner

Deed of Sale of Land John CARTER to James CARTER proved by the oath of Charles EURE &c

Ordered that James MASSEY orpan of James MASSEY about the age of (blank) years be bound to James BARNES to learn the Buisiness of a Farmer

Ordered that William LASSITER about 17 years of Age be bound as an Appe to George LASSITER to Learn the Buisiness of a Cooper

Willis BROWN Guardian to Nancy GARRETT orpan of Jas GARRETT decd exhibited his accot with said Orphan on Oath &c

Ordered that Charles ROBBINS Son of Thaney ROBBINS about Seven years of age be bound as an Appe to Wm HINTON (Indian Neck) to learn the Buisiness of a Cooper

Ordered that Jethro SUMNER, Jethro BALLARD Kedar BALLARD & Miles BENTON or any three of them Audite State & Settle the Accots of Jesse BENTON with the Estate of John BENTON decd

Tuesday evening the Court adjourned until tomorrow morning 10 oClock

(11) 186 Wednesday morning the Court met
    Present Christopher RIDDICK)
                Joseph RIDDICK   ) Esqrs.
                Jethro BALLARD   )
                William GOODMAN   )
                David RICE   )

Ordered that Edward PILAND be appointed Overseer of the Road instead of Moor CARTER resigned &c

Ordered that Francis SPEIGHT Henry SPEIGHT James RANSOM & William GOODMAN or any three of them Audite State & Settle the Accots.. of William KING Admr of Charlotte KING decd and that they also divide the Estate among the Heirs agreeable to Law.

Thomas HUNTER, Jo RIDDICK Thomas BOUKILL & James BAKER who were appointed to Audite

State & Settle the accots of William KING Admr of John PURNELL decd. made report of their proceedings &c

Joseph RIDDICK Esquire Guardian to Joseph Love & Willis TROTMAN Orphans of Thomas TROTMAN decd exhibited his Account seperately with said Orphans as also an accot. Jointly with the above said Orphans on oath &c

James GATLING Deputy Sheriff exhibited the account of Sales of the Estates of John GATLING Edwd GATLING, John ROUNTREE & Samuel Heath JAMESON on oath &c

Accot of Sales of a Negro Boy belonging to the Orphans of Abner BLANSHARD decd was exhibited into Court on oath by James GATLING D Shff

(12) Bill of Sale Demsey JONES to William BAKER for four Negroes vizt. SARAH, WINNEY, ROZELLA & VENUS proved by the oath of Jethro BALLARD Esquire &c

Bill of Sale Charles LAWRENCE to William BAKER for four Negroes vizt SARAH WINNEY ROZELLA & VENUS proved by the oath of Jethro BALLARD Esquire &c

Ordered that the Sheriff of this County Summon James KNIGHT, Jacob GORDON, William DAUGHTY & Charles EURE personally to be and appear as Jurymen at the next ~~County~~ Supr Court to be held at Edenton for the District of Edenton on the Sixth day of Apl next

Jethro BALLARD, James NORFLEET & Benjamin GORDON three of the Gentlemen who were appointed to settle the accounts of Daniel POWELL & James POWELL Exors of Jacob POWELL exhibited their proceedings thereon &c

Thomas HUNTER Job RIDDICK & Timothy LASSITER three of the Gentn. who were appointed to Audite State & Settle the Accounts of David RICE & Isaac COSTEN Exors of James COSTEN decd exhibited thereon there proceedings &c

William LEWIS Guardian to James HODGES orphan of James HODGES decd. exhibited his account with said Orphan ~~of~~ where there appears to be a Balan__ due the said Orphan the sum of two hundred & fourteen ~~Shillings~~ pounds fourteen Shillings & one farthing &c

Ordered that William LEWIS, David HARRELL Kedar HINTON James FREEMAN, James BAKER, Aaron HOBBS Abraham HURDLE John SMALL, Moses DAVIS, Thomas PARKER, John POWELL Luke SUMNER, William MATTHIAS Amos PARKER, Abraham MORGAN John ARNOLD, Micajah RIDDICK, James PRUDEN Philip LEWIS Bray SAUNDERS, Benjamin BARNES Thos BARNES

(13) 188 John ODOM, Stephen EURE, Demsey ODOM, James BRADY Willis BROWN, Thomas SMITH Henry SPEIGHT & Isaac LANGSTON be summoned to appear at this Court at next Term as Jurors &c

Ordered that Thomas HURDLE Constable be allowed the sum of two pounds Eight Shillings for Services summoning the Inhabitants of Captn HUNTERs Capty to give list Taxables & Taxable property &c

Ordered that Lawrence BAKER Clerk of this Court be allowed the sum of Eighteen pounds ten Shillings for axtra Services performed by him the year passed.

Ordered that a Tax of One Shilling & Six pence on each poll & and Six pence on each hundred Acres Land be levied on the Inhabitants of this County for a County Tax &c

Feb. 1794

John B WALTON Guardian to Guy HILL Orphan of Kedah HILL decd. exhibited his account with said Orphan on Oath &c

Deed of Sale Thomas HUNTER to John B WALTON proved by the oath of Timothy WALTON &c

Bond Joseph HOLLAND, Joseph HOLLAND & Demsey SUMNER to Mills LEWIS proved by the oath of Luten LEWIS &c

(14)   Thursday morning the Court met
          Present Jos RIDDICK   )
                   William GOODMAN) Esquires Justices
                   Henry GOODMAN   )
                   William BAKER   )

Ordered that Humphry HUDGINS be appointed Ranger for this County and that the Executors of James COSTEN decd deliver up to the said HUDGINS all the Book or Books relatave to that Buisiness

Ordered that John BAKER William BAKER Christopher RIDDICK & George WILLIAMS or any three of them Audite State & Settle the accounts of Jesse SPIVEY Exr. of Mosess SPIVEY decd & that they make Division of the Estate of the Dec agreeable to Law the Will &c

Thomas MARSHALL Guardian to John HILL orphan of Guy HILL decd. exhibited his accot. with said Orphan wherein there appears to be a Bale. due the said Orphan the sum of £34.13.9. &c

Francis SPEIGHT came into Court and mooved for Administration on the Estate of James BOON decd which was accordingly granted Ordered that he give Secy in the sum of One hundred pounds at same time Philip LEWIS & John WARREN came into Court and offered themselves as security, who were approved of &c at same time the said Exr Admr came into Court and quallified himself for that office &c

Inventory of the Goods & Chattels Rights & Credits which were of the Estate of James BOON decd was exhibited into Court by Francis SPEIGHT on Oath &c

Charles POWELL Guardian to Richard FREEMAN Orphn of Demsey FREEMAN decd. exhibited his acct with said Orphan on oath wherein there appears to be a Bale due the said Orpn the sum of £17.18.1 3/4

(15) 190 Ordered that Britain WILLS an Illegitimate Child about Ten years of old be bound as An Apprentice to Hillory WILLEY to learn the Buisiness of a Farmer &c

Ordered that Jesse Hiatt ROGERS & Timothy HIATT Orphan of Jesse HIATT decd the former about Ten years of Age & the latter about Eight years old be bound as an apprentice to Richard BARNES to learn the Buisiness of a Black smiths. &c

Ordered that Henry WINBORN orphan of Philip WINBORN decd about Fourteen years of age be bound as an Appe to James GATLING to learn the Buisiness of a Cooper

Account of Sales of a Negro Girl & a feather Bid & furniture belonging to the Eliza KING Orphan of Henry KING decd was exhibited his account into Court by James GATLING Depy Sheriff

Benjn GORDON came into Court and resigned his appointedment as Entry taker of this

County &c
    Jo RIDDICK
    Henry GOODMAN
    Wm GOODMAN

(16)   State of No.. Carolina   May 19th: 1794 2/5_?
        Gates County

At a Court of Pleas and Quarter Sessions begun and held for the County of Gates at the Court House on the third Monday May in the Eighteenth year of American Independence and in the year of our Lord one thousand seven hundred and Ninety four

    Present
    Jethro SUMNER   )
    David RICE   ) Esquires Justices
    William GOODMAN)

William GOODMAN Henry SPEIGHT & James RANSOM three of the Gentlemen who were appointed to Audit State & Settle the accots of William KING Admr of Charlotte KING decd. made report of their proceedings thereon &c

The following Gentlemen were drawn as Grand Jurors for this term who were quallified. agreeable to Law vizt. Philip LEWIS Foreman. Luke SUMNER, John ODOM, Isaac LANGSTON Aaron HOBBS, Henry SPEIGHT, John ARNOLD, Demsey ODOM Moses DAVIS, Micajah R__-DICK jr. Thomas PARKER Willis BROWN, John POWELL, James BRADY & Abraham MORGAN

Ordered that James BRADY jr. be appointed Overseer of the Road instead of Henry SPEIGHT resigned

William FREEMAN Guardian to the Heirs of John ROUNTREE decd exhibited an Accot of Sales of that part of the Orphans Estate which fell to them at the Death of Mary ROUNTREE their Grandmother &c

(17) 192 Simon STALLINGS, James FREEMAN & Timothy WALTON three of the Gentn who were appointed to Audite State & Settle the accounts of Micajah BLANSHARD Adm of Priscilla PARKER decd made report of their proceedings &c

Simon STALLINGS James FREEMAN & Timothy WALTON three of the Gentn who were appointed to make a Division of the Estate of Priscilla PARKER decd made report of their proceedings thereon &c

Ordered that James GREGORY Esquire be appointed (instead of Wm BAKER Esquire who is unable to attend) with Persons formerly appointed to audit State and settle the accounts of Willis RIDDICK Admr of James RIDDICK decd and also to make a division of the said Estate agreeable to Law &c

Present Thomas HUNTER & Simon STALLINGS Esqui___ Justices

Additional Account of Sales which were of the estate of Mary ROUNTREE decd was exhibited into Court by Joseph RIDDICK Admr on oath &c

Ordered that Hardy HOWARD orphan of Hardy HOWARD decd about Eleven years of age be bound as an Apprentice to Amos DILDAY to learn the buisness of a House Carpenter &c

Inventory of the Goods & Chattels rights & Credits which were of the Estate of John WEATHERLEY decd was exhibited into Court by John WEATHERLEY Admr on oath &c

Miles ROUNTREE Guardian to Josiah ROUNTREE orphan of Charles ROUNTREE decd exhibited his account with said Orphan wherein there appears to be a Balance due the said Orphan the sum of Seventy Eight pounds fourteen Shillings & two pence &c

(18) Isaac COSTEN came into Court and mooved for Administration on the Estate of William GORDON decd. which was accordingly granted Ordered that he give Bond and Security in the sum of One thousand two hundred pounds at same time James COSTEN & Jethro MILTEAR came into Court and offered themselves as Security, who were approved of &c

Ordered that Jethro SUMNER Esquire Exr. of Moses HARE jr decd sell as much of the personal Estate of the decd as will pay the just Debts of the decd &c

Inventory of the Goods & Chattels rights & Credits which were of the Estate of William GORDON decd was exhibited into Court by Isaac COSTEN Admr on oath &c

Simon STALLINGS Moses HILL William VOLINTINE & James WALTON who were appointed to make a Division of the Estate of Mary ROUNTREE decd made report of their proceedings thereon &c

Simon STALLINGS Moses HILL William VOLINTINE & James WALTON the Gentlemen who were appointed to make a Division of Audit State and settle the accounts of Joseph RIDDICK Esquire Admr of Mary ROUNTREE decd with the Estate of the decd made report of their proceedings thereon &c

Simon STALLINGS Moses HILL William VOLINTINE & James WALTON who were appointed to Audite State & Settle the Accounts of Joseph RIDDICK Esqr. Exr of Rachel TROTMAN decd with the Estate of the decd made report of their proceedings thereon &c

Deed of Sale of Land Richard BOND & Uxr to John Benbury WALTON ackd in open Court in due form of Law private Examination of Mary BOND taken by Jethro SUMNER Esqr.

(19) 194 Account of Sales of the Estate of Joseph WARREN was exhibited into Court which was proved by the oath of William WARREN Admr before William BAKER Esquire &c

Ordered that Charles EURE, Stephen EURE Cyprian CROSS and Asa HARRELL or any three of them Audite State & Settle the accounts of Israel BEEMAN Admr of Hardy BROWN decd with the Estate of the decd

Deed of Sale of Land with a receipt thereon Richard BRIGGS to John RIDDICK proved by the oath of William HARRISS &c

Deed of Sale of Land James WALTON to George OUTLAW ackd in open Court &c

Deed of Sale of Land David CROSS & Uxr to John ROCHELL proved by the oath of William WATSON &c

Deed of Sale of Land Zacherias COPELAND & Henry COPELAND to Jethro SUMNER proved by the oath of Demsey SUMNER &c

Deed of Sale of Land John KITTRELL to Isaac WALTERS proved by the oath of Winborn JENKINS &c

Bill of Sale for a Negro Man DEMSEY Luke SUMNER to James KNIGHT proved by the oath of Demsey KNIGHT &c

May 1794

Bill of Sale for a Negro Woman PATT John DARDEN to James KNIGHT proved by the oath of Demsey KNIGHT &c

Deed of Sale of Land Solomon PHILLIPS to Demsey ODOM proved by the oath of Benjamin ODOM &c

(Entire entry crossed-out.) Account of Sales of the Estate of Tris?tram BETHEY decd which was left in his Last Will to his Wife-entd on the other side-and sold after her decease was exhibited into Court by John BETHEY Exr on oath &c

(20)   Account of the Sales of the Estate Trestram BETHEY decd was exhibited into Court by John BETHRY who says he is Exr on oath &c

Joseph RIDDICK Esqr. & Patrick HEGERTY Surveyor of this Cot?y who were appointed to make plotts of Certain Lands now in dispute between John ELLIS & Benjn BARNES exhibited their proceedings &c

Deed of Sale of Land Henry HILL to Demsey JONES proved by the oath of John DARDEN &c

Ordered that James NORFLEET be appointed Guardian to Mary ROUNTREE orphan of Charles ROUNTREE decd and that he give Bond & Security in the sum of One thousand pounds at same time Joseph RIDDICK & Simon STALLINGS came into Court and offered themselves as Securitys &c

Bill of Sale of Land Nathl RIDDICK & David RIDDICK for a Negro Man TOM to Isaac MILLER proved by the oath of Jos GRANBERY

Deed of Sale of Land William LEWIS & Samuel HARRELL to Holladay WALTON proved by the oath of Charles EURE &c

Bill of Sale for a Negro Girl ROSE George EASON & Betsey EASON to John B WALTON proved by the oath of Thomas LEDSAM &c

Deed of Sale of Land Jacob GORDAN to Elisha NORFLEET proved by the oath of Nathl RIDDICK &c

Deed of Sale of Land Elisha NORFLEET to Jacob GORDON proved by the oath of Nathl RIDDICK &c

Deed of Sale of Land Demsey ODOM to Elisha HARE proved by the oath of Patrick HEGERTY &c

(21) 196 Deed of Sale of Land Jethro BALLARD & David RICE to Richard MITCHELL proved by the oath of Luke SUMNER &c

The Last Will and Testament of Moses HARE decd was exhibited into Court by Jethro SUMNER Esquire Exor therein appointed and was proved by the oath of Andrew MATTHEWS one of the subscribing Witnesses thereto at the same time the said Exor came into Court and quallified himself for that Office &c

Inventory of the Goods and Chattels rights and Credits which were of the Estate of Moses HARE decd was exhibited into Court by Jethro SUMNER Exor &c

Bill of Sale of Land for a Negro Girl LIDIA John DARDEN to Joseph HARE proved by the oath of Jethro SUMNER &c

Inventory of the Goods & Chattels Rights & Credits which were of the Estate of Michel LASSITER was exhibited into Court by Jethro LASSITER Exor on oath &c

The Sheriff having returned the pannel of a Jury with the Verdict thereof in a Certain Caviat made by Wm KING against an entry made by Abel CROSS (to wit), North Carolina Gates County. Agreeable to an order of Court I summoned a Jury of Twelve free houloulders of the aforesaid County, after being sworn they proceeded on the disputed Tract of Land that Abel CROSS entered in the entry Book No 17. and William KING entered a Caveat against the said CROSS entry, and it is the Opinion of the Subscribers Jurors that the KING Caveat shall stand and have all the Land that Henry KING held in BARNES Patent at his decease it appears to be the same land that the said CROSS entered and it is mos? appear to us that the said patent lines has been prosessioned by lawful processioners and the said Henry KING held the said Land, in quiet possession many years before his decease, and it is the opinion of us the Juriors that Abel CROSS shall pay all Costs and Charges &c   John ODOM LS. Isaac LANGSTON LS. Demsey LANGSTON LS John PARKER LS Henry SPEIGHT LS Jesse his J mark SAUNDERS LS Isaac his J (or I) mark CARTER LS Wm WARREN LS John LEWIS LS John PARKER LS Philip LEWIS LS. Mills LEWIS LS James GATLING Depy Shff

(22) Tuesday morning May the 20th 1794 the Court met
   Present
   Joseph RIDDICK
   David RICE
   Simon STALLINGS

Ordered that William GLOVER have a License to keep a Public House at the House where he now lives at Gates Court House & that he give Bond & Security in the sum of (blank) pounds at same time Henry FORREST & Joseph John SUMNER came into Court and offered themselves as Securitys &c

Thomas PARKER Guardian to Kinchen NORFLEET orphan of Jacob NORFLEET exhibited his accot current with said Orphan on oath wherein there appears to be a Balance due the said Orphan the sum of Forty Seven pounds Six Shillings & two pence

Ordered that Kedar HINTON be appointed Overseer of the Road where William GORDON decd. formerly acted as Overseer of the said Road &c

Ordered that William DRAPER be exempt from the payment of a Poll Tax for the year 17943

Ordered that William GOODMAN Henry GOODMAN Philip LEWIS & Francis SPEIGHT or any three of them Audite State and settle the accounts of John BETHEY Exr. of Tristram BETHEY with the Estate of the decd. and that they also make a Division of the said Estate agreeable to the Will &c

Ordered that Richd BOND be summoned by the Sheriff to be & appear at this Court at next Term to shew cause why he hath stoped the pass way to and from Timothy WALTONs Mill

(23) 198 Samuel EURE Guardian to Nancy EURE orphan of Enos EURE decd exhibited his account Current against the said Orpan wherein there appears to be a ballance due the said orphan the sum of Thirty five pounds fifteen Shillings & five pence &c

Ordered that John VANN son of Jesse be appointed Inspector instead of John WEATHERLEY decd and that he give Bond & Secy in agreeable to Law at same time John ODOM &

Demsey BARNES (blank) came into Court and offered themselves as Securitys who were approved.

Deed of Sale of Land Benjamin BARNES to Demsey BARNES ackd &c

Ordered that Jethro MILTEAR be allowed the sum of One pound four Shillings for his services summoning the Inhabitants of Captn Jonathan ROBERTS's Captaincy to return a list of their Taxables & Taxable property &c

Ordered that Lewis SPARKMAN Constable be allowed the sum of One pound four Shillings for summoning the Citizens in Capt Charles EURE's district, to return a list Taxables & Taxable property &c

Ordered that William ELLIS be exempt from the payment of five Shillings it being the price for the said his Stud Horse covering the Season Abraham HURDLE having inlisted the said Horse and paid the Tax before &c

Ordered that a Road be Cut from Seth EASONs in this County through the great Dismal Swamp to (blank) DAVIS's in Pasquotank County.

(24) Wednesday morning the Court met.
        Present Christopher RIDDICK)
                 Joseph RIDDICK   )
                 David RICE   ) Esquires Justices
                 Henry GOODMAN   )
                 Thomas HUNTER   )

Ordered that the following Gentlemen take the list Taxables in the Districts of this County to wit, David RICE Esquire in Captn. Jethro SUMNERs Captaincy, Joseph RIDDICK Esqr in the district of Capt. Jonathan ROBERTS Capty. James GRAGORY Esqr. in Captn. Isaac HUNTERs Capty, Christopher RIDDICK Esqr in Captn Wm HARRISS's Capty Henry GOODMAN in Captn John BETHEYs Capty. William BAKER Esquire in Captn Jesse BENTONs Capty. & that William GOODMAN Esqr. in the District of Capt. Charles EUREs Captaincy

Ordered that James GATLING be allowed Twenty four Shillings for summoning the Inhabitants in Captn John BETHEYs Captaincy to give lists Taxables and Taxable property in the year 17943.

The State vs Jeremiah SPEIGHT Jury impannelled & Sworn to try Issue of Truverce? vizt. Stephen EURE, Kedar HINTON Amos PARKER David HARRELL, John SMALL, James PRUDEN William MATTHIAS James FREEMAN William LEWIS, Thomas BARNES Benjamin BARNES, John LANG.

Charles JOHNSON vs James B SUMNER & Edward LIGGETS, Jury impannelled & Sworn to try Issue vizt. Thomas SMITH Stephen EURE Kedar HINTON, Amos PARKER, David HARRELL, John SMALL James PRUDEN, William MATTHIAS, James FREEMAN William LEWIS Thos BARNES & Benjamin BARNES

(25) 200 In the Suit Jacob GORDON against Seth EASON, Jury Impannelled and sworn vizt. Thomas SMITH, Stephen EURE, Kedar HINTON Amos PARKER, David HARRELL, John SMALL, James PRUDEN William MATTHIAS, James FREEMAN William LEWIS Thomas BARNES & Benjamin BARNES

In the Suit Thomas DUNN Admr of George DUNN decd against Riddick HUNTER & Miles

BENTON, Jury Impannelled & Sworn vizt. Thomas SMITH, Stephen EURE, Kedar HINTON, Amos PARKER, David HARRELL, John SMALL, James PRUDEN William MATTHIAS, James FREEMAN, William LEWIS Thomas BARNES & Benjamin BARNES

Ordered that Thomas PARKER be appointed Overseer of the Road in the stead of William ARNOLD resigned

The Court taking into Consideration the Act of the Genl Assembly at their Sessions in December last relative to the Classing the Justices of the peace in this County, after delibration thereon Classed the said Court in the following manner (to wit) first Class Wm BAKER Esqr Chairman, David RICE, Jethro BALLARD, Jethro SUMNER Henry GOODMAN, & William GOODMAN Esquires Second Class Thomas HUNTER Esqr. Chairman, James GRAGORY Simon STALLINGS John BAKER Christopher RIDDICK & Joseph RIDDICK Esquires Justices &c

Ordered that Isaac COSTEN Admr of William GORDON decd. sell as much of the personal Estate of the decd as will pay his Debts

James GATLING Deputy Sheriff exhibited an account of the Sales of the Estate of James BOON decd on oath &c

Accot of the Sales of the perishable Estate of John WEATHERLEY decd was exhibited into Court by James GATLING Depy. Sheriff on oath &c

(26) The Court taking into Consideration the Act of the General Assembly relative to the appointment of Sheriffs after mature delibration Simon STALLINGS Esquire was appointed Sheriff in this County Ordered that he give Bond & Security agreeable to Law at same time Thomas HUNTER Esqr & James GATLING came into Court & offered themselves as Securitys who were approved off &c Thomas HUNTER Joseph RIDDICK, Henry GOODMAN & David RICE Esqrs were on the Bench when the above order passed

In Suit, Pasco TURNER against Isaac HUNTER Jury Impannelled and Sworn (to wit) Thomas SMITH, Stephen EURE, Kedar HINTON, Amos PARKER, David HARRELL, John SMALL, James PRUDEN, William MATTHIAS, James FREEMAN, William LEWIS Thomas BARNES & Benjamin BARNES.

Ordered that the Sheriff of this County Summons the following persons to serve this Court at next sitting as Patit & Grand Jurors (to wit) Demsey BARNES, David CROSS, John LANG William KING, Mills LEWIS, Charles EURE, David LEWIS Samuel EURE, James CARTER, Elisha CROSS, Jonathan ROGERS, Jonathan WILLIAMS, Hillory WILLEY, Abraham HURDLE, Moses BRIGGS, Jacob HOBBS, Jacob EASON, James BAKER, William HUNTER Abraham SPIVEY, William VOLLENTINE, John B WALTON, Timothy WALTON, Henry FORREST, Isaac HUNTER, Isaac COSTEN, William HARRISS, Demsey JONES Richard BOND & Jeremiah SPEIGHT.

Ordered that Humphry HUDGINS Constable be allowed the sum of Seven pounds four Shillings for Services attending this Court and for summoning the Citizins of Captn William HARRISS's Capty &c

(27) 202 Ordered that William WALTERS Constable be allowed the sum of Seven pounds four Shillings as pr his Accot exhibited for his Services attending this Court and for warning the Citizens of Capn. Jesse BENTONs Captaincy to return lists of their Taxables & Taxable property &c

                                              Jo RIDDICK
                                              Henry GOODMAN
                                              Thos. HUNTER

(28)   State of North Carolina   August 18. 1794
         Gates County)ss
                    At a Court of Pleas and Quarter Sessions begun
and held for the County of Gates at the Court House on the third Monday in August
in the Nineteenth year of the Independence of the said State Anno Dom 1794
         Present.
         Christopher RIDDICK)
         James GREGORY   ) Esquires Justices
         Henry GOODMAN   )

Ordered that William BAKER Esquire be permitted to turn the main Road at Knotty pine Chappel or alter the same in any manner that he may think propper provided it does not in any ma_ner incommode the public good

Ordered that Reuben MILLER Orphan of John MILLER about thirteen years old be bound as an apprentice to James JONES (of David) to Learn the Buisiness of a Cooper & Wheelright &c

Ordered that William MILLER orphan of John MILLER about Eight years of Age be bound as an Apprentice to John SMALL to learn the Buisiness of a Shoemaker,

Ordered that William KING be appointed Guardian to Sarah KING orphan of Henry KING decd, and that he give Bond and Security in the sum of Five hundred pounds at same time Francis SPEIGHT & Francis SAUNDERS (blank) came into Court and offered themselves as Securitys &c

(29) 204 Ordered that Thomas MARSHALL George WILLIAMS, Robert PARKER & Charles EURE or any three of them Audit State & Settle the accounts of James PILAND Admr of Thomas PILAND decd &c

An Additional Inventory of the Goods & Chattels rights & Credits which were of the Estate of Dorcas VANN was exhibited into Court by Luke LANGSTON Exor &c

Deed of Sale of Land Luke SUMNER to Daniel FRANKLIN proved by the oath of John BROTHERS &c

Deed of Sale of Land Henry FORREST to Demsey PHELPS Ackd &c

Deed of Sale of Land Luke SUMNER to Kedar BALLARD proved by the oath of Patrick HEGERTY &c

Cyprian CROSS, Charles EURE, & Asa HARRELL, three of the Gentn who were appointed to Audit State and settle the Accots of Israel BEEMAN Admr of Hardy BROWN decd made report of their proceedings

The Last Will and Testament of James PHELPS deceased was exhibited into Court by Humphry HUDGINS & James PRUDEN Exors therein appointed and was proved by the oath of Lodowick PRUDEN one of the subscribing Witnesses thereto and on motion was ordered to be recorded at the same time the said Exor's came into Court and quallified themselves for that office &c

Inventory of the Goods and Chattels rights and Credits which were of the Estate of James PHELPS decd was exhibited into Court by Humphry HUDGINS & James PRUDEN Exors on oath. &c

(30) The Last Will and Testament of James BRADY decd was exhibited into Court by William GOODMAN Exor one of the Exors therein appointed and was proved by the oath of William VANN, one of the subscribing Witnesses thereto and on motion was ordered to be Recorded at same time the said Exor came into Court and quallified himself for that office &c

Inventory of the Goods & Chattels rights & Credits which were of the Estate of James BRADY decd was exhibited into Court by William GOODMAN on oath &c

Deed of Sale of Levin DURE to Josiah GRANBERY Ackd &c with a receipt in the back thereof also ackd

An Additional account of Sales of part of the Estate of Thomas PILAND was exhibited into Court by James PILAND Exor

Additional Inventory of the Estate of Thomas PILAND was exhibited into Court by James PILAND Admr on oath &

Deed of Sale of Land Job FELTON to Uriah EURE proved by the oath of Luke LANGSTON &c

Bill of Sale William BAKER to William LEWIS proved by the oath of Jno BAKER &c

Grand Jury Impannelled & Sworn for Augt Term 1794 vizt. John B WALTON Foreman Timothy WALTON, Samuel EURE, Jonathan WILLIAMS, Jonathan ROGERS, Abraham SPIVEY Demsey BARNES, Charles EURE, Isaac HUNTER, Hillory WILLEY Henry FORREST, Moses BRIGGS William HUNTER & James BAKER

Then the Court adjourned untill tomorrow morning 10 oClock

(31) 206 Tuesday morning the Court met agreeable to adjournment
Present
Christopher RIDDICK)
William GOODMAN) Esqrs Justices
David RICE)
Henry GOODMAN)

The Last Will and Testament of Moses HARE decd was exhibited into Court by Honour HARE Administratrix and was proved by the oath of Kedar BALLARD one of the subscribing Witnesses thereto and on motion was ordered to be Recorded at the same time the said Extx came into Court and quallified herself for that office &c

Inventory of the Goods and Chattels rights & Credits which were of the Estate of Moses HARE decd was exhibited into Court by Honour HARE Extrix on oath &c

Ordered that Francis SAUNDERS pay unto Mary PARKER the sum of five pounds for expenses of the said Mary's lying in and also five pounds a year for Seven years for the maintenance of an Illegitimate the said SAUNDERS begot on the Body of the said Polly PARKER

Accot Current William WARREN with the Estate of Joseph WARREN decd was exhibited into Court by Wm BAKER &c

Accot Current William WARREN with Patience WARREN Eliza WARREN, Josey ELLIS in right of his Wife Mary, Olive WARREN Edward WARREN, and Etheldred WARREN who were Orphans of Joseph WARREN decd, was exhibited into Court by William BAKER Esquire in behalf of William WARREN who was Admr. of Joseph WARREN decd

(32)   In a Suit Admr. of Matthew OMALLEY decd against Admr of Samuel H. JAMESON Jury impannelled & Sworn (to wit) William KING, David CROSS, David LEWIS, Jeremiah SPEIGHT Mills LEWIS, William VOLINTINE, Richard BOND, John LANG Demsey JONES, Elisha CROSS, James CARTER, & John POWELL say the Defendants Intestate did assume and Assess the Plaintiffs damage L67..6..4 with 9..1..8 Interest & further say that the defendant has a right to detain for Debts of equal Nature with the Plaintiffs for his own demand.

Ordered that Jacob EASON Jacob HOBBS, & Isaac COSTEN be fined five pounds each N?iss for their Nonattendance at this Court as Jurymen, &c

Ordered that John BAKER late Sheriff of this County be allowed in the Settlement of his accounts with the public Treasurer the Tax on Bray WARREN two poll Evin JONES one poll, William SMALL one poll, Robert CLEAVES one pole, Saml H JAMESON three poll & Six Wheels of Pleasure, Aaron LASSITER one poll, Joseph BENNETT one poll, James GREGORY one poll & on Claiborn OSTIN two poll

Ordered that John BAKER Esquire late Sheriff of this County be allowed the sum of Sixteen pounds Ten Shillings for Extra services by him performed while he was Sheriff

Deed of Sale of Land William CRAFFORD to Jesse VANN & Benjn BARNES ackd &c

Ordered that Moses HILL, James WALTON, William VOLINTINE & Simon STALLINGS or any three of them make a Division of the Estate of Rachel TROTMAN, decd agreeable to her Last Will & Testament of the deceased

Ordered that William GOODMAN, Henry GOODMAN, Jesse VANN & John ODOM or any three of them make a division of the Estate of Dorcas VANN agreeable to her last Will & Testament &c

(33) 208 ~~Bill of Sale~~ Deed of Gift Elisha NORFLEET, to John BENTON for a Negro Boy named JACOB proved by the oath of Jethro SUMNER Esq &c

Deed of Sale Henry COPELAND to ~~Josiah GRANBERY~~ John ODOM proved by the oath of William HARRISS &c

Henry GOODMAN Esquire who was appointed to take a List of Taxable property in this County for the year 1794 exhibited his proceedings thereon &c

Ordered that William GOODMAN Henry GOODMAN, Jesse VANN & John ODOM or any three of them audite State and settle the accounts of the Executors of Dorcas VANN with the Estate of the decd &c

Ordered that Joseph RIDDICK, David RICE, Jethro SUMNER & Christopher RIDDICK Esquires Contract and agree with John BAKER Esquir for as much Land whereon the Court House of this County now stands as will be sufficient to erect the Public Buildings, for the use of said County and that they take a deed for the same and also that they secure a priviledge to some certain and convenient part of said John BAKER's plantation as will be sufficient for the Perading the Militia on at General Musters &c

In a suit Josiah GRANBERY against Lemuel POWELL Jury Impannelled and Sworn (to wit) William HARRISS, William KING, David CROSS David LEWIS, Jeremiah SPEIGHT, Mills

LEWIS William VOLINTINE Richard BOND, John LANG Demsey JONES Elisha CROSS & James CARTER, say the Obligation declared on is the Act and Deed of the Deft and that there are no setts of and that the Defendant is of full age & ~~that the Defendant is of full age and~~ that he is not an unlettered person and that there is no fraud or circumvention, say that the money therein mentioned is of the Value of ₤25..0..0 ~~Damage~~ with 5..7..6 Damage & 6 Costs

(34)   (Entire entry crossed out.) In a Suit Thomas WHITE against Seth EASON, Jury Impannelled and sworn ~~say~~ (to wit) William HARRISS, William KING, David CROSS, David LEWIS, Isaac CARTER, Mills LEWIS William CRAFFORD Richard BOND,-Entered below- John LANG, Demsey JONES, Elisha CROSS & James CARTER ~~Say~~ Dfse?

Then the Court adjourned until tomorrow morning 9 oCloct

        Wednesday morning the Court met
        Present the Worshipfull Justices

William GOODMAN & David RICE Esquires two of the Gentn. who were appointed to receve lists of Taxables and Taxable property in the Districts of Jethro SUMNER & David LEWIS made report of their proceedings thereon &c

Joseph RIDDICK Esqr. & James GREGORY Esqr. who were appointed to take a List Taxables and Taxabl_ property in the districts of Isaac HUNTER & Jonathan ROBERTS Captains made report of their proceedings &c

In a Suit Thomas WHITE against Seth EASON the Jury being impannelled and sworn to wit William HARRISS William KING David CROSS, David LEWIS Isaac CARTER, Mills LEWIS, William CRAFFORD Richard BOND, John LANG, Demsey JONES, Elisha CROSS, James CARTER, Assess the plaintiffs damage one hundred & three pounds & Six pence Costs.

Ordered that William W RIDDICK, Jethro WILLIAMS, Henry SMITH Thos. SMITH junr. & James B SUMNER be appointed to Patroll in the District of Captn William HARRISS

Christopher RIDDICK, Esquire who was appointed to take a List of the Taxables in the District or Captny of Captn William HARRISS made report of his proceedings &c

(35) 210 Ordered that James COSTEN, David RIDDICK, Riddick TROTMAN, John GORDON, & Noah HARRELL, act as a patroll in Captn Isaac HUNTER's Captaincy

Ordered that Timothy WALTON, Demsey JONES (Odom) Seth ROUNTREE, Timothy FREEMAN & David HARRELL, Act as a Patroll in Captain Jonathan ROBERTS's Captaincy.

Ordered that John VANN, of Jesse, Luten LEWIS, William WARREN junr, Isaac PIPKIN, junr & Bryant SAUNDERS act as a patroll in Captain BETHEYs District.

The State against John BETHEY, Jury Impannelled & Sworn to wit, William HARRISS William KING, David CROSS, David LEWIS, Jeremiah SPEIGHT Mills LEWIS, William VOLINTINE Richard BOND, Francis SPEIGHT, Demsey JONES, John ODOM & James CARTER, say the Deft. is Guilty, Fined by the Court Five pounds

In the Action the State against Miles PARKER, Jury Impannelled and sworn ---- (to wit) William HARRISS, William KING, David CROSS, David LEWIS, Jeremiah SPEIGHT, Mills LEWIS William VOLINTINE, Richard BOND, Francis SPEIGHT Demsey JONES, John ODOM, & James CARTER ~~say the Deft is~~ Miss Trial

Ordered that James SMALL, James JONES, John ELLIS, Robert RIDDICK & Daniel DUKE act as a patroll in the Captaincy of Captn Jethro SUMNER

William BAKER County Trustee of this County of Gates exhibited his account current with the County of Gates aforesaid wherein there appears to be a balance of Sixty Nine pounds three Shillgs & 3½ due the said County &c

(36)   Deed of Sale of Land Joseph RIDDICK to James BAKER acknowledged &c

Deed of Sale of Land Abner ROUNTREE Sarah ROUNTREE his Wife and Priscilla SPIVEY to Lawrence BAKER and John BAKER proved by the oath of Samuel BROWN one of the Subscribing Witnesses thereto &c

Grand Jury discharged

Ordered that the Sheriff Summons, James WALTON, Timothy WALTON, Seth ROUNTREE & Richard BARNES personally to be and appear as Jurymen at the Supr. Court to be held at Edenton for the district of Edenton on the Sixth day of Octr next

Ordered that the Sheriff of this County Summons Henry LEE, Philip LEWIS, Henry SPEIGHT, Thomas BARNES, Abel CROSS, Stephen EURE, Isaac LANGSTON, Levi EURE, William CRAFFORD Cyprian CROSS, Philip ROGERS, William DOUGHTY Demsey WILLIAMS Joel FOSTER, Jesse PARKER, William CLEAVES Abraham MORGAN, Thomas SMITH George WILLIAMS (Clk) Willis BROWN, Aaron HOBBS, William HURDLE, William BERRYMAN, Jacob EASON, Benjamin GORDON, Nathl RIDDICK James SMALL, John SMALL John RIDDICK & George BROOKS personally be and appear at this Court at next term to serve as Jurymen

In a Suit Solomon ROUNTREE against Joseph John SUMNER Jury Impannelled & Sworn, to wit James JONES, James BETHEY John LEWIS, James BRADY, Benjamin BARNES Willis BROWN James CURLE Henry SMITH, Patrick HEGERTY, Demsey WILLIAMS John VANN, Robt PARKER junr. say, the Deft is Guilty & Assess the Plaintiffs damage Twelve pounds & Six pence Costs.

(37) 212 Ordered that Jno PARKER (Gatling) James CARTER Mills LANDING, David HARRELL, Mills EURE, & Lewis SPARKMAN be appointed to Act as a Patroll in the District of Capt David LEWIS

Deed of Sale John BAKER to Thos HUNTER Chairman of Court ackd &c

In a Suit Josiah GRANBERY against Josiah COLLINS Admr of of Saml H JAMESON Jury Impannelled & Sworn to wit John LANG William KING, David CROSS David LEWIS Jeremiah SPEIGHT Mills LEWIS William VOLINTINE, Richard BOND Frans SPEIGHT, Demsey JONES, John ODOM, James CARTER say the Defts.. intestate did assume and assess the Plaintiffs damage Seventy four pounds four? Shillings & Six pence Costs and further say that the Deft. has fully administered and that he has a right to retain in his own hands for debts of a Supr nature.

Presentment made by the Grand Jury against Seth EASON fined 5/.-fee of 6/ paid

Presentment made by the Grand Jury against Joseph John SUMNER fined 5/. fees paid 6/.

Then the Court adjourned until Court in Course
       By Order of the Court
          Test Law BAKER CC

(38) State of No.. Carolina
At a Court of Pleas and Quarter Sessions begun and held for the County of Gates at the Court House on the third Monday in November in the year of our Lord one thousand Seven hundred and Ninety four and Nineteenth year of the Independence of the said State.
Present.
Christopher RIDDICK
William BAKER
David RICE

Ordered that ~~Joseph WEATHERLEY~~ William MILLING ~~orphan of John WEATHERLEY~~ decd be appointed Guardian to Joseph WEATHERLEY orphan of John WEATHERLEY decd and that he give Bond and Security in the sum of Five hundred pounds at the same time William BAKER Esquire came into Court and offered himself as Secy who was approved of &c

William GOODMAN Henry GOODMAN Jesse VANN & John ODOM the Gentlemen who were appointed to audit State and settle the accounts of the Executors of Dorcas VANN decd made report of their proceedings thereon &c

Ruth MORGAN came into Court and mooved for Administration on the Estate of Abraham MORGAN decd which was accordingly granted Ordered that she give Bond & Security in the sum of three thousand pounds at same time Thomas PARKER and Humphry HUDGINS came into Court and offered themselves as Securitys who were approved of &c

(39) 214 Inventory of the Goods and Chattels Rights and Credits which were of the Estate of Abraham MORGAN decd was exhibited into Court by Ruth MORGAN Extx on oath &c

William GOODMAN Henry GOODMAN Philip LEWIS & Francis SPEIGHT three of the Gentlemen who were appointed to Audit State and settle the accounts of John BETHEY Exor of Tristram BETHEY decd made report of their proceedings thereon &c

William VOLINTINE, Simon STALLINGS & James WALTON three of the Gentlemen who were appointed to make a division of the Estate of Rachel TROTMAN decd made report of their proceedings thereon &c

William UMFLEET came into Court and mooved for Administration on the Estate of David UMFLEET decd which was accordingly granted Ordered that he give Bond & Secy in the sum of Five hundred pounds at same time Israel BEEMAN & Josiah HARRELL came into Court and offered themselves as his Securitys who were approved of &c

Inventory of the Goods & Chattels Rights & Credits which were of the Estate of David UMFLEET decd was exhibited into Court by William UMFLEET Admr on oath &c

James GOODMAN came into Court and mooved for Administration on the Estate of Timothy GOODMAN minor Orphan of Joel GOODMAN decd Ordered that he give bond & Security in the sum of Five hundred pounds at same time Henry GOODMAN & Richd BARNES came into Court and offered themselves as Securitys &c

(40) Sarah LASSITER and Isaac COSTEN came into Court and mooved for Administration on the Estate of Timothy LASSITER decd whicch was accordingly granted Ordered that they give Bond & Security in the sum of Six thousand pounds at same time David RICE & James COSTEN came into Court and offered themselves as Securitys &c

Inventory of the Goods & Chattels Rights & Credits which were of the Estate Timothy LASSITER decd was exhibited into Court by Sarah LASSITER Extx & Isaac COSTEN Exor on oath &c

Ordered that Elisha CROSS, Jonathan ROGERS, Hillory WILLEY, Noah FELTON & Richard BARNES be appointed Searchers or patrollers in the Captaincy of Captain Jesse BENTON

Ordered that William ELLIS be appointed Overseer of the Road instead of James SMALL who was appointed patroller

Lease of Land Renthy PHELPS to Clement R. MATTHEWS proved by the oath of Anthony MATTHEWS &c

Deed of Sale of Land Demsey JONES & Uxr to John B. WALTON proved by the oath of Richard BOND &c

Deed of Sale of Land John B WALTON & Uxr to Richard BOND Ackd by Jno B WALTON

The Last Will & Testament of William ODOM decd was exhibited into Court by John ODOM Exor therein appointed and was proved by the Oaths of Francis SAUNDERS & David WATSON the subscribing Witnesses thereto and on motion was Ordered to be Recorded at the same time the said Exor came into Court and quallified himself for that office and prayed an order for letters Testamentary thereon &c And at same time Doctr KEY, Attorney

(41) 216 for the Widdow of the decd and disented to the said Will under the Act of Assembly &c

Inventory of the Goods & Chattels, Rights & Credits which were of the Estate of William ODOM decd was exhibited into Court by John ODOM Exor on oath &c

Ordered that Sarah LASSITOR Admx & Isaac COSTEN Admr.. of the Estate of Timothy LASSITER decd sell as much of the Estate of the decd. as will pay his just Debts &c

Ordered that David RICE James GREGORY & Thomas HUNTER Esquires and Humphry HUDGINS or any three of them make a division of the Estate of Timothy LASSITER decd agreeable to Law

Ordered that Charles CARTER orphan of Charles CARTER about the age of (blank) years be bound as an Apprentice to Richd BARNES to Learn the Buisiness of a Blacksmith &c

Last Will and Testament of Jacob WALTERS decd was exhibited into Court by Mary WALTERS Extx. therein appointed and was proved by the oath of Patience WARREN one of the subscribing Witnesses thereto and on motion was ordered to be Recorded at the same time the said Executrix came into Court and quallified herself for that office and prayed an order for Letters Testamentary thereon &c

Inventory of the Estate of Jacob WALTERS decd was exhibited into Court by Mary WALTERS Executrix on oath &c

(42) The Last Will and Testament of Moses SPEIGHT deced was exhibited into Court by Moses SPEIGHT Executor therein appointed and was proved by the oath of Richard BRIGGS one of the Subscribing Witnesses thereto and on motion was ordered to be Registered at same time the said Exor came into Court and quallified himself for that office & prayed an order for Letters Testamentary thereon &c

Inventory of the Estate of Moses SPEIGHT decd was exhibited into Court by Moses

SPEIGHT Exr. on oath &c

The Last Will of Sarah ALLEN decd was exhibited into Court by William CLEAVES Exor therein appointed and was proved by the oath of George WILLIAMS a Subscribing Witness thereto and on motion was ordered to be Registered at the same time the said Exor came into Court and quallified himself for that office &c

Inventory of the Estate of John GORDON decd was exhibited into Court by Benjn GORDON one of the Exors on oath &c

Deed of Sale of Land Demsey SUMNER to Solomon KING proved by the oath of Jethro SUMNER &c

Deed of Sale of Land John JONES to David HARRELL proved by the oath of Jonathan ROBERTS &c

Deed of Sale of Land Robert NAPPER to William DILDAY ackd &c

Deed of Sale of Land Thomas VANN to William BAKER Acknowledged &c

Deed of Sale of Land Mills RIDDICK Nathl RIDDICK & & David RIDDICK to Moses BRIGGS Proved by the oath of Rachel BRIGGS &c

Bill of Sale David RICE to Abraham RIDDICK Ackd

(43) 218 Deed of Sale of Land James KNIGHT to John DARDEN ackd

Bill of Sale Seth EASON to John KNIGHT proved by the oath of John GORDON &c

Deed of Gift Eliza COSTEN to Peggy SAMESON proved by the oath of Jno CUNNINGHAM & William HARRESS &c

Deed of Gift Eliza COSTEN to Wm HARRISS proved by the oath of John CUNNINGHAM &c

    Then the Court adjourned untill tomorrow morning 10 oClock

    Tuesday Morning the Court met
        Present
        Joseph RIDDICK   )
        David RICE   ) Esquires Justices
        William GOODMAN   )
        Henry GOODMAN   )

Deed of Sale Stephen EURE to Lemuel KEEN Ackd &c

Grand Jury Impannelled to wit. Philip LEWIS Foreman William DOUGHTIE, Levi EURE, John SMALL, George BROOKS Henry SPEIGHT'S, Benjamin GORDON, Philip ROGERS Henry LEE, Thomas BARNES, William BERRIMAN Thomas SMITH Joel FOSTER & Abel CROSS

(44)   Accot of Sales of the Estate of James BRADY was exhibited into Court by William GOODMAN Exr. on oath &c

Ordered that the Sheriff of this County Summons the following persons to attend at this Court the next Term as Patit & Grand Jurors (to wit) John B WALTON James OUTLAW, James FREEMAN, Nathaniel TAYLOR, David HARRELL (of Isaac) Kedar HINTON, Amos

LASSITER Bond MINSHEW, Abraham GREEN, Reuben RIDDICK Richd BRIGGS, Moses DAVIS, John POWELL, James KNIGHT Thomas PARKER, William HARRISS, Jeremiah SPEIGHT John ARNOLD, Micajah RIDDICK jr. Wm BROOKS, Jesse BENTON John LANG, John LEWIS, William KING Benjn BARNES, Charles EURE, Josiah HARRELL, David LEWIS, Jonathan WILLIAMS & Halan WILLIAMS

Ordered that William UMFLEET Admr of David UMFLEET decd sell the perishable part of the Estate of the decd. to make a division

Deed of Sale of Land Demsey JONES & Uxr to John B WALTON proved by the oath of Abraham HURDLE &c

William GOODMAN, Henry GOODMAN John ODOM & Jesse VANN who were appointed to make a Division of the Estate of Dorcas VANN decd made report of their proceedings &c

Ordered that Willie JONES Son of Priscilla JONES about, Twelve years of age be bound as an Apprentice to James SMALL to Learn the Buisiness as a Cooper

(45) 220 Ordered that Miles BENTON Admr of John MORGAN decd. sell as much of the Estate of the decd as will pay his just debts &c

Abraham HURDLE came into Court and mooved for Administration on the Estate of Eliza HURDLE decd which was granted Ordered that he give Bond & Security in the sum of One thousand pounds at the same time Reubin RIDDICK & Thomas HURDLE came into Court and offered themselves as Secys who were approved off &c

Account of Sales of part of the Perishable Estate of William GORDON decd was exhibited into Court by James GATLING Depy Shff on oath &c

In the Action Thomas HURDLE and others against the Last Will of Eliza HURDLE decd, The Jury being impannelled & Sworn to inquire a letter the paper writing exhibited to the Court purporting to be the last Will & Testament of the said Elizabeth HURDLE decd do say that the said writing doth not contain the true last Will & Testament of the said Eliza HURDLE deceased she not being of sound & disposing mind & memory at the time of making & executing the same (Jury to wit) Willis BROWN, William CRAFFORD Stephen EURE, William CLEAVES, Demsey WILLIAMS Aaron HOBBS, William HURDLE, Jacob EASON, James BRADY John LANG, Jesse VANN Francis SPEIGHT & David LEWIS

Thomas MARSHALL Charles EURE & George WILLIAMS three of the Gentlemen that were appointed to Audit State and settle the Accounts of James PILAND Admr of Thomas PILAND decd made report &c

(46) Then the Court adjourned until tomorrow morning 10 oClock

    Wednesday morning the Court met
        Present
        Thomas HUNTER)
        William BAKER)
        Joseph RIDDICK)
        John BAKER)

Ordered that Jesse ROOKS a Mallato Boy Son of Edith ROOKS about five years of Age be bound as an Apprentice to Mills LEWIS to learn the Buisiness of a Cooper

Ordered that Thomas HUNTER & James GREGORY Esqrs William VOLENTINE and Moses HILL or any three of them make a Division of the Estate of Eliza HURDLE decd

Ordered that the County Trustee pay to Wm CUMMING Esqr. Twelve pounds current money of this State for one Years Service as Atto for this County.

The Court taking into consideration the Act of the Genl Assembly relative to the appointment of an Entry taker after delibration thereon William Right RIDDICK was unanimusly elected Entry of Lands in this County Ordered that he give Bond & Secy agreeable to Law at same time Humphry HUDGINS & William HARRISS came into Court and offered themselves his Securitys who were approved of at the same time the said Entry taker quallified himself for that office

(47) 222 Deed of Sale of Land Henry HILL and Himbrick to William LEWIS proved by the oath of Joseph RIDDICK &c

Ordered that Abraham HURDLE Guardian to Jacob SUMNER Sun of Abraham SUMNER sell the said Jacob's part of his Grandmother Elizabeth HURDLEs Estate

Jethro SUMNER, Jethro BALLARD & Kedar BALLARD Esqrs three of the Gentlemen who were appointed to Audit State, and settle the accounts of Jesse BENTON Executor of John BENTON decd, made report of their proceedings &c

Ordered that William GOODMAN Henry GOODMAN Francis SPEIGHT and Benjamin BARNES or any three of them make a Division of the Estates of John GATLING & Edward GATLING deceased &c.

Ordered that Cyprian CROSS Isaac LANGSTON Demsey LANGSTON & Jno PARKER with the surveyor of this County make a Division of the Real Estate of David UMFLEET decd &c

          Jo RIDDICK
          Wm BAKER
          Tho HUNTER

(48) State of North Carolina Feby 16th 1795
    At a Court of Pleas and Quarter Sessions begun and held for the County of Gates at the Court House on the third Monday in February in the year of our Lord one thousand seven hundred & Ninety five
    Present
    Thomas HUNTER)
    Joseph RIDDICK) Esquires Justices
    William GOODMAN)

William GATLING came into Court and mooved for Administration on the Estate of James CANNON decd which was accordingly granted Ordered that he give Bond & Security in the sum of One hundred pounds at same time William BAKER Esquire came into Court and offered himself as his Security who was approved off &c

Ordered that William GATLING Admr of James CANNON decd. sell the Estate of the decd to pay his debts &c

Ordered that Jonathan ROBERTS Admr of Henry FORREST decd sell as much of the Estate of the deceased as will pay his just Debts &c

Ordered that John B WALTON Richd BOND Thomas MARSHALL, & William VOLENTINE or any three of them make a Division of the Estate of Henry FORREST decd &c

(49) 224 Jonathan ROBERTS came into Court and mooved for Adm. on the Estate of Henry FORREST decd which was accordingly granted. Ordered that he give Bond & Security in the sum of Five thousand pounds at same time Samuel HARRELL and David HARRELL came into Court and offered themselves as Securitys who were approved of &c

Inventory of the Goods and Chattels rights and Credits which were of the Estate of Henry FORREST decd was exhibited into Court by Jonathan ROBERTS Admr on oath &c

The Last Will and Testament of Joseph FIGG decd was exhibited into Court by James FIGG one of the Exors therein appointed and was proved by the oath of Robt CUSTESS one of the subscribing Witnesses thereto and on motion was ordered to be Recorded at the same time the said Exor came into Court and quallified himself for that office &c

Inventory of the Goods and Chattels Rights and Credits which were of the Estate of Joseph FIGG was exhibited into Court by James FIGG Exor on oath &c

Deed of Sale Solomon ROSS & Uxr. to Ebron SEARS proved by the oath of William VANN &c

Samuel HARRELL Guardian to Thomas WALTON, John WALTON Melison WALTON, Emelia WALTON & William WALTON Orphans of Thomas WALTON decd exhibited his account current with said Orphans &c

William HINTON Guardian to Robert & Whitmell Orpns of Kedar HILL decd exhibited his accot current with said orpns wherein there appears to be a Bale due Robt HILL the sum of £87..4.1 and to Whitmell HILL the sum of £89..8 5½

(50)   Deed of Sale Thomas BARNES to William WARREN proved by the oath of James GATLING &c

Richard BOND Guardian to Eliza HILL orpn of Guy HILL decd exhibited his accot current with said Orphan wherein there appears to be a bale due the Orpn the sum of £23.13..3½

Inventory of the Goods and Chattels rights and Credits which were of the Estate of Eliza HURDLE decd was exhibited into Court by Abraham HURDLE Admr on oath &c.

Accot of Sales of the Estate of Joel GOODMAN decd was exhibited into Court by James GOODMAN Exor on oath

Accot of Sales of the Estate of Timothy GOODMAN decd was exhibited into Court by James GOODMAN Admr on oath &c

Inventory of the Goods and Chattels Rights and Credits which were of the Estate of Timothy GOODMAN decd was exhibited into Court by James GOODMAN Admr on oath &c

Ordered that Richard BOND Exor of Guy HILL decd sell the property that the Deceased lent his Wife during her life &c

Ordered that David UMFLEET about Sixteen years of Age be bound to Jethro HASLETT to learn the Buisiness of a House Carpenter &c

William BERRYMAN Guardian to James FREEMAN Orphan of Richard FREEMAN decd exhibited his account current with said Orphan wherein there appears to be a Bale due the said

Orphan the sum of £71.0 7½.

(51) 226 Deed of Sale of Land, Job FELTON & Sarah FELTON to Jonatha_ CULLINS proved by the oath of Nathan CULLINS &c

Deed of Sale of Land Abraham RIDDICK to John SIMONS with a receipt on the back was ackd &c

Deed of Sale of Land John HUNTER to Theopholis HUNTER proved by the oath of Joseph ALPHIN &c

Ordered that William HARRESS Humphry HUDGINS Jeremiah SPEIGHT & James B SUMNER or any three of them Audite State and settle the accounts of William CLEAVES Exor of Sarah ALLEN decd &c

Deed of Sale of Land William ARNOLD to Andrew MATTHEWS proved by the oath of John ARNOLD &c

Bill of Sale George BROOKS to Henry COPELAND for a Negro Man MILES proved by the oath of Richd R SMITH &c

Deed of Sale of Land James PHELPS to Noah FELTON proved by the oath of John ARNOLD &c

Deed of Sale of Land Elisha LANDING & Uxr to John PARKER with private examination ef taken by Jos RIDDICK Esqr acknowledged &c

Deed of Sale of Land Charles SMITH to Seth ROUNTREE proved by the Oath of Thomas HUNTER &c

Deed of Sale of Land William WALLIS & Uxr to David CROSS proved by the oath of Benjn HARRELL &c

Deed of Sale of Land Lemuel KEEN to Josiah HARRELL proved by the oath of John ODOM &c

(52) Deed of Sale of Land James LASSITER & Ux to Demsey JONES ackd by James LASSITER

Deed of Sale of Land Silas COPELAND to William GATLING proved by the oath of William GOODMAN &c

Deed of Sale of Land Benjamin EURE & Uxor to Jesse TAYLOR Ackd by Benjn EURE & the signature of Ruth EURE proved by the oath of Mills EURE &c

Deed of Sale of Land John CARTER to Isaac LANGSTON proved by the Oath of John PARKER &c

Deed of Sale of Land Jacob SPIVEY Joseph TAYLOR & Lidia TAYLOR to William VOLINTINE proved by the oath of Moses HILL &c

Deed of Sale of Land John SIMONS & Uxr to John ARNOLD Ackd by John SIMONS

Deed of Gift of Land James OUTLAW to George OUTLAW Junr proved by the oath of Seth ROUNTREE &c

Mary SPIVEY Guardian to Frederick BLANSHARD William BLANSHARD & Mary BLANSHARD Orphans of Absolom BLANSHARD exhibited her account current with said Orphans, wherein there appears to be a balance due Frederick BLANSHARD the sum of £125.17.10. & to William BLANSHARD the sum of £108.10..11 & to Mary BLANSHARD £111.18.6. &c

Elisha HARE Guardn of Mourning NORFLEET orphan of Jacob NORFLEET decd exhibited his accot current with said Orpn wherein there appears to be a bale due her of the sum of £22.15.9

(53) 228 George EASON Guard to Samuel HOBBS orphan of (blank) exhibited his account with said Orphan wherein there appea__ to be a bale due the said Orphan of £24..17..6½

Joseph TAYLOR Guardian to Sally SPIVEY Orphan of Thomas SPIVEY decd exhibited his account Current wth said Orphan wherein there appears to be a balance due her of £49.3.5

Moses HOBBS Guardian to William HOBBS & Jesse HOBBS orpns of Guy HOBBS decd exhibited his account with said Orpns. wherein there appears to be a Bale due William HOBBS the sum of £41..2 10 & to Jesse HOBBS the sum of £31.2.3.

William VOLINTINE Guardian to Henry BAGLEY & Trotman BAGLEY orphans of Jacob BAGLEY & Miles HILL orphan of Kedar HILL decd exhibited his accot Current with said Orphans wherein there appears to be balances due the said Orphans as follows to wit to Henry BAGLEY 0..0 0 to Trotman BAGLEY 144 8.10 & to Miles HILL £83 1.10

Inventory of the Goods and Chattels rights and Credits which were of the Estate of Sarah ALLEN decd was exhibited into Court by William CLEAVES Exor on oath &c

Then the Court adjourned until tomorrow morng 10 oClock

(54)   Tuesday morning the Court met   Feby 17th 1795
         Present
         Thomas HUNTER   )
         James GREGORY   ) Esqrs Justices
         Joseph RIDDICK)

In the suit Miles PARKER against John BETHEY Jury impannelled and sworn (to wit) Abraham GREEN John B WALTON John ARNOLD Bond MINSHEW James FREEMAN William BROOKS Raseter RIDDICK Halan WILLIAMS, David HARRELL Moses DAVIS, John POWELL & Richard BRIGGS say the Deft is Guilty and Assess for the Plaintiffs damag_ Thirty Seven pounds ten Shillings & 6d Costs

Grand Jury Impannelled & Sworn for this term (to wit) William HARRISS Foreman Amos LASSITER, Benjamin BARNES William KING, John LEWIS James KNIGHT Jonathan WILLIAMS Thomas PARKER, Josiah HARRELL, Charles EURE, Jesse BENTON, Kedar HINTON, Jeremiah SPEIGHT John LANG, & Micajah RIDDICK

Demsey TROTMAN Guardian to Joseph SCOTT, Sarah SCOTT & Christian SCOTT Orphans of Sarah SCOTT decd exhibited his accot with said Orphans wherein there appears to be a Balance due the said Orphans as follows (to wit) to Joseph SCOTT £51.3.3 to Sarah SCOTT L38.7.10½ & to Christian SCOTT L44..5.1½

(55) 230 Demsey JONES Guardian to Selah BOND Orphan of Demsey BOND decd on oath&c

Deed of Sale of Land William WALLIS & Uxr to Demsey BARNES proved by the oath of

Jesse VANN &c

William HAYS came into Court and mooved for Administration on the Estate of Wright HAYSE decd which was granted Ordered that he give Bond & Security in the sum of two thousand pounds at same time Jacob HAYS & Holladay WALTON came into Court and offered themselves as Secys who were approved off

Inventory of the Goods and Chattels rights & Credits which were of the Estate of Wright HAYSE decd. was exhibited into Court by William HAYSE Admr on oath &c

Bill of Sale Kedar BALLARD to Isaac HARRELL Junr for a Negro Boy proved by the oath of Josiah GRANBERY one of the subscribing Witnesses &c.

Ordered that George WILLIAMS Robert PARKER senr Humphry HUDGINS & Christopher RIDDICK or any three of them Audite State and settle the accounts of James FIGG Exor of Joseph FIGG decd with sd Estate &c

Ordered that George WILLIAMS Robert PARKER senr Humphry HUDGINS & Christopher RIDDICK or any three of them make a Division of the Estate of Joseph FIGG deceased agreeable to the Will

Seth ROUNTREE Guardian to Peney ROUNTREE orphan of Thom__ ROUNTREE decd. exhibited his accot with said Orphan where there appears to be a balance due the said Orphan the sum of 84:12.__ &c.

(56)   In a suit William WALTERS vs Patrick HEGERTY to wit David LEWIS, William CRAFFORD, George BROOKS, Demsey ODOM, Francis SPEIGHT Henry SPEIGHT, James BRADY Wm HAYSE Demsey JONES (Odom) Abraham HURDLE, Jesse SAUNDERS & John PARKER, On motion of Mr. KEYS the Council of the Plff that this appeal should be dismissed 1st because the Court have not any Jurisdiction of the Court 2d that no appeal from the sentence of the Justice. On agreement the Court were of opinion that they had no jurisdiction & that no appeal did lie from the sentence of the Justice out of Sessions

Thomas PARKER Guardian to Kinchen NORFLEET orphan of Jacob NORFLEET decd. exhibited his account current with said Orphan wherein there appears to be a Balance due the said Orphan the sum of L48..1..6

David KELLY Guardian to Seth SPIVEY orphan of William SPIVEY exhibited his account Current with said Orphan wherein there appears to be a bale due the Orphan the sum of L30..4..7 3/4

Isaac COSTEN & James COSTEN Guardians to Thomas Nathl Benjn Demsey & Eliza. & Polly COSTEN orphans of Demsey COSTEN decd exhibited their account with said Orphans wherein their appears to be a bale due the said Orps the sum of L332.6..8 3/4

Isaac COSTEN & James COSTEN Guardians to Thomas COSTEN Orphans of Demsey COSTEN decd exhibited their accot with the said Orphan their appears to be a balance due the said Orphan the sum of L41..0..7?

Abraham HURDLE Guardian to Jacob SUMNER Son of Abraham SUMNER exhibited his accot current with the said Jacob SUMNER wherein there was a Bale due him the sum of L74..3..1½

(57) In a Suit John LAWRENCE surviving partner of SPARLING & LAWRENCE against Henry SPEIGHT & Francis SPEIGHT Jury impannelled & Sworn (to wit) David LEWIS William CRAF-

FORD, George BROOKS Demsey ODOM John VANN, James BRADY, William HAYSE Demsey JONES (Odom) Abraham HURDLE, Jesse SAUNDERS Seth EASON, & John PARKER, say (End of entry.)

William WALTERS Guardian to Bray BAKER orphan of Samuel BAKER decd. exhibited his account current with said Orphan where there appears to be a balance due the Orphan the sum of £104 19..5½

William WALTERS for Susanna BAKER Guardian to Peggy BAKER orphan of Samuel BAKER decd exhibited her accot on oath of said WALTERS wherein there appears to be a balance due said Orpn the sum of £21..2.4½.

Deed of Sale of Land David SMALL James SMALL & John SMALL to William ELLIS proved by the oath of Patrick HEGERTY &c

Ordered that James GREGORY, Thomas HUNTER David RICE & Isaac HUNTER Esquires or any three of them mak_ a Division of the Estate of Demsey COSTEN decd agreeab__ to the Will &c

Ordered Christopher RIDDICK, William HARRISS Humphry HUDGINS & William WALTERS or any three of them make a Division of the Estate of Edwin SUMNER decd agreeable to his will &c.

Ordered that Christo RIDDICK William HARRISS Humphry HUDGINS & William WALTERS or any three of them Audit Sta__ and Settle the Accots of Jethro SUMNER Admr of Edwin SUMNER ___

(58) Ordered that Hance HAYSE & Howell HAYSE orphans of Wright HAYSE decd be bound as Apprentices to Holloday WALTON to learn the Buisniss of House Carpenters & Wheel Wrights &c

Ordered that Jesse PHELPS orphan of James PHELPS decd. be bound an Apprentice to John SIMONS to learn the Buisiniss of a Wheel Right

Ordered that Thomas HUNTER James GREGORY Moses HILL & William VOLINTINE or any three of them audit State & Settle the accots of Abraham HURDLE Admr of Eliza HURDLE with sd Estate

Then the Court adjourned until tomorrow morning 10 OClock

Wednesday morning the Court met Present Thos HUNTER Joseph RIDDICK Christo RIDDICK Davd RICE Wm GOODMAN & Jas? BAKER Esqrs

Cyprian CROSS, John PARKER, Isaac LANGSTON three of the Gentn who with the Surveyor Patrick HEGERTY was appointed to make a Division of the Estate Real of David UMFLEET made report of their proceedings thereon &c

Ordered that Lawrence BAKER Clerk of this Court be allowed the sum of Eighteen pounds ten Shillings for Extra Services by him performed the year passed

Willis BROWN Guardian to Nancy GARROTT Orphn of James GARROTT decd exhibited his account current with said Orpn wherein there appears to be a Bale due said Orphan the sum L1007.2.11

Ordered that Mills BENTON be appointed Overseer of the Road instead of Moses HARE decd

(59) 234 John B WALTON Guardian to Guy HILL Orphan of Kedar HILL decd exhibited his account Current with said Orphan where in there appears to be a balance due said Orphan the sum of 84.5.9½

James GATLING Guardian to Hillir?y ROGERS orphan of Stephen ROGERS decd exhibited his accot current with said Orphan where in there appears to be a bale due the said Orphan the sum of of L57..4..11½

James GATLING Guardian to John ROGERS orphan of Stephen ROGERS decd. exhibited his accot current with said Orphan --- wherein there appears to be a balance due the said Orph__ the sum of £15.1.3½

Ordered that the Sheriff of this County Summons Benjn GORDON Patrick HEGERTY Joseph RIDDICK Esq & Demsey JONES (Odom) personally to be and appear as Jurymen at the Supr Court in Apl next

Ordered that the Sheriff of this County Summons Jacob PEIRCE William BOND, James JONES, William PEARCCE Levi EASON Solomon EASON, James BAKER, William HUNTER Noah HARRELL, James COSTEN, James BARNES Miles ROUNTREE James WALTON, Jacob HOBBS Henry LEE Thomas BARNES Abel CROSS Stephen ROGERS, James BRADY Levi EURE Cyprian CROSS Isaac LANGSTON, Elish HARRELL James B SUMNER, James FIGG Thomas SMITH Demsey WILLIAMS William DAUGHTIE & Peter PARKER personally be and appear at this Court next Term as Jurymen

(60) Jacob BENTON Orphan of Isaac BENTON came into Court and made choice of David BENTON for his Guardian Ordered that he give Bond & Security in the sum of One hundred pounds at same time the said Thomas PARKER and William ELLIS came into court and offered themselves as Secys. &c

Ordered that the Admr of Timothy LASSITER sell the perishable property of the decd &c

Ordered that John SMALL be appointed Overseer of the Road from the Folly to POWELLs Mill

James BAKER Guardian to Thomas TROTMAN Orphan of Thomas TROTMAN decd exhibited his account current with said Orphan wherein there appears to be a balance due said Orphan the sum of £127..14.11

Thomas MARSHALL Guardian to John HILL orpn of Guy HILL decd exhibited his account with said Orpn wherein there appears to be a balance due said Orphan the sum of 34.13.9

Stephen ROGERS appointed Guardian to William ROGERS orphan of Stephen ROGERS decd. Ordered that he give Bond & Security in the sum of Five hundred pounds at same time James GATLING & Patrick HEGERTY came into Court and offered themselves as secys &c

Stephen ROGERS appointed Guardian to John ROGERS Orpn of Stephen ROGERS decd Ordered that he give Bond & Security in the sum of Five hundred pound at Same time James GATLING & Patrick HEGERTY came into Court and offered themselves as secys &c

(61) 236 Ordered that Jethro SUMNER, Miles BENTON, William HINTON John RIDDICK, & John DARDEN with the Surveyor of this County make a Division of the Real Estate of Isaac BENTON decd, agreeable to the prayer of the Patition

By Order
Law BAKER CC

Feb. 1795

(62) State of No.. Carolina   May 18th 1795

At a Court of Pleas and Quarter Sessions begun and held for the County of Gates at the Court House on the third Monday in May in the year of our Lord one thousand Seven hundred and Ninety five & Nineteenth year of the Independence of the said State

Present
Thomas HUNTER)
Christopher RIDDICK)
William GOODMAN) Esquires Justices
Henry GOODMAN)

James FIGG appointed Guardian to Willis FIGG orphan of Joseph FIGG decd. Ordered that he give Bond & Security in the sum of Five hundred pounds at the same time William James B SUMNER & Jas TUGWELL came into Court and offered them selves as Securitys who were approved off &c

Ordered that John HOFFLER be appointed Overseer of the Road instead of Jas WALTON Resigned &c

Ordered that the County Surveyor attend Jesse VANN, John ODOM, Cyprian CROSS, Demsey HARRELL, & Isaac LANGSTON in the Division of a Certain Tract of Land on Chowan River between Hardy MURFREE and (blank) DUNN Orpn of George DUNN decd

Bill of Sale for a Negro Girl SUE Elisha NORFLEET to Abraham HARRELL ackd &c

(63) 238 Bill of Sale John RICHARDS to William DOUGHTIE proved by the oath of Humphry HUDGINS &c

Deed of Sale of Land Francis SPEIGHT to Isaac PIPKIN ackd

Bill of Sale for a Negro Girl NANCY Peter FOSTER & Thos RANSONS to Isaac HARRELL junr proved by the oath of Humphry HUDGINS &c

Bill of Sale of Land for a Negro Boy ROBIN George EASON senr to Abraham HARRELL proved by the oath of Humphry HUDGINS &c

Deed of Sale of Land James DAVIS & Ux to James HODGES with a rect. on the back thereof proved by the oath of George BROOKS &c

Deed of Sale of Land Daniel ELLIS to William CRAFFORD proved by the oath of David HARRELL &c

Ordered that Jesse TAYLOR be appointed Overseer of the Road instead of Elisha LANDING resigned

Ordered that Andrew SAVAGE Orphan of William SAVAGE about Ten years of age be bound as an apprentice to Elisha HARRELL to Learn the Buisiness of a Cooper.

Deed of Sale for Land James HAYSE to William HAYSE proved by the oath of Holloday WALTON &c

Accot of Sale of the Estate of Wright HAYSE decd was exhibited into Court by William HAYSE on oath

Additional Inventory of the Goods & Chattels Rights & Credits which were of the Estate of Wright HAYSE decd was exhibited into Court by Wm HAYSE Admr &c

(64) Lease of Land Jas B SUMNER to William HALL ackd.

Bill of Sale ~~of Land~~ for a Negro Boy JIM Elisha NORFLEET to John DARDEN proved by the oath of Jethro SUMNER &c

Inventory of the Goods & Chattels rights & Credits which were of the Estate of James A CANNON decd was exhibited into Court by William GATLING Admr. on oath &c

Account of Sales of the Estate of ~~James~~ A CANNON decd was exhibited into Court by William GATLING senr. Admr. on oath &c

James NORFLEET Guardian to Mary ROUNTREE orphan of Charles ROUNTREE exhibited his account current with said Orphan wherein there appears to be a Balance due the said Orphan the sum of £2076..6..4.

Accounts of Sales of the Estate of John MORGAN decd was exhibited into Court by Miles BENTON Admr on oath &c

Saml EURE Guardn. to Nancy EURE orphan of Enos EURE decd exhibited his account current with said Orphan wherein there appears to be a Bale due said Orpn of £28..6..2½.

Deed of Sale of Land Lodowick BROOKS to Edward PILAND proved by the oath of William BROOKS &c

Ordered that Joseph RIDDICK, James GREGORY, James BAKER, & Isaac HUNTER or any three of them (End of entry.)

Deed of Sale of Land William SAUNDERS to John LANG proved by the oath of Jno ODOM & Uriah ODOM &c

Account of Sales of the Estate which was left by Guy HILL decd to his Wife during her Life, was exhibited into Court by Richd BOND Exr of said Guy HILL

(65) 240 (Entire entry crossed out.) Agreeable to the Patition of Sarah LASSITER Relict of Timothy LASSITER decd Ordered that the Sheriff of this County Summons a Jury and Lay off the dower of the said Widow ----- Josiah GRANBERY & Isaac HUNTER & Jos RIDDICK or any three of them with the Sheriff & Surveyor lay off the Dower agreeable to Law

Robert POWELL came into Court and mooved for Administration on the Estate of James POWELL decd which was accordingly granted Ordered that he give Bond and Security in the sum of One thousand pounds at the same time Daniel POWELL and Moses DAVIS came into Court and offered themselves as Securitys &c

William BAKER Esquire County Trustee exhibited his accot current with said County wherein there appears to be a Balance due the County the sum of £87.3..2½

Deed of Sale of Land Luke SUMNER to Joseph Jno ___? SUMNER Ackd

James GREGORY, Isaac HUNTER & David RICE three of the Gentn who were appointed to make a Division of the Estate of Demsey COSTEN decd made report of their proceedings thereon &c

James GREGORY Thomas HUNTER & William VOLINTINE three of the Gentn who were appointed to make a Division of the Estate of Eliza HURDLE decd made report of their proceedings thereon

James GREGORY, Thos HUNTER, & William VOLINTINE three of the Gentlemen who were appointed to Audite state & Settle the accounts of Abraham HURDLE Admr of Eliza HURDLE with the Estate of the Decedent

(66)   Ordered that the sum of two Shillings be levied on each poll __ this County and Eight pence on each hundred Acres of Land, for a County Tax for the year 1794.

Ordered that the Sheriff of this County sell the old Jail of this County tomorrow three oClock at Six Months Credit

Inventory of the Goods & Chattels rights and Credits which were of the Estate of James POWELL decd. was exhibited into Court by Robert POWELL Admr on oath &c

(Entire entry crossed out.) Saml WILLIAMS came into Court and mooved for Admin__

Saml WILLIAMS appointed Guardian to Mills WILLIAMS Jonathan WILLIAMS & Frederick WILLIAMS his own Children Ordered that he give Bond & Security in the sum of Fifty pounds at same time Jonathan WILLIAMS & Demsey WILLIAMS came into Court and offered themselves as Securitys &c

Ordered that David COPELAND orphan of Jesse COPELAND about Thirteen years of age, be bound as an Apprentice to Levin DEURE to learn the Buisiness of a Taylor.

Ordered that Robt POWELL sell as much of the perishable part of the Estate of James POWELL decd as will pay his just Debts.

Ordered that Kedar BALLARD Robt RIDDICK Samuel HARRELL & Richd BRIGGS or any three of them make a Division of the Estate of James POWELL decd agreeable to Law

        Then the Court adjourned until tomorrow morning 10 oClock

(67) 242   Tuesday morning the Court met
            Present James GREGORY   )
                    Joseph RIDDICK   ) Esquires Justices
                    David RICE   )
                    William GOODMAN)

Account of Sales of part of the Estate of James BRADY decd exhibited into Court by William GOODMAN Exr on oath

Grand Jury impannelled for this Term to wit James BAKER Foreman, Isaac LANGSTON, Elijah HARRELL James JONES James BRADY, Solomon EASON, Stephen ROGERS James WALTON Miles ROUNTREE, Cyprian CROSS, Abel CROSS Levi EURE, Thomas BARNES, Levi EASON, & Jacob HOBBS

Deed of Sale of Land John BAKER late Sheriff of this County to John DORLON ackd &c

Accot. of Sales of the Estate of James PHELPS senr. decd was exhibited into Court by Humphry HUDGINS one of the Exors on oath &c

In the Action Thomas HIATT against John BETHEY Jury impannelled & Sworn (to wit)

May 1795

James B. SUMNER, Henry LEE. Jacob PIERCE, James BARNES, Peter PARKER, Thomas SMITH. William HUNTER, Demsey WILLIAMS, James FIGG, John POWELL David LEWIS, & Francis SPEIGHT, say the Defendant is not Guilty. Justices on the Bench when the above Action was on trial John BAKER, Joseph RIDDICK & Davd RICE Esqrs.

(Entry crossed out.) Ordered that Demsey WILLIAMS be fined ___

(68)   William LEWIS came into Court and mooved for Administration on the Estate of William GLOVER? decd. which was accordingly granted Ordered that he give Bond & Security in the sum of One thousand pounds at the same time Thomas MARSHALL & Leven DURE came into Court and offered themselves as Securitys who were approved off &c

Ordered that William LEWIS Admr of William GLOVER decd sell so much of the Estate of the Decedent as will pay his just Debts &c

Deed of Sale of Land Willis SPARKMAN & Uxr to Nathan CULLENS proved as to Willis SPARKMAN by David LEWIS &c

Deed of Sale of Land Edward BERRYMAN to James BAKER proved by the oath of Joseph DAVIS &c

In the Action Henry MERONEY against Elisha NORFLEET Jury impannelled & Sworn to wit James B SUMNER Henry LEE Jacob PIERCE, James BARNES, Peter PARKER, Thomas SMITH William HUNTER, James FIGG, John POWELL, David LEWIS Francis SPEIGHT & William CRAFFORD, say Plaintiff called & Nonsuit

Ordered that Lewis SPARKMAN Constable be allowed Twenty four Shillings for his services Summoning the Citizens in the Captaincy of Captn David LEWIS &c to return lists of their Taxables & Taxable propy

Ordered that Jethro MILTIAR Constable be allowed Twenty four Shillings for his Services summoning the Citizens in this Captaincy of Captn Jonathan ROBERTS's Capty &c

Agreeable to an order of this Court made yesterday for selling the Jail of this County the Sheriff made his report of his proceedings to wit that he had sold the said Jail to John BAKER for £7.5.6 at 6 Months Credit

(69) 244 Account of Sales of part of the perishable Estate of Timothy LASSITER decd sold Decr. 16 1794 was exhibited in to Court On oath by James GATLING Depy Sheriff

Account of Sales of the perishable Estate of David UMFLEET decd sold 27 Nov 1794 was exhibited into Court on oath by James GATLING, Depty Shff

Account of Sales of the Estate of William ODOM decd Sold by John ODOM was exhibited into Court by James GATLING Depy Sheriff Dep on Oath &c

On Motion of Doctr. Ebinezer GRAHAM praying from the Court a Certificate of his Citizenship. Ordered that the Clerk of this Court do grant to the said Ebinezer GRAHAM a Certificate under the Seal of the County Certifying that this Court hath received Satisfactory information that the said Ebinezer GRAHAM is a Native Born within the Limits of the United States of America and that he hath resided in this County since the Month of August in the year of our Independence the 13th and of our Lord one thousand Seven hundred & Eighty Eight during which time the said Ebinezer GRAHAM has Conducted himself with honesty & Sobriety.

Bill of Sale for a Negro Man HARRY Micajah RIDDICK to Moses HINES proved by the oath of William HARRISS &c

In the Action the Admrs. of Saml H JAMESON against Luke SUMNER Jury impannelled and Sworn (to wit) James B SUMNER Henry LEE, Jacob PIERCE, James BARNES, Peter PARKER Thomas SMITH William HUNTER, James FIGG John POWELL, David LEWIS Francis SPEIGHT & William CRAFFORD say the Defendant did assum_ and Assess for the Plaintiffs Damage Thirty pounds & Six pence Costs, &c

Agreeable to the Peto of Sarah LASSITER Relict of Timothy LASSITER decd Ordered that the Sheriff of this County Summons a Jury and lay off the Dower of out of the Estate of the decd agreeable to Law

(70)   Joseph RIDDICK Esquire Guardian to Joseph TROTMAN Love TROTMAN & Willis TROTMAN and his account account with Joseph Love & Willis TROTMAN, was exhibited into Court on oath by the said Joseph RIDDICK

The Court taking into consideration the Act of the Genl Assembly respecting the appointment of a Sheriff after mature delibration thereon Henry GOODMAN was unaminously appointed to that office Ordered that he give Bond & Security agreeable to Law, at same time William GOODMAN & John BAKER Esqr came into Court and qualified offered themselves as Securitys who were approved off &c at the same time the said Sheriff took and subscribed the oath of office &c Majistrates on the Bench Thomas HUNTER William GOODMAN John BAKER Christo RIDDICK William BAKER

   Then the Court adjourned until tomorrow morning 10 oClock

   Wednesday Morning the Court met
      Present
      Christopher RIDDICK)
      Joseph RIDDICK   )
      William GOODMAN   ) Esquires Justices
      James GREGORY   )
      John BAKER   )

(71) 246 Ordered that the Sheriff of this County Summons Isaac PIERCE Nathaniel RIDDICK John HOFFLER, Abraham HURDLE, Richard MITCHELL Thomas HOBBS, William BERRYMAN, Thomas HOFFLER Amerias BLANSHARD John RIDDICK, Jethro BENTON Elisha BRINKLEY, Mills BENTON, William MATTHIAS, Elisha HARE, James KNIGHT John ARNOLD Noah FELTON Philip ROGERS, Micajah RIDDICK junr Moor CARTER Robert PARKER junr. Willis BROWN, John WARREN Demsey LANGSTON Charles EURE Josiah HARRELL, David CROSS Richd BARNES Binj BARNES John LEWIS personally be and appear before the Justices of this Court at Next Term to Serve as petit and Grand Jurors

Ordered that the following Justices of the peace of this County receive Lists of the Taxables and Taxable property from the Citizens of this County (to wit) William GOODMAN Esquire in Captn John BETHEYs Captaincy Jethro SUMNER Esquire in Captain Jesse BENTONs Captaincy Christo RIDDICK in Captn William HARRISS's Captaincy, John BAKER in Captain David LEWIS's Captaincy, David RICE in Captain Jethro SUMNERs Captaincy, Thomas HUNTER Esquire in Captain Isaac HUNTERs Captaincy & Simon STALLINGS Esquire in Captn. Jonathan ROBERTSs Captaincy, and that they make report to this Court next Term &c

In the Action James ROBBINS against John ODOM & William WATSON Jury impannelled & Sworn (to wit) James B SUMNER, Henry LEE Jacob PIERCE, James BARNES, Peter PARKER,

Thomas SMITH William HUNTER James FIGG, Demsey WILLIAMS, William HARRISS Reubin RIDDICK & Francis SPEIGHT, say the Deft is Guilty of the Assault & Battery charged in the plaintiffs Declaration & assess four pounds Damage & Six pence Costs

(72)   Ordered that Thomas HUNTER, John B WALTON, Simon STALLINGS & James WALTON or any three of them Audite State and settle the Accounts of the Admr of John ROUNTREE decd. with the Estate of the Decadent.

Ordered that Reubin RIDDICK be appointed Constable in the room of Thomas HURDLE resigned

Ordered that William SUMNER an Illegitimate Child Son of Martha SUMNER be bound as an Apprentice to Bray SAUNDERS to learn the Buisiness of a Cooper

Deed of Sale of Land Ebinezer GRAHAM to James GATLING proved by the oath of James B SUMNER

Account of Sales of part of the perishable Estate of Henry FORREST decd was exhibited into Court by James GATLING Deputy Sheriff on oath &c

Humphry HUDGINS Constable exhibited his account current (written over) Against the County for Services done in his office Ordered that the County Trustee pay him the sum of Six pounds &c

William WALTERS Constable exhibited his account with this County wherein there appear: to be a Balance due him of Six pounds Ordered that the County Trustee pay the same.

Agreeable to the Petition of James BROWN and Willis BROWN Ordered that William GOODMAN Christopher RIDDICK & Joseph RIDDICK with the Surveyor of this County make a Division of Lay off the Legacies in a Certain Tract of Land left in the last will and Testament of Moses SPIVEY to James BROWN Willis BROWN & Sarah DANIEL & her two Daughtes: &c By Order Law BAKER CC

(73) 248 State of No.. Carolina
         Gates County) ssts?
                     At a Court begun and held at the Court House in the County of Gates on the fifth day of June in the Nineteenth year of the Independence of the said State and in the year of our Lord one thousand seven hundred & Ninety five, summoned for the purpose of trying MIKE a Negro Man Slave named MIKE the property of James B SUMNER accused of Felony, (to wit)

          William BAKER   )
          Christopher RIDDICK)
          John BAKER   ) Esquires Justices
          William GOODMAN   )

MIKE the prisoner was brought to the Bar who pleaded not Guilty, Jonathan PARKER the prosecutor after being duly sworn as a Witness in behalf of the State sayath that on Satturday Night llast preeeeding the 30th of May last passed his smoke House was broken open and Six Midlings of Bacon stolen therefrom, (Remainder of line blank.) CAMBRIDGE a Negro Man belonging to the Estate of Edwin SUMNER decd. after being Charged to tel the truth and nothing but the truth, sayeth that on Satterday night last he met the prisoner at the Bar at the Corner of Mrs. Busheba SUMNERs Kitchen & that he the prisoner asked him if he knew where he could get some meat his answer to him was no, he the prisoner further asked him if Jonathan PARKER's smoke house was covered with Shingles or Punching &? he he told him it was covered with punchings, he then asked the

(74) Witness if the door was locked he told him it was tied with a string yes they then parted that night, on the next morning he the Witness met the prisoner and that he told him he had been and got some Meat

Jury being impannelled & Sworn to wit Philip LEWIS James BRADY, Francis SPEIGHT, Mills LEWIS, John VANN, Cyprian CROSS David CROSS David LEWIS, Thomas BARNES, Joseph BRADY, Robert PARKER, & Willis BROWN all owners of Slaves say the Prisoner at the Bar is (form the circumstantial proof that has been given) is that he is Guilty The Court then proceeded to pass Judgment which is in the following words Ordered that the Sheriff MIKE Receive thirty Nine lashes well laid on his bare back by the Sheriff

By order of the Court
Law BAKER C

(75) 250 State of North Carolina   August 17th.. 1795
         Gates County) ss.
                        At a Court of Pleas and Quarter Sessiones begun and held for the County of Gates at the Court House on the third Monday of August in the Twentieth year of the Independence of the State aforesaid and in the year of our Lord one thousand seven hundred and Ninety five.
         Present
         John BAKER   )
         William GOODMAN)
         David RICE   )

Grand Jury Impannelled & Sworn to this Tarm (to wit) Charles EURE Foreman Elisha HARE, Philip ROGERS, Noah FELTON, Elisha BRINKLEY, William BERRYMAN, Mills BENTON, John LEWIS, Josiah HARRELL, Nathl RIDDICK Demsey LANGSTON, Thomas HOFFLER Willis BROWN & Thos HOBBS.

Deed of Gift Isaac HARRELL sr to Isaac HARRELL jr ackd, &c

Ordered that William GOODMAN Esqr. Isaac PIPKIN, Francis SPEIGHT & Hillory WILLEY or any three of them Audit State & Settle the accounts of James GOODMAN Exor of Joel GOODMAN decd and also that they make a Division of the Estate of the Testator agreeable to his Will

(76) Ordered that William GOODMAN Esqr. Isaa PIPKIN jr Francis SPEIGHT & Hillory WILLEY Audit State and settle the Accounts of James GOODMAN Admr of Timothy GOODMAN decd and that they also make a Division of the Estate of the Decedent agreeable to Law

Deed of Sale of Land Henry Ebron SEARS & Uxr. to Hardy CROSS Ackd by Henry E SEARS and signature of Mary SEARS proved by the oath of Danl DUKE &c

Deed of Sale of Land Augustin MINSHEW to George LASSITER proved by the oath of Moses LASSITER &c

Deed of Sale of Land James MATTHEWS & Uxr to Jacob PRUDEN Ackd by James MATTHEWS &c

Deed of Gift Easther MATTHEWS to James MATTHEWS proved by the oath of James PRUDEN &c

Bill of Sale for Negro Girl CHERRY John WARREN to John PARKER proved by the oath of

William WARREN jr &c

Bill of Sale for a Negro Boy JACK John WARREN to William WARREN proved by the oath of John PARKER &c

Last Will & Testament of Sarah LASSITER decd was exhibited into Court by Isaac HUNTER & James COSTEN Executors therein appointed and was proved by the oath of Isaac COSTEN one of the subscribing Witnesses thereto and on motion was ordered to be Recorded at the same time the said Exrs. came into Court and quallified themselves for that office &c

(77) 252 Inventory of the Goods & Chattels Rights & Credits which were of the Estate of Sarah LASSETER decd was exhibited into Court by Isaac HUNTER & James COSTEN Executors on oath &c

Last Will & Testament of Joel GOODMAN decd was exhibited into Court by William GOODMAN one of the Exrs. therein appointed and was proved by the oath of William GOODMA_ Esquire one of the subscribing Witnesses thereto and on motion was ordered to be Recorded at the same time the said Exor came into Court and quallified himself for that office &c

Inventory of the Goods & Chattels Rights & Credits which were of the Estate of Joel GOODMAN decd was exhibited into Court by William GOODMAN Exr. on oath &c

Deed of Sale of Land Moses BRIGGS to Josiah BRIGGS proved by the oath of Nathl RIDDICK &c

Bill of Sale for Negro Man JAMES Thomas BILLUPS to John B WALTON proved by the oath of Willis BROWN &c

Ordered that Robert RIDDICK Esqr. be appointed Guardian to Demsey BOND & Thomas BOND orphans of Demsey BOND decd and that he give Bond & Security in the sum of one thousand pounds at the same time John B WALTON & Richard BOND came into Court and offered themselves as as Securitys who were approved of &c

Isaac PIPKIN Esqr. Guardian to Sarah ROGERS orphan of Stephen ROGERS decd exhibited his account with said Orphan &c

(78)   James GREGORY Simon STALLINGS & Jethro SUMNER Esquires present

Bill of Sale for Negro Woman CLARISSA & Child RANDELL James B SUMNER to Lawrence BAKER with a Receipt on the back thereof, ackd &c.

Ordered that the Sheriff of this County Summon a Jury and allot & lay off to Ruth MORGAN Relict of Abraham MORGAN decd her Dower in the Real Estate of the decd &c agreeable to her Patition

Deed of Gift of Land Jeremiah SPEIGHT to William SPEIGHT Ackd &c

Ordered that Jethro SUMNER Kedar BALLARD, William HARRISS & Miles BENTON or any three of them make a Division of the Estate of Abraham MORGAN decd &c

James FIGG Guardian to Willis FIGG exhibited an account of the Sales of the perishable part of the Estate of the said Orphan amounting to £71..16.2.

Deed of Sale of Land Jethro BALLARD & David RICE Exors of James SUMNER decd. to Charles POWELL ackd

Bill of Sale for a Negro Boy TOM Sarah LASSITER Green STEED Jean LASSITER Sarah LASSITER & Frederick NEWBY to Aaron LASSITER proved by the oath of Charles POWELL &c

Deed of Sale of Land Enos ROGERS to Jonathan ROGERS proved by the oath of Jonathan WILLIAMS &c

Deed of Sale of Land John KITTRELL & Uxr. to Jonathan WILLIAMS Acknowledged by John KITTRELL &c

(79) 254 Ordered that James KNIGHT pay a Tax on five hundred & Sixteen Acres Land instead of five thousand & Sixteen which was returned by mistake for the year 1794 &c

Jesse VANN Cyprian CROSS John ODOM & Isaac LANGSTON With Patrick HEGERTY the surveyor of this County who were appointed to make a Division of a Certain Tract of Pecoson Land on Chowan River between Colo Hardy MURFREE & Susanna DUNN orphan of George DUNN decd made report of there proceedings thereon &c which is as follows (to wit) Pursuant to an order of Court we the Subscribers met on Tract of Pocoson Land surveyed for Colonel MURFREE & George DUNN on the east side of Chowan River & and made the following Division (to wit) Allotted to Colo MURFREE No 2 according to the Survey thereof begining at a Cypress on the side of the River a Corner in the patent then down the River to a mark'd Cypress thence through the pocoson a North west Course or thereabouts to Buckhorn Creek, thence up sd Creek & with the patent bounds to the first Station for one hundred Acres Allotted to Susanna DUNN orphan of George DUNN No 1. according to the survey thereof Begining lat a mark'd Cypress on the side of the River thence down the River to the mouth of Buckhorn Creek thence up sd Creek to the dividing Line thence to the begining for one hundred Acres Given under our hands & Seals this 13th Augt. 1795 Jesse VAN LS. Cypn CROSS LS John ODOM LS Isaac LANGSTON LS. Pa HEGERTY Surveyr.

Isaac PIPKIN jr Francis SPEIGHT Henry SPEIGHT & Philip LEWIS the Gentn, who were appointed to Audit State & Settle the Accot, of Fereby PARKER Executrix of Francis PARKER decd and also to make a Division of the Estate of the Desedent made report of their proceedings &c

(80) Bond James CARTER to John CARTER & Uxr proved by the oath of John ODOM &c

Willis WIGGINS came into Court and mooved for Administration on the Estate of Stephen MASON decd, Ordered that he give Bond & Security in the sum of Thirty pounds at same time Jethro SUMNER Esquire & Lewis WALTERS came into Court and offered themselves as Securitys &c

Inventory of the Goods & Chattels rights & Credits which were of the Estate of Stephen MASON decd was exhibited into Court by Willis WIGGINS Administrator on oath &c

Ordered that Jacob JOHNSON be exempt from paying a Poll Tax for the year 1794.

Ordered that Miles BENTON, Jethro SUMNER, Kedar BALLARD William HARRISS & Micajah RIDDICK jmr with the surveyor of this County make a Division of the E (written over) Real Estate of Abraham MORGAN decd agreeable to Law.

Ordered that the Sheriff of this County be allowed in the Settlement of his Accounts for the following Insolvents for the year 1794 Hardy REID Hardy ROBINS Lewis SUMNER John DAVIS William CARTER Menney MITCHELL John ROBBINS Elisha ROBBINS Samuel ROBBINS Benjn REID Ann HARRELL Edward KELLY &c

Ordered that the Sheriff of this County (say Simon STALLINGS) be allowed the sum of Sixteen pounds ten Shillings for extra Services by him performed the year passed &c

(81) 256 Then the Court adjourned until tomorrow morning 10 o Clock

   Tuesday Morning the Court met
    Present James GREGORY
        Jethro BALLARD
        David RICE
        Jethro SUMNER

Ordered that James GATLING Constable be allowed the sum of one pound four Shillings for 3 days warning the Inhabitants in Captn BETHEYs Capty to return a list of their Taxable property &c

Ordered that Henry GOODMAN, Isaac PIPKIN junr Francis SPEIGHT & Henry COPELAND or any three of them audit state & settle the accounts of William GOODMAN Exr. of James BRADY decd & also that they make a Division of the Estate of the Decedent agreeable to the Will

Ordered that Isaac MILLER Senr. be appointed Constable in the room Humpy HUDGINS resigned.

Inventory of the Goods and Chattels right & Credits which were of the Estate of William GLOVER decd was exhibited into Court by William LEWIS Admr. on oath &c

Acco. Sales of the Estate of William GLOVER decd was exhibited into Court by William LEWIS Admr on oath &c

Deed of Sale of Land Francis SPEIGHT & Henry SPEIGHT to William CRAFFORD proved as to Francis SPEIGHT by Benjn BARNES & Henry SPEIGHT ackd in open Court &c

(82) Jethro SUMNER Esqr who was appointed to receive lists of the Taxable property from the Citizens in Captn Jesse BENTONs Capty made report of his proceedings &c

Thomas HUNTER Esqr. who was appointed to receive lists of the Taxable property from the Citizens in Captn Isaac HUNTERs Captaincy made report of his proceedings &c

Deed of Sale of Land Patrick HEGERTY to Noah FELTON Ackd &c

Aaron BLANSHARD came into Court and mooved for Admn on the Estate of Demsey BLANSHARD decd which was accordingly granted, Ordered that he give Bond & Security in the sum of One thousand pounds at same time Palatiah BLANSHARD & James HODGES came into Court and offered themselves as Securitys who were approved of &c

In the Action Josiah COLLINS Admr of Saml H JAMESON against Jethro BALLARD Jury Impannelled & Sworn (to wit) James KNIGHT William MATTHIAS John RIDDICK, John ARNOLD, Abraham HURDLE Micajah RIDDICK jr. Moor CARTER Richd MITCHELL John HOFFLER Amerias BLANSHARD Richard BARNES & William GATLING Junr. say the Deft. did assume and assess

Aug. 1795

for the Plaintiffs damage the sum of ₤23.10..6 & 6d Costs

David RICE Esquire who was appointed to receive lists of the Taxable property from the Citizens of Capt. Jethro SUMNERs Captaincy made report of his proceedings &c

(83) 258 Willis FIGG Orphan of Joseph FIGG decd came into Court and made Choice of George WILLIAMS Clerk for his Guardian ordered that he give Bond & Security in the sum of Six hundred pounds at same time William HARRISS & Jonathan ROBERTS came into Court and offered themselves as Securitys &c

Inventory of the Goods & Chattles Rights & Credits which were of of the Estate of Demsey BLANSHARD decd was exhibited into Court by Aaron BLANSHARD Admr on oath &c

Ordered that Aaron BLANSHARD Admr of Demsey BLANSHARD decd sell so much of the Estate of the Decadent as will pay his just Debts

In an Action Josiah COLLINS Admr of Saml H JAMESON against William WALTERS, Jury impannelled & Sworn (to wit) James KNIGHT, William MATTHIAS, John RIDDICK John ARNOLD Abraham HURDLE Micajah RIDDICK jr. Moor CARTER Richd MITCHELL John HOFFLER, Amerias BLANSHARD Richard BARNES & William GATLING Junr. say that the defendant did assume and Assess for the Plaintiffs Damage to the sum of ₤7..4..4 & 6 d Costs.

In an Action Thomas LENORE against William WILLIAMS Jury Impannelled & Sworn to wit James KNIGHT, William MATTHIAS John RIDDICK John ARNOLD Abraham HURDLE Micajah RIDDICK Junr. Moor CARTER Richard MITCHELL John HOFFLER Amerias BLANSHARD Richd BARNES & Wm GATLING say the Obligation declared on is the Act & Deed of the Defendant & that there are no payments or set offs, and Assess the Plaintiffs Dame?. by way of Interest ₤2..10..0. & 6d Costs

(NOTE: Page 259 was omitted in the original page numbering.)

(84) 260 Ordered that John BAKER & James GREGORY & Lawrence BAKER or any two of them Audit State & Settle the Accounts of Josiah COLLINS Admr of Samuel H JAMESON &c

Ordered that William BAKER Esquire be appointed Overseer of the Road in the room & stead of James BROWN

Ordered that Moses HILL Overseer of the Road from James BAKER's to the swamp run Kedar Moses HILLs, take charge and keep the said Road from said Swamp to the Bennetts Creek Road near John B WALTONs Plantation with the hands under his direction

Ordered that the Sheriff of this County Summons James B SUMNER, James WALTON, Timothy WALTON & Demsey BARNES personally to be and appear as Jurymen at the Supr Court to be held for the District in Octr. next,

Ordered that the Sheriff of this County Summons George BROOKS Stephen ROGERS, Isaac LANGSTON Elisha HARRELL Demsey JONES (Odom) James JONES of David Miles ROUNTREE Thomas BARNES John B WALTON, Thomas HURDLE, Solomon EASON Benjamin GORDON, Isaac COSTEN, William VOLINTINE Demsey TROTMAN James BROWN, William BROOKS, Wm BOYCE Robert PARKER, John PILAND David BRINKLEY Amos PARKER John POWELL William ARNOLD, Richd BRIGGS Jethro BENTON Elisha BRINKLEY (son of John) Levi LEE, Levi EASON & James THOMAS? personally to be and appear at this Court at next Term as Jurymen,

Ordered that Luten LEWIS be appointed Constable instead of James GATLING resigned Ordered that he give Bond & Security agreeable to Law at same time Abel CROSS John

Aug. 1795

LEWIS & James GATLING came into Court and offered themselves as Securitys &c

(85)　　In the Action the Exrs. of Pleasant TWINE against Seth EASON Jury impanelled & Sworn (to wit) James KNIGHT, Wm MATTHIAS John RIDDICK, John ARNOLD, Abraham HURDLE Micajah RIDDICK Jr. Moor CARTER Richard MITCHELL John HOFFLER, Amerias BLANSHARD Richard BARNES & Abel CROSS, say that the Deft, hath made no payments nor set off's nor shewn any satisfaction or release & assess the Plffs Damage to 6d, &, 6d Costs they further say that the value of a Dollar is 10s

On Motion Ordered that Joseph RIDDICK James GREGORY Isaac HUNTER & Jethro SUMNER or any three of them Audit state and settle the accounts of Jethro BALLARD & David RICE Esquires ~~or any three of them Audit~~ Exors of James SUMNER decd and as Admrs. of Luke SUMNER decd &c

Simon STALLINGS who was appointed to receive a List of Taxables and Taxable property in Captn ROBERTS Capty made report of his proceedings &c

Ordered that Sarah HUGHS ~~be exempt~~ f pay a Tax only on one poll instead of four which was returned to her

　　　　　　　　　　　　　Jo RIDDICK
　　　　　　　　　　　　　David RICE
　　　　　　　　　　　　　James GREGORY

(86)　262　State of No Carolina
　　　　　　　　　　At a Court of Pleas and Quarter Sessions begun and held for the County of Gates at the Court House on the third Monday in Novr. in the Twentieth year of the Independence of the said State Anno Domini 1795

　　　　　　　Present
　　　　　　　Christopher RIDDICK)
　　　　　　　John BAKER　　　　　) Esquires Justices
　　　　　　　William GOODMAN　　)

Bill of Sale for a Negro Girl ABB Charles KING to Thomas BARNES proved by the oath of Thomas PARKER &c

Deed of Sale of Land Abraham RIDDICK to John SIMONS proved by the oath of William BOYCE

Release Isaac POWELL to William POWELL proved by the oath of John ARNOLD &c

Grand Jury impannelled & Sworn to wit Benjn GORDON James BROWN, Levi LEE, James THOMAS, John PILAND Stephen ROGERS, George BROOKS Miles ROUNTREE Levi EASON, Wm VOLINTINE Thomas BARNES, William BROOKS William BOYCE Jno B WALTON, & Isaac COSTEN

　　　　　Then the Court adjourned until tomorrow morning 10 oClock

(87)　　Tuesday Morning the Court met
　　　　　　　Present
　　　　　　　David RICE　　　)
　　　　　　　William GOODMAN) Esquires Justices
　　　　　　　Simon STALLINGS)

Bill of Sale Thomas PHILLIPS to Demsey LANGSTON for a Negro Man named DAVEY proved by the oath of Isaac LANGSTON &c

Deed of Sale of Land James LASSITER to Charles Matthew SMITH proved by Joel FOSTER &c

Deed of Sale Joel FOSTER & Uxr, to Charles SMITH Ackd __ &c by Joel FOSTER

Deed of Sale of Land John POWELL to Nicholas MINOR Ackd __ &c

Deed of Sale of Land Luke SUMNER to John BRINKLEY -- Ackd. __ &c

Lease of Land David WATSON to Mary BEASLY proved by the oath of John ELLIS one of the subscribing Witnesses thereon &c

Last Will and Testament of Richard BOND decd was exhibited into Court by William BOND & Richard BOND Executors therein appointed and was proved by the oath James GREGORY and David RICE Esquires two of the Witnesses thereto and on motion was ordered to be Recorded at the same time the said Exrs. quallified themselves for that office &c

Inventory of the Goods & Chattels Rights & Credits which were of the Estate of Richd BOND decd was exhibited into Court by Wm BOND & Richd BOND Exrs. &c

(88) 264 Last Will & Testament of Demsey TROTMAN decd was exhibited into Court by Ezekial TROTMAN Exr. therein appointed and was proved by the oath of Thomas TWINE & Noah TROTMAN two of the Witnesses thereto and on motion was ordered to be Registered at the same time the said Exor came into Court and quallified himself for that office &c

Inventory of the Goods and Chattels Rights and Credits which were of the Estate of Demsey TROTMAN decd was exhibited into Court by Ezekial TROTMAN Exr on oath &c

William GOODMAN I PIPKIN junr. & Hillory WILLEY three of the Gentn. who were appointed, to Audit State and settle the Accounts of James GOODMAN Admr of Timothy GOODMAN and Also a Division made by the above Gentn &c

William GOODMAN I PIPKIN jr. Hillory WILLEY three of the Gentn.. who were appointed to Audit State & Settle the accounts of James & John GOODMAN Exrs. of Joel GOODMAN decd and also to make a Division of the Estate of the decadent made report of their proceedgs thereon &c

Isaac PIPKIN Junr, Henry COPELAND & Francis SPEIGHT three of the Gentn who were appointed to Audit State & Settle the accounts of William GOODMAN Exor of James BRADY decd & also to make a Division of the Estate of the decedent made report of their proceedings thereon

Deed of Gift Isaac HARRELL to Levin DEURE for one Negro Girl named PLEASANT and one Negro woman named MOLL proved by the oath of Saml HARRELL &c

(89) Deed of Sale of Land with a Rect thereon William ELLIS & Uxr to Levin DEURE Ackd by William ELLIS in person & the Signature of Mary ELLIS proved by the oath of Jethro BALLARD &c

Ordered that Judith SUMNER wife of Luke Willis WIGGINS & Patty WILKINSON & Tresey BROTHERS be summoned Nisa?

Bill of Sale with a Rect thereon James NORFLEET to Robert DICKINS for a Negro Woman

FRANK & Child ISAAC proved by the oath of Jethro BALLARD &c

Ordered that Jonathan ROBERTS be appointed Guardian to Thomas FORREST Henry FORREST Ann FORREST & Susanna FORREST orphans of Henry FORREST decd and that he give Bond & Security in the sum of Three thousand pounds (blank) at the same time John B WALTON & Timothy WALTON came into Court and Offered themselves as Securitys who were approved of

Ordered that Ezekial TROTMAN Exr. of Demsey TROTMAN decd sell so much of the Decedent's Estate as will pay his just Debts &c

Deed of Sale of Land Abraham RIDDICK to Thomas RIDDICK proved by the oath of James HODGES &c

Deed of Sale of Land Abraham RIDDICK to Bond MINSHEW proved by the oath of James HODGES &c

Deed of Sale of Land Henry SPEIGHT to Francis SPEIGHT proved by the oath of Philip LEWIS &c

Deed of Sale of Land Jesse BENTON to Robt F BENTON proved by the oath Pa HEGERTY &c

Deed of Gift Jesse SAUNDERS to Bray SAUNDERS ackd.

(90) 266 Deed of Sale with Rect thereon Luke SUMNER & Uxr to William ELLIS Ackd by Luke SUMNER,

Deed of Sale of Land Luke SUMNER to William ELLIS Ackd.

Kedar BALLARD Samuel HARRELL & Richd BRIGGS three of the Gentn.. who were appointed to make a Division of the Estate of James POWELL decd made return of their proceedings thereon &c

Robt POWELL Admr of James POWELL decd exhibited an account of Sales of the decedent on oath &c

Deed of Sale of Land John KITTRELL to Demsey WILLIAMS proved by the oath of Wm BAKER Esqr &c

        Then the Court adjourned until tomorrow morning 10 o Clock

        Wednesday morning the Court met
            Present
        James GREGORY)
        David RICE   ) Esquires Justices
        John BAKER   )
        William GOODMAN)

Jethro SUMNER Esquire appointed Guardian to David Edwin SUMNER orphan of Edwin SUMNER decd Order'd that he give Bond with Security in the sum of three thousand pounds at same time William GOODMAN & Miles BENTON came into Court and offerd themselves as Security &c

(91) Ordered that William CUMMING Esqr Atto for the State in this County be allowed the sum of Twelve pounds for one years Services the year passed and that the

County Trustee pay the same &c

The State against John HAMILTON
Ordered that Colo Jno HAMILTON be fined the sum of Twenty five pounds for a Contempt to the said Court for committing an Assault on Seth EASON before this Court and that he give Security for better behaviour until this Court in the sum of two hundred pounds & each Security in the sum of one hundr? pounds at next Term, at same time Josiah GRANBERY & Thos HUNTER Esquires came into Court and offered themselves as Securitys who were approved off &c

Ordered that William BAKER Esqr repair the Windows and Window Shutters of the Court House for this same County and that he be allowed for the same

Agreeable to the Pato of Barshiba SUMNER Ordered that the Sheriff of this County Summons a Jury and lay off and Allot to the said Barshiba SUMNER Relict of Edwin SUMNER decd her Dower &c

Last Will and Testament of Solomon KING decd was exhibited into Court by Henry GOODMAN one of the Executors therein appointed and was proved by the oaths of William GOODMAN & James GATLING two of the subscribing witnesses thereto and on motion was ordered to be Recorded at same time said Exr. came into Court and quallified themselves himself for that office &c

Deed of Sale of Land Moses WILLIAMS to Thomas SMITH proved by the oath of Isaac MILLER sr? &c

(92) 268 Agreeable to the Pato. of Sally FORREST Relict of Henry FORREST Ordered that the Sheriff of this County summon a Jury and lay off the Dower of the said Sally FORREST agreeable to Law &c

Agreeable to an order of the County Court made last Term to lay off the Dower of Ruth MORGAN relict of Abraham MORGAN decd the Sheriff made the following return (to wit) Gates County, agreeable to an order hereunto annexed we the Subscribers Jurymen after being summoned Quallified for that purpose have laid off Ruth MORGAN right of Dower of Land as follows viz.. begining at a Stake in the dividing line between Seth MORGAN & Abraham MORGAN thence runing to a Parsimmon tree thence to a sliped pine thence along a sliped line to two sliped Rid oaks, thence runing Northwestwardly to William ARNOLDs line then binding on said ARNOLDs line to the dividing line between Seth MORGAN & Abraham MORGAN thence runing their dividing line to a Red oak from thence to a Chinkapin Tree and thence to a Stake in a Ditch thence runing said Ditch to a Dead oak a corner tree, thence runing a straight to a live white oak thence runing a sliped line to a sweet Gum standing in a branch thence along said branch to run of Bennetts Creek thence runing up Bennetts Creek to the dividing line between Seth MORGAN & Abraham MORGAN thence along the dividing line to the first Station Septr 3d day 1795 Hillory WILLEY Henry GRIFFIN Halon WILLIAMS, Jonathan WILLIAMS Wm MATTHEWS Anthony MATTHEWS, Noah FELTON Micajah RIDDICK John ARNOLD Miles BENTON Lewis WALTERS & Jethro BENTON

(93) Ordered, that Willis BROWN Thomas MARSHALL, Thomas HUNTER & William VOLINTINE or any three of them audit state and settle the accounts of William WILLIAMS Admr of Abner BLANSHARD decd &c

Ordered that Miles BENTON be appointed Overseer of the Road wher_ Moses HARE decd was formerly overseer &c

Ordered that Elijah HARRELL be appointed Overseer of the road instead of Edwd PILAND Resigned. &c

Ordered that John TAYLOR orphan of Jonas TAYLOR decd about thirteen years of Age be bound as an Apprentice to Miles ROUNTREE to learn the Buisiness of a Cowper &c

Ordered that the Sheriff of this County Summons Robert PARKER, Jeremiah SPEIGHT William CLEAVES Thomas SMITH Moor CARTER Kedar BALLARD Thomas PARKER, Mills BENTON, Elisha HARE, Robert RIDDICK James BARNES, James COSTEN, Noah HARRELL Timothy WALTON, James WALTON, Amos LASSITER, James FREEMAN Hillory WILLEY, William DOUGHTIE, John ARNOLD Jonathan ROGERS, Micajah RIDDICK John LEWIS Mills LEWIS Francis SPEIGHT, Richard BARNES John Parker GATLING Demsey LANGSTON Cyprian CROSS & Asa HARRELL personally to be and appear at this Court next Term as Jurymen

(94) 270 Ordered that Isaac PIPKIN junr be appointed as Deputy Sheriff of this County at the same time he came into Court and quallified himself for that office &c

Ordered that Reuben PILAND orphan of Peter PILAND decd about Eight years of age be bound as an Apprentice to Edward PILAND (of Edwd) to learn the Buisiness of a Farmer.

Then the Court adjourned until Court in Course

> David RICE
> Wm GOODMAN
> Simon STALLINGS

(95) State of North Carolina 15 Feby 1796
Gates County

At a Court of Pleas and Quarter Sessions begun and held for the County of Gates at the Court House on the third Monday in February in the year of our Lord one thousand seven hundred & ninety Six & twentieth year of the Independence of the State aforesaid.

Present
William BAKER)
John BAKER) Esquires Justices
Jethro SUMNER)

Deed of Sale of Land William LEWIS to John BAKER for a Tract of Land in the County of Tenassee in the Cumberland Settlement proved by the oath of Mary GLOVER &c

Agreeable to an order of this Court at last Term, to lay off the Dower of Sally FORREST Relict of Henry FORREST decd the Sheriff made the following return (to wit) Agreeable to an Order of Court hereunto annexed, we the subscribers herein? alotted and laid off Sally FORREST Relict of Henry FORREST decd right of Dower which is bounded as follows vizt Begining at a Hickery standing in Captn Jonathan ROBERTS' line, thence a SWest Course to a white Oak standing in the head of a Bottom then to a stake standing in the Orchard then a SWest Course to a Stake on the other side the Orchard, thence a SEast course to a Persimn Tree, thence a Straight Course to D FULKS's line thence down said FULKS's line to the Creek thence up the Creek to the Pocoson then

(96) 272 up the Pocoson to ROBERTS's line then along the said ROBERTS's line to the first Station John B WALTON, Seth ROUNTREE Willis BROWN, Aaron HOBBS, James FREEMAN, David HARRELL, Josiah his X mark PARKER Ameriah BLANSHARD Timothy WALTON

Agreeable to an order of this Court at last Term, to lay of the Dower of Bathsheba SUMNER Relict of Edwin SUMNER decd the Sheriff made the following Return (to wit) Agreeable to an order of Court hereunto annexed we the Subscribers have met and laid off Bathsheba SUMNERs Dower Relict, Widow of Edwin SUMNER decd which is bounded as follows vizt Begining at Demsey PARKERs line where it Crosses HUGHES read Old Road, thence along the said Road to the Poly Bridge Branch near the old Plantation, thence down the said Branch to the little Percoson Branch, thence up that Branch to H GRIFFITHs line thence along the said GRIFFITHs line to Sally WILLEYs line thence along her line to the Knotty pine swamp then down the said Swamp to VANNs line thence along VANNs line to I PARKER's line thence along said I PARKERs line to D PARKERs line thence along D PARKERs line to first Station Mills LEWIS, James BRADY Ebron SEARS, William DOUGHTIE Daniel PARKER, Henry COPELAND Henry GRIFFIN Elisha CROSS Isaac PARKER, Demsey PARKER Jonathan ROGERS Cyprian GOODMAN.

Grand Jury impannelled & Sworn (to wit) Kedar BALLARD Foreman, Thomas SMITH, Jonathan ROGERS Demsey LANGSTON, William DOUGHTIE, Micajah RIDDICK Richard BARNES Robert PARKER Asa HARRELL, Hillory WILLEY John Parker GATLING, Mills LEWIS, James FREEMAN Cyprian CRO__ Amos LASSITER & Moor CARTER

(97)   The Commissioners for leting the building of a Jail in this County reported that John BAKER became the undertaker and had built the said Jail agreeable to contract it is therefore Ordered that the County Trustee pay the said John BAKER the sum of One hundred & thirty three pounds that being the sum it was undertaken at

Ordered that the Negroes which belonged to Edward RIDDICK decd orphan decd of James RIDDICK decd be sold at Public Sale and the money arising from such sale to be equally divided between those who have a right to receive the same

Ordered that the Sheriff of this County Summon a Jury and lay off the Dower of Sally FORREST Relict of Henry FORREST

Christian MORRISS came into Court and mooved for Administration on the Estate of Ephraim MORRISS decd, which was accordingly granted Ordered that she give Bond & Security in the sum of Five hundred pounds at same time James FREEMAN & Henry HILS? (blank) came into Court and offered themselves as Securitys who were approved off &c

Mary HARRELL Orphan of Lemuel HARRELL decd came into Court and made choice of Lewis SPARKMAN as her Guardian ordered that he give Bond & Security in the sum of Five Hundred pounds at same time Moor CARTER & Stephen EURE came into Court & quallified & offered themselves as Secys &c

(98) 274 Ordered that the Indentures of Charles CARTER orphin of Charles CARTER who was bound to Richd BARNES be delivered up to his Mother Ann RITTER & ---- BARNES? &c

Ordered that John BRINKLEY act as overseer of the Road in the district & stead of Wm MATTHIAS resignd

Ordered that Robert RIDDICK act as Overseer of the Road in the Dastrict and stead of Moses DAVIS resigned

Abraham HURDLE Guardian to Jacob SUMNER Son of Abraham SUMNER exhibited his account with said Jacob wherein there appears to be a balance due him the sum of Ninety five pounds three Shillings & Eleven pence

Inventory of the Goods and Chattles Rights and Credits which were of the Estate of

Ephraim MORRIS decd was exhibited into Court by Christian MORRIS Administratrix on oath &c

Deed of Sale of Land William HAYSE & Jacob HAYSE to Joseph DAVIS, acknowledged &c

William HINTON Guardian to Robert & Whitmell HILL orphans of Kedar HILL decd. exhibited his account Current with said Orphans wherein there appears to be a Balance of Eighty Nine pounds two Shillings & 7½ due Robert HILL & the sum of One hundred pounds one Shilling & 1 3/4 due to Whitmell HILL.

Agreement Lott ROGERS to Demsey ODOM proved by the oath of William GOODMAN &c

(99)   Deed of Sale of Land John LANG James LANG and Elizabeth LANG to Henry LEE proved by the oath of Hillory WILLEY

Miles ROUNTREE Administrar of John ROUNTREE decd exhibited into (written over) an account of Sales of the Estate of the deceased on oath &c

Thomas HUNTER, John B WALTON, & James WALTON three of the Gentlemen that were appointed to audit state & settle the accounts of the Administrator & Administratrix, made report of there proceedings &c

Bill of Sale for a Negro Man JACK Luke SUMNER to Simeon BRINKLEY ackd. &c

Deed of Sale of Land Richard FREEMAN to Charles POWELL Ackd &c

Deed of Sale of Land Moore CARTER to Elee? GREEN & Martha GREEN proved by the oath of Israel GREEN BEEMAN &c

Deed of Sale of Land Stephen ROGERS to Levi EURE Ackd.

William BERRIMAN Guardian James FREEMAN orphan of Richard FREEMAN exhibited his accot with said Orphan wherein there appears to be a Balance due the said orphan the sum of L89.16.6

Bill of Sale for two Negroes VIOLET & WINNEY Wm CARTER to William MATTHIAS ackd.

The Last Will and Testament of James OUTLAW decd was exhibited into Court by Seth ROUNTREE George OUTLAW & Isaac COSTEN Executors therein appointed and was proved by the oath of James FREEMAN one of the subscribing Witnesses thereto and on motion was ordered to be Recorded at the same the said Executors came into Court and quallified themselves for that office &c

(100) 276 Inventory of the Goods and Chattels Rights and Credits which were of the Estate of James OUTLAW was exhibited into Court by Seth ROUNTREE George OUTLAW & Isaac COSTEN Exors on oath

William HARRISS, Humphry HUDGINS William WALTERS & Christo RIDDICK the Gentn who were appointed to make a Division of the Estate of Edwin SUMNER decd made report of their proceedings &c

Deed of Sale of Land Seth MORGAN & Ux to John ARNOLD proved by the oath of John HUDGINS &c

Account of Sales of the personal Estate of Demsey TROTMAN decd was exhibited into

Court by Ezakial TROTMAN Exr on oath

Deed of Sale Isaac HARRELL to David HARRELL proved by the oath of Henry MERONEY &c

William VOLENTINE, Guardian to Henry BAGLEY, Trotman BAGLEY orphan of Jacob BAGLEY decd. & Miles HILL orphan of Kedar HILL decd exhibited his account with said Orphan wherein there appears to be a Balance due Henry BAGLEY the Guardian from H BAGLEY the sum of £8..5.0 and there appears to be a Balance due Trotman BAGLEY the sum of £146..1.1. & to Miles HILL the sum of £77..14.10

Joseph TAYLOR Guardian to Sally SPIVEY orphan of Thos SPIVEY exhibed his account with said Orphan wherein there appears to be a Balance due said Orphan the sum of £49..4..5

Deed of Sale of Land Richard BRIGGS to Robert RIDDICK proved by the oath of Humphry HUDGINS &c

Deed of Sale of Land John VARNELL to Demsey BARNES provd by the oath of John VANN &c

William JAMES Guardian to Wm BLANSHARD & Mary BLANSHARD exhibited his accounts with said Orphan wherein there appears to be a Bale due to William the sum of £108..10.11 & to Mary the sum of £111..18.6.

(101)   Deed of Sale Gift of Land James HAYSE to John HAYSE proved by the oath of Abraham RIDDICK &c

Deed of Sale of Land Abraham RIDDICK to James HAYSE ackd

Lease of Land Francis SAUNDERS to Thomas RITTER proved by the oath of Uriah ODOM &c

Last Will of Zilpha ROGERS was exhibited into Court by Jonathan ROGERS one of the Executors therein appointed & was proved by the oath of William GOODMAN one of the subscribing witnesses thereto and on motion was ordered to be Recorded at same time the said Exr. came into Court and quallified himself for that office &c

Inventory of the Goods and Chattels Rights and Credits which were of the Estate of Zilpha ROGERS decd was exhibited into Court by Jonathan ROGERS Exr.

Last Will of Moses WILLIAMS was exhibited into Court by Henry SMITH one of the Exrs. therein appointed and was proved by the oaths of Jonathan SMITH & Thomas SMITH junr. two of the Witnesses thereto and on motion was ordered to be Registered at the same time the said Executor came into Court and quallified himself for that office &c

Inventory of the Goods and Chattels Rights and Credits which were of the Estate of Moses WILLIAMS decd was exhibited into Court by Henry SMITH Exr on oath &c

Deed of Sale of Land Samuel SMITH to Moses WILLIAMS was Ackd &c

    Then the Court adjourned untill tomorrow morning &c

(102) 278 Tuesday Morning the Court met
    Present James GREGORY)
        David RICE   ) Esqrs Justices
        Simon STALLINGS)

Inventory of the Goods & Chattels rights & Credits of Solomon KING decd was exhibited into Court by Hy GOODMAN Executor &c

Demsey JONES (Odom) Guardian to Selah BOND Orphan of Demsey BOND decd exhibited his account with said Orphan wherein there appears to be A Balance due said Orpn £5..15.0

Agreeable to an Order of this Court at February Term last Jethro SUMNER, Miles BENTON, William HINTON, John RIDDICK & John DARDEN with the surveyor of this County were appointed Commissioners to make a Division of the Real Estate of Isaac BENTON decd who made report of their proceedings &c

In the Action of Ejectment Jno ELLIS against Benjamin BARNES Jury impannelled & Sworn to wit, James BARNES, Timothy WALTON, Jeremiah SPEIGHT, James COSTEN, Elisha HARE, James WALTON, John LEWIS John ARNOLD, Robert RIDDICK, Mills BENTON Noah HARRALL & Francis SPEIGHT say that the Plaintiff Defendant is Guilty &c

(Note: Approximately three lines have been left blank between these two entries.)

Ordered that Jno B WALTON Kedar HINTON, Jonathan ROBERTS & Miles ROUNTREE or any three of them make a Division of the Perishable Estate of Demsey BLANSHARD decd agreeable to Law

(103)   Seth ROUNTREE Guardian to Peny ROUNTREE Orphan of Thomas ROUNTREE decd exhibited his Account with said Orphan wherein there appears to be a Bale due said Orpn the sum of £87.4.5

Ordered that Seth ROUNTREE Geo OUTLAW & Isaac COSTEN Executors of James OUTLAW decd sell as much of the perishable Estate of the decedent as will pay his just Debts &c

Deed of Sale of Land Charity MORRIS & David HILL to William LEWIS proved by the oath of Thos MARSHALL

Deed of Sale of Land Jonathan NICHOLS & Mary NICHOLS to James BAKER proved by the oath of John HARE

Deed of Sale of Land William LEWIS to Levin DURE proved by the oath of Thomas MARSHALL

Deed of Sale of Land William LEWIS to James BAKER proved by the oath of Jonathan ROBERTS &c

Deed of Sale of Land Levin DURE to James BAKER Ackd, &c

Deed of Sale of Land Stephen ROGERS to John PARKER Ackd.

Deed of Sale of Land Asa UMFLEET to William UMFLEET proved by the oath of John PARKER &c

The Last Will of William LEWIS decd was exhibited into Court by Joseph RIDDICK Noah HARRELL & Jonathan ROBERTS Executors therein appointed and was proved by the oath of Levin DURE one of the subscribing witnesses thereto and on motion was ordered to be Recorded at the same time the said Exrs. quallified themselves for that office &c

Ordered that a Commission Issue to the County of Nansd Virga to take the private examination of Eliza ALLEN Wife of Edwd ALLEN to a Deed passed by them and Katey REID to Wm HARRISS &c

Feb. 1796

(104) 280 Account of Sales of the Estate of Sarah LASSITER decd was exhibited into Court by Isaac HUNTER Executor on Oath &c

Demsey WILLIAMS Guardian to Saml BAKER Orphan of Saml BAKER decd exhibited his accot with said orphan wherein there appears to be a Bale due the Orphan the sum of £61.14..6½

Jonathan WILLIAMS Guardian to Blake BAKER orpn. of Saml BAKER decd exhibited his accot wherein there appears to be a Bale due to the sd Orphan £39..4..8 3/4

John B WALTON Guardn. to Guy HILL orphan of Kedar HILL decd exhibited his account wherein there appears to be a bale. due the said Orpn the sum of £87..11..1½

James BAKER Guardn. to Thoms TROTMAN orphan of Thos TROTMAN decd. exhibited his account, wherein there appears to be a balance due the said orphan £135.0.9.

Account of Sales of the Estate of John DAVIS decd was exhibited into Court with a certificate thereon of his making oath to the sum

James RAWLS Admr. of William BOOTH decd exhibited his accot with the orphans of said BOOTH wherein there appears to be a Bale due them £26..18. 4 3/4

Jonathan ROBERTS Guardian to John PARKER, Kedar PARKER James PARKER Nancy PARKER & Prissey PARKER orphans of Jos PARKER decd exhibited his accot wherein there appears to be a Bale due John the sum of £16.14.6 to Kedar £16..14.6 and to James Nancy & Prissey L16..14..6 each

Joseph RIDDICK Esqr. Guardn. to Joseph TROTMAN Love TROTMAN & Willis TROTMAN & to Joseph Love & Willis TROTMAN jointly wherein there appears to be Balances due the said Orps as follows (to wit) To Joseph £83.15.0 To Love £68.13.4½ to Willis £323..6..5½ & to Joseph Love & Willis jointly £179..12.8

Ordered that William BAKER John ODOM Cyprian CROSS & Israel BEEMAN with the surveyor of this County make a Division of the Real Estate of Lemuel HARRELL decd.

(105)   Ordered that Seth ROUNTREE be appointed Inspector of the County in the stead of James OUTLAW Deceased.

       Then the Court adjourned until to morrow morning 10 oClock

          Wednesday Morning the Court met
          Present
          James GREGORY)
          John BAKER   ) Esquires Justices
          David RICE   )

Ordered that Christopher RIDDICK, William W. Wright RIDDICK James SUMNER & Robert PARKER or any three of them make a Division of the Estate of Wright HAYSE de_d

The State against Abel CROSS Jury impannelled & Sworn (to wit) James BARNES, Timothy WALTON, James COSTEN Elisha HARE, John ARNOLD, Robert RIDDICK, Mills BENTON Noah HARRELL Francis SPEIGHT, Patrick HEGERTY HEGERTY Demsey ODOM & Stephen ROGERS, say the Defendant is Guilty of the Assault & Battery charged in the Bill of Indictment.

Feb. 1796

Ordered that Ezekial TROTMAN Exr. of Demsey TROTMAN decd sell the Estate of the decd as a division of the said Estate may be made &c

Ordered that Henry HOBBS be appointed Overseer of the Road instead of William BERRIMAN Al Moses HILL resigned &c

(106) 282 Ordered that the Sheriff Summons Samuel EURE, William BROOKS, David LEWIS, Stephen EURE, John ODOM, John PILAND William VOLENTINE, Moses HILL, Aaron HOBBS Thomas HOFFLER Willis BROWN, James BAKER, Thomas HURDLE, Isaac COSTEN Nathl RIDDICK, James JONES (of Lewis David) John RIDDICK, Richd BRIGGS, David BENTON, William ARNOLD, James KNIGHT Simeon BRINKLEY, William MATTHIAS, George BROOKS Jethro BENTON, Thomas PARKER, Micajah PHELPS, Moses DAVIS, William BOND, & Richard BOND, &c as Jurors.

Ordered that the Sheriff Summons, William HARRISS Miles BENTON David HARRELL & Richard MITCHELL to serve as Jurors at the Supr. Court at Edenton &c

Ordered that Lawrence BAKER Clerk of this Court be allowed the sum of Eighteen pounds Ten Shillings for extra Services performed by him the year passed

Ordered that Daniel RIDDICK DUKE be appointed Constable in the Captaincy of Jethro SUMNER instead of William ELLIS decd Ordered at the same time that he give Bond & Security agreeable to Law, at the same time Jonathan ROGERS & James B SUMNER came into Court and offered themselves as his securitys who were approved of &c

Ordered that the Sheriff of this County Summons a Jury & allot and lay off to Zelpha POWELL Relict of James POWELL decd her dower in Lands which the decedent died siezed and possessed

Ordered that Aaron BLANSHARD Admr to the Estate of Demsey BLANSHARD decd, sell the perishable Estate of sd deceased that a Division may be made

(107)   Bill of Sale Law & William BAKER for a Negro Boy JACOB to John PARKER Ackd. &c

John ELLIS came into Court and mooved for Administration on the Estate of William ELLIS decd, which was accordingly granted Ordered that he give Bond & Security in the sum of Two Thousand pounds at the same time Kedar BALLARD & James SMALL came into Court and offered themselves as Securitys &c

Ordered that William SPEIGHT be appointed Guardian to Anna FORREST & Susanna FORREST orphans of Henry FORREST decd and that he give Bond & Security in the sum of Five hundred (blank) pounds current money at same time Jeremiah SPEIGHT & James COSTEN came into Court and offered themselves as Securitys &c

Bill of Sale for a Negro man JUCOB Miles TURLINGTON to James GATLING proved by the oath of Wm BAKER

Deed of Sale of Land Stephen ROGERS to James GATLING Ackd.

Stephen ROGERS Guardian to John ROGERS & William ROGERS, orphans of Stephen ROGERS decd exhibited his accounts wherein there appears to be a Balance due William ROGERS the sum of £66..19..7 3/4 & to John ROGERS the sum of £21..11.4½.

Ordered that William BAKER Esquire belowed the sum of Nine pounds three Shillings & 4d the amount of his Account for repairing the Court House &c

Feb. 1796

Deed of Sale of Land John BAKER to William BAKER ackd.

Lease of Land William BAKER to Seasbrook WILSON Ackd

(108) 284 Deed of Sale of Land Jethro BALLARD & David RICE to Joseph RIDDICK proved by the oath of Lawrence BAKER

Ordered that John ELLIS Admr of the Estate of Wm ELLIS decd sell as much of the perishable Estate of the decedint as will pay his Debts

    Then the Court adjournad until tomorrow morning

    Present
    William BAKER)
    Joseph RIDDICK) Esquires Justices
    John BAKER   )

Ordered that Jonathan ROGERS Executor of Zilpha ROGERS decd sell the Estate of the said decedent in order to make a Division thereof.

William WALTERS Guardn to Bray BAKER orphan of Saml BAKER decd. exhibited his account with said Orphan where in there appears to be a Balance due the Orphan the sum of £106.37.3.

Ordered that the Hands of Levi EURE John EURE senr Samuel TAYLOR (blank, ___, __) David LEWIS & ~~Benjamin~~ Abraham BEEMAN work on the Road under Jesse TAYLOR Overseer &c

William BLANSHARD came into Court and made choice of Friderick BLANSHARD his Brother as his Guardian Ordered that he give Bond & Security in the sum of Five hundred pounds at same time James COSTEN & Timothy WALTON as Secys &

(109)   James COSTEN came into Court and mooved for Administration on the Estate of Nathl COSTEN which was considered of & granted Ordered that he give Bond & Security in the sum of Five hundred pounds at same time Jeremiah SPEIGHT & Frederick BLANSHARD came into Court and offered themselves as securitys &c

Inventory of the Goods & Chattels rights & Credits which were of the Estate of Nathaniel COSTEN decd was exhibited into Court on oath by James COSEN &c

Thomas MARSHALL, Guardian to ~~Guy~~ Thos. HILL orphan of ~~Themas~~ Guy HILL decd exhibited his accot wherein there appeared to be a Balance due the orphan the sum of £34..13..0

Ordered that, James GATLING Lewis SPARKMAN Israel BEEMAN & Abraham BEEMAN or any three of them audite State & settle the accounts of the Exr or Admr. of David UMFLEET decd, and that they make a Division of the Estate of the decedent

Ordered that John ROBBINS & (One-half of line left blank.) Indian or Molatto Boys which was formerly bound to William LEWIS now decd be now bound to Henry LEE to learn the Buisiness of a House Carpenter & Joiner

Joseph RIDDICK Jonathan ROBERTS & Noah HARRELL Executors of William LEWIS decd came into Court and mooved for the Administration on the unadministered part of the Estate of William GLOVER decd which was ----ing not Administered on by the above said Wm LEWIS decd. which was granted Ordered that they give Bond & Security in the sum of one hundred pounds at same time James GATLING & Jeremiah SPEIGHT offered themselves as Secys &c

(110) 286 Ordered that Christian MORRISS Admr. of Ephraim MORRIS decd sell so much of the Estate of the decd as will pay his just Debts

Ordered that William GOODMAN Henry GOODMAN Richd BARNES & Elisha CROSS or any three of them make a Division of the property belonging to the Estate of Robert ROGERS decd agreeable to his Will, which was left his Wife in his last Will and Testament during her natural life.

Ordered that William GOODMAN Henry GOODMAN & Benjamin BARNES & Francis SPEIGHT or any three of them Audite State and settle the accounts of James GATLING Admr. of John GATLING & Edward GATLING decd &c

Ordered that Jonathan ROBERTS Admr of Henry FORRIST decd sell the perishable part of the Estate of the decd which has not been sold, &c

Bill of Sale Demsey ROOKS to William BAKER proved by the oath of James GATLING ----

Ordered that Jonathan ROGERS Executor of Zilpha ROGERS sell the Estate of Robert ROGERS decd if a Division of the said Estate cannot be conveniantly be made

```
            Jo RIDDICK
            Wm.. BAKER
            Wm.. GOODMAN
```

End of Book

Vol.: Not numbered   Years: May 1796-Feb. 1803   Pages: 1-278

(111) 1 State of North Carolina   May 16 1796
At a County Court of Pleas and Quarter Sessions begun and held for the County of Gates at the Court House on the third Monday in May in the Twentieth year of the Independence of the above said State and in the year of our Lord one thousand seven hundred and Ninety Six.

```
    Present  James GREGORY
             David RICE
             Jethro SUMNER
             William GOODMAN
```

Inventory of the Goods and Chattels Rights and Credits which were of the Estate of William ELLIS decd was exhibited into Court on oath by John ELLIS Admr.

Account of Sales of the Estate of William ELLIS decd. was exhibited into Court by John ELLIS Administrator on oath &c

Deed of Sale of Land James JONES of David & Uxr to Jacob Parker JONES proved by the oath Jethro BALLARD &c

Deed of Gift of Land John MORAN to his Son John MORAN proved by the oath of David HARRELL &c

Deed of Sale of Land George PILAND to Willis BROWNE proved by the oath of Seasbrook WILSON &c

Bill of Sale for a Negro Boy TONEY Seth EASON to William HUNTER ackd.

(112) 2 Account of Sales of the Estates of Robert ROGERS & Zelpha ROGERS deceased was exhibited into Court by Jonathan ROGERS Executor of Zelpha ROGERS decd

Deed of Sale William PERRY & Uxr to Kedar HINTON proved by the oath of Joseph PARKER &c

Deed of Sale of Land Paletiah BLANSHARD to John B WALTON ackd.

Deed of Sale of Land Stephen HARRELL to John PILAND provd by the oath of Willis PILAND &c

Account of Sales of the Estate of Moses WILLIAMS decd was exhibited into Court by Henry SMITH Admr on oath &c

Ordered that James JONES a Molatto Boy Son of Milley JONES about Eight years old be bound to Demsey HARRELL to learn the Buisiness of a Cooper

Ordered that William DANIEL a Child of Elizabeth DANIEL G? About Ten years old be bound as an Apprentice to Paletiah BLANSHARD to Learn the Buisiness of a Cooper

Account of Sales of part of the Estate of Henry FORREST decd. was exhibited into Court by Jonathan ROBERTS Admr on oath

The Last Will & Testament of George LASSITER decd was exhibited into Court by Moses LASSITER Executor therein appointed and was proved by the oath of James HODGES one of the subscribing witnesses thereto and on motion was ordered to be Recorded at the same time the said Executor came into Court and quallified himself for that office.

Ordered that Humphry PARKER orphan of William PARKER decd about Eighteen years of age be bound as an Apprentice to Charles JONES to learn the Buisiness of a Taylor &c

(113) 3 Samuel EURE Guardian to Nancy EURE orphan to Enos EURE decd exhibited his account with said Orphan where there appears to be a balance of Thirty pounds & two pence

Account of Sales of part of the Estate of Demsey TROTMAN decd was exhibited into Court by Ezekiel TROTMAN Executor on Oath &c

Leah LEWIS Relict of William LEWIS decd, exhibited a petition for her right of Dower in Certain Lands which her decd Husband died seized and possessed agreeable to Law, the said Leah LEWIS at same time dissented to the Will of her said Husband.

Selah BOND orphan of Demsey BOND decd came into Court and made choice of her Brother Elisha Hance BOND as her Guardian Ordered that he give Bond & Security in the sum of Five hundred pounds at the same time Richard BOND & John HARE came into Court and offered themselves as Secys &c

Ordered that Herman HAYSE orphan of Wright HAYSE decd about thirteen years of age be bound to John SIM?ONS to learn the Buisiness of a Wheel Wright.

May 1796

Bill of Sale James B SUMNER to Jethro SUMNER for Sundry Negros &c. Ackd.

William VALLENTINE came into Court and mooved for Administration on the Estate of Henry HILL deceased which was considered of & granted Ordered that he give Bond & Security in the sum of one hundred and fifty pounds at same time Moses HILL & Aaron HOBBS came into Court and offered themselves as Securitys &c

Ordered that Kedar BALLARD Miles BENTON, James KNIGHT, & Jethro BENTON or any three of them Audite State and Settle the Accounts of Amos PARKER Exr. of William PARKER Senr decd

(114) 4 Ordered that Kedar BALLARD Miles BENTON, James KNIGHT & Jethro BENTON or any three of them settle the accounts of Amos PARKER Admr of William PARKER Junr decd and that the same persons make a Division of the Estates of William PARKER senr & William PARKER junr decd &c

Ordered that Benjamin BARNES, James GATLING Abrah BEEMAN Isaac LANGSTON & David LEWIS be appd with the Surveyor to make a Division of the Real property of Lemuel HARRELL decd between the Heirs

Account of Sales of the Estate of Amos Wm PARKER deceased was exhibited into Court by Amos PARKER Exr. on Oath &c

Deed of Sale of Land Charles SMITH to Demsey JONES son of Hardy, proved by the oath of Joel FOSTER &c

Eliza KITTRELL Guardian to William KITTRELL George KITTRELL Elizabeth KITTRELL & Charity KITTRELL Exhibited her accounts with said Orphans on oath &c

Deed of Sale of Land James HODGES to Demsey JONES proved by the oath of Jonathan LASSITER &c

Deed of Sale of Land David WATSON & Uxr to Abel CROSS proved by the oath of John VANN &c

Deed of Sale of Land Samuel PITMAN to Benjamin CROWELL proved by the oath of Demsey KNIGHT &c

Deed of Sale Uriah ODOM & John ODOM to Jethro SUMNER proved by the oath of Francis SAUNDERS &c

Account of Sales of the Estate of Ephraim MORRISS decd was exhibited into Court by Christian MORRISS Admrtx on oath &c

Bill of Sale for four Negros PHEBE, AMY ISAAC & JACOB John BAKER to George PILAND proved by the oath of William HAYSE &c

(115) 5 The Last Will and Testament of James NORFLEET decd was exhibited into Court by Sarah NORFLEET Executrix therein appointed and was proved by the oaths of Jethro BALLARD Esquire and Kinchen NORFLEET two of the subscribing Witnesses thereto, and on motion was ordered to be Registered at the same time the said Executrix came into Court and quallified herself for that office and prayed an order for Letters Testamentary thereon &c

William GOODMAN, Benjamin BARNES & Francis SPEIGHT three of the Gentn. who were appointed ~~Guardian~~ to make a Division of the Estate of John GATLING decd made report of their proceedings thereon &c

William GOODMAN Benjamin BARNES & Francis SPEIGHT three of the Gentn who were appointed to make a Division of the Estate of Edward GATLING decd. made report of their proceedings thereon &c

James GATLING Lewis SPARKMAN Israel BEEMAN & Abraham BEEMAN the Gentlemen who were appointed to make a Division of & Audite State & Settle the accounts of William UMFLEET Admr of David UMFLEET decd made report of their proceedings thereon &c

Grand Jury drawn & impannelled for this Term (to wit) John RIDDICK Foreman, Willis BROWN, Micajah ~~RIDDICK~~ PHELPS, William BOND Stephen EURE, James JONES (of David) William BROOKS, Isaac COSTEN, Saml EURE, David LEWIS, William ARNOLD, Thomas HOFFLER Nathl RIDDICK

Then the Court adjourned until tomorrow morning 10 oClock

(116) 6 Tuesday morning the Court met.
Present
James GREGORY)
David RICE) Esquires Justices
William GOODMAN)
Simon STALLINGS)

Ordered that the Sheriff of this County Summon the Following persons to serve at next Term as Petit & Grand Jurors to wit Thomas BARNES, Henry LEE Richard BARNES, David CROSS, William KING Charles EURE Demsey LANGSTON, Josiah HARRELL Moor CARTER Jonathan PARKER (of Isaac) Micajah RIDDICK jr. William RIDDICK James B SUMNER Micajah RIDDICK senr. James PRUDEN, John POWELL James KNIGHT James SMALL Moses SPEIGHT Leven DURE David DAVIS Hardy EASON Abraham HURDLE, James HODGES, Kedar HINTON Joseph PARKER Timothy WALTON, David HARRELL Noah HARRELL & Reuben LASSITER,

Ordered that the following Gentlemen receive List of Taxables and Taxable property in this County from the Citizens thereof to wit William BAKER in the District of Captn David LEWIS's William GOODMAN in the District of Captn SPEIGHT Cristo RIDDICK Esquire in Capt HARRISS's District, Jethro SUMNER in Capt. ~~Jethro SUMNERS Dis~~ Jesse BENTONs District, Simon STALLINGS in Captn. WALTONs District, Thomas HUNTER in Captn Isaac HUNTERs District Jethro BALLARD in the District of Captn Jethro SUMNER &c

(117) 7 Account of Sales of Part of the Estate of Demsey BLANCHARD decd was delivered into Court by Aaron BLANSHARD Admr on oath &c

Inventory of the Estate of Henry HILL decd was exhibited into Court by William VOLLINTINE Admr on oath &c

Joseph RIDDICK & Jonathan ROBERTS Executors of William LEWIS decd exhibited an Inventory of the Estate of the deceased on oath &c

Account of Sales of part of the Estate of William LEWIS decd. was exhibited into Court by Joseph RIDDICK & Jonathan ROBERTS Executors on oath &c

Ordered that Joseph RIDDICK Jonathan ROBERTS & Noah HARRELL Executors of William LEWIS decd sell so much of the Personal Estate of the Decd as will pay his just Debts

May 1796

Ordered that William VOLLINTINE Admr of Henry HILL decd sell the perishable Estate of the Decd to pay debts &c

Aaron HOBBS came into Court and mooved for Administration on the Estate of Jacob HOBBS decd which was accordingly granted Ordered that he give Bond & Security in the sum of Five hundred pounds at same time Simon STALLINGS & Moses HILL came into Court and offered themselves as Securitys who were approved off &c.

Inventory of the Goods & Chattels rights & Credits which were of the Estate of Jacob HOBBS decd was exhibited into Court by Aaron HOBBS Admr on oath &c

(118) 8 Ordered that Job RIDDICK, Isaac HUNTER, William HARRIS, Humphry HUDGINS or any three of them Audite State and settle the Accounts of Isaac COSTEN Admr to the Estate of William GORDON decd.

William WALTERS exhibited his account as Constable ordered that the County Trustee pay him Six pounds &c

Ordered that the County Trustee pay Jethro MILTEAR the sum of two pounds the amount of his Account against the County as Constable

Ordered that the County Trustee pay Luten LEWIS two pounds Sixteen Shillings the amount of his Accot against the County as Constable.

Ordered that the County Trustee pay Lewis SPARKMAN the sum of Twenty four Shillings the amount of his Account against the County as Constable

Ordered that Aaron HOBBS Admr of Jacob HOBBS decd sell as much of the Estate of the decd as will pay his just Debts &c

Deed of Sale of Land Simon STALLINGS Sheriff of this County to James BAKER Ackd.

On the Petition of James BAKER to cut a Cannel into the Bennetts Creek through the Lands of William FREEMAN George OUTLAW, & Others, it is Ordered that the Jury whose names are hereunto (blank) be summoned by the Sheriff to go on the premisses and lay off the strip of Land under act of Assembly Which the Canel is to be cut & Where; and Assess such Damages, if any as they may think proper and report what Bridges and other Conveniances if any, are Neccessary to be made for the Benefit of the Neighbouring proprietors of Lands to wit Moses HILL John HOFFLER Jacob SPIVEY Josiah PARKER, Miles ROUNTREE Amerias BLANSHARD, George BROOKS Henry HOBBS Willis BROWN John HAIR, Daniel POWELL James HODGES Demsey JONES of Demsey or any twelve of them

(119) 9 Ordered that there be Levied on each poll in this County one Shilling & Six pence & Six pence on each hundred Acres of Land for County Tax.

Ordered that Jethro MELTEAR be appointed Guardian to James GORDON & Elizabeth GORDON Orphans of William GORDON decd & that he give Bond & Security in the sum of five hundred pounds for each? Orphan at same time Jonathan ROBERTS & William VOLLINTINE came into Court and offered themselves as Securitys &c

Ordered that David HARRELL junr. be appointed Constable in the room & stead of Lewis SPARKMAN resigned, & that he give Bond & Secy and take the oath of Government agreeable to Law.

The Court taking into Consideration the act of the General Assembly relative to the

May 1796

appointment of a Sheriff for this County; and after maturely considering the same unanimously appointed Isaac PIPKIN junr Sheriff, Ordered that he give Bond & Security agreeable to Law at same Henry GOODMAN & Lawe BAKER as Securitys who were approved off &c the Gentlemen Justices of the peace at the time the Bonds were assigned & Appointment made were James GREGORY David RICE, Simon STALLINGS Joseph RIDDICK William GOODMAN Esquires.

Ordered that Christopher RIDDICK Esqr let to the lowest bidder such necessary repairs that he may think Necessary to the Bridge below Lawrence BAKER's ~~Bridge~~ Mill.

        Jo RIDDICK   Wm GOODMAN   David RICE

(120) 10   State of No.. Carolina   August 15. 1796
                    At a County Court of Pleas and Quarter Sessions begun and held for the County of Gates at the Court House on the third Monday in August in the Twenty first year of the Independence of the said State and in the year of our Lord one thousand Seven hundred & Ninety Six

                Present   Christopher RIDDICK)
                        David RICE   ) Esquires
                        William GOODMAN   )

Deed of Sale of Land Esther PARKER to Riddick HUNTER proved by the oath of Elisha PARKER one of the Subscribg Witnesses

Bill of Sale John SMALL to Joseph HARE proved by the oath of James SMALL &c

Pannel of Grand Jury at August Term 1796 vizt Henry LEWIS? Foreman, Moses SPEIGHT Timothy WALTON, Josiah HARRELL, James HODGES, David HARRELL, Abraham HURDLE, James B SUMNER Thomas BARNES Moor CARTER, John POWELL, Hardy EASON, Reuben LASSITER Levin DUER Joseph PARKER William WALTERS Constable to attend

Ordered that Nicholas TEABOUT who is and has been for some time almost blind be exempt from paying Taxes working on the Road &c until he should get better &c.

Deed of Sale of Land Wm BAKER (of Samuel) to Joseph BRADY proved by the oath of Luten LEWIS &c

Deed of Sale of Land John BURGES & Uxr to John VANN proved by the oath of Joseph BRADY

Deed of Sale of Land Isaac HUNTER to Samuel HARRELL Acknowledged &c

(121) 11 Ordered that Cyprian CROSS be appointed Overseer of the Road in the room and stead of William CRAFFORD resigned

Ordered that Abraham BEEMAN be appointed Overseer of the Road in the room and Stead of Jesse TAYLOR resigned

Job RIDDICK Isaac HUNTER & Hy HUDGINS three of the Gentn who were appointed to audite state and settle the accounts of Isaac COSTEN Admr of William GORDON decd, exhibited their proceedings thereon &c

Inventory of the Goods & Chattels Rights & Credits which were of the Estate of George LASSITER decd was exhibited into Court by Moses LASSITER Exr. &c

Account of Sales of the Estate of Jacob HOBBS decd was exhibited into Court by Aaron HOBBS Admr &c

Deed of Sale of Land William FRYER to John LEWIS proved by the oath of James GATLING &c

Isaac HUNTER Guardian to John H RIDDICK orphan of Seth RIDDICK decd exhibited his account current with said orphan wherein there appears to be a Balance due the said orpn. the sum of 55..18..4..

Deed of Sale of Land Halladay WALTON to Bond MINSHEW with a Receipt thereon Ackd

Thomas HUNTER Esquire who was appointed to take a List Taxables and Taxable property in Captain Isaac HUNTER's Captaincy, made report of his proceedings thereon &c

Ordered that Kedar BALLARD be appointed Guardian to Mary ROUNTREE orphan of Charles ROUNTREE decd and that he give Bond and Security in the sum of Two thousand pounds at same time James SMALL & James B SUMNER came into Court and offered themselves as Security &c

(122) 12 Ordered that Samuel HARRELL Constable be allowed the sum of Twenty Shillings for his Services warning the Citizens of Captn Isaac HUNTERs Capty to return list's of their Taxables &c

Ordered that Reuben RIDDICK Constable be allowed the sum of Forty Shillgs for warning the Citizens of Captain HUNTERs District to return Inventorys of their Taxables &c

Ordered that Stephen EURE & Thos HARRELL be exempt from paying a poll Tax on themselves for the year 1795 they being upwards of Sixty years of Age

Ordered that James GREGORY Thomas HUNTER Moses HILL & Joseph RIDDICK or any three of them make a Division of the Estate of Demsey TROTMAN decd agreeable __ (faded) his Will

Ordered that James GREGORY, Thomas HUNTER Joseph RIDDICK & Moses HILL or any three of them audite State and settle the accounts of Ezekiel TROTMAN Exr of Demsey TROTMAN decd &c

Bill of Sale George EASON to Betsey EASON for a Negro Girl MILLEY, proved by the oath of Isaac PIPKIN &c

Lease of Land Keziah BLANSHARD to Joseph ALPHIN ackd. &c

Jethro SUMNER William HARRISS & Micajah RIDDICK junr who with the Surveyor of this County exhibited a Division of the Real Estate of Abraham MORGAN decd &c

Ordered that Stephen HARRELL be appointed Overseer of the Road instead of William BAKER resigned

Account of Sales of the Estate of Henry HILL decd was exhibited into Court by William VALENTINE Admr &c

(123) 13 Deed of Sale Gift of Land Joseph RIDDICK to Isaiah RIDDICK acknowledged &c

Account of Sales of the Perishable Estate of James OUTLAW, deceased was exhibited into Court by Seth ROUNTREE Isaac COSTEN & George OUTLAW Executors made report of their proceeding &c

Ordered that Francis SAUNDERS be appointed Overseer of the Road instead of John ODOM, resigned

Leah RIDDICK Guardian to Eliza RIDDICK orphan of Seth RIDDICK decd. exhibited her accot (by Isaac HUNTER on oath) ~~her acect current~~ wherein there appears to be a Balance due the said Orphan the sum of 84.13..2. &c

Ordered that Reuben RIDDICK be exempt for the payment of a Tax for the future on a Negro Boy STEEL, unless the said Negro should get into a better State of Health &c

Ordered that Benjn BARNES, James GATLING Abraham BEEMAN Isaac LANGSTON and David LEWIS with the Surveyor of this County make a Division of the Real Estate of Lemuel HARRELL decd agreeable to a petition exhibited into this Court &c

In a Suit brought on a Warrant Levin DUER against James B SUMNER, ---- Judgment was entered up against the said James B SUMNER for the sum of Thirteen pounds two Shillings & Six pence with (Half of next line is blank.) costs on said Warrant & Samuel HARRELL Constable returned on said Execution that there was no property to be found except Land which he had levied on, Ordered that Execution be issued from this Court for the above Judgment & Costs

        Then the Court adjourned until tomorrow morng 10 oClock

(124) 14 Tuesday Morning the Court met
    Present
    James GREGORY)
    David RICE) Esquires Justices
    Jethro BALLARD)

Deed of Sale of Land Mariam WHITEHEAD Extx of John WHITEHEAD to John & William COWPER proved by the oath of Hardy MURFREE Esqr. &c

Deed of Sale of Land Luke SUMNER & Uxr.. to John COWPER proved by the oath of John COWPER junr &c

Mortgage Deed for Land Josiah GRANBERY to Josiah COLLINS Junr with a receipt on the back thereof proved by the oath of Alexander MILLEN &c

Mortgage Deed for Twelve Negroe Slaves Josiah GRANBERY to Josiah COLLINS Junr. proved by the oath of Alexander MILLEN &c

Deed of Sale of Land Josiah GRANBERY to Josiah ~~GRANBERY~~ COLLINS proved by the oath of Alexander MILLEN &c.

Deed of Sale of Land with a Receipt thereon Wm ARNOLD to John COWPER Ackd..

A Contract or Bargain William ARNOLD, to John COWPER Ackd &c

Ordered that Charney EURE an Illegitimate Child Son of Sarah EURE about Eighteen years of age be bound as an Apprentice to Timothy FREEMAN to learn the Buisness of a Planter &c

Aug. 1796

(125) 15 Deed of Lease Henry COPELAND to Sarah WINBORN Ackd.

Release Sarah WINBORN to Henry COPELAND Ackd

Deed of Sale of Land John ODOM to Jethro SUMNER provd by the oath of Henry SPEIGHT &c

Inventory of the Goods & Chattels, Rights and Credits which were of the Estate of James NORFLEET decd was exhibited into Court for the Extx of the Decd by Jethro BALLARD Esqr which was proved before him

Bill of Sale for a Negro Man PATER William BOND to Levin DUER proved by the oath of William HARRISS &c

Ordered that Bond MINSHEW be appointed Overseer of the Road instead of Kedar HINTON resigned

Jethro BALLARD Esquire who was appointed to receive a list of Taxables from the Citizens in Capt Jethro SUMNERs Capty returned his proceedings &c

Deed of Sale of Land Jesse EASON to James GORDON proved by the oath of Nathl. RIDDICK

Ordered that the Sheriff of this County Summons Jeremiah SPEIGHT, Thomas SMITH, John ARNOLD William DOUGHTIE, Willis BROWN, Robert PARKER Elisha CROSS, Hillory WILLEY, Asa HARRELL, Henry SPEIGHT, Isaac LANGSTON, William BROOKS, Demsey ODOM, William CLEAVES, William MATTHIAS, Simeon BRINKLEY David BRINKLEY, John SMALL, William ARNOLD, Robert RIDDICK, William BERRIMAN Ezekiel TROTMAN, William HUNTER Bond MINSHEW Geo BROOKS John HAIR Wm HINTON Indian Neck Demsey JONES of Dem Jesse BENTON, Benjamin GORDON personally to be and appear at next Term as Jurymen

(126) 16 Ordered that the Sheriff of this County Summons David HARRELL (of Isaac) Patrick HEGERTY John ODOM Demsey BARNES & William VOLENTINE to attend the Supr. Court to be held for the District of Edenton at Edenton on the Sixth day of Octr next

Deed of Sale of Land Samuel HARRELL to James HODGES proved by the oath of Josiah GRANBERY &c

Accounts of Sales of the Estate of William LEWIS decd was exhibited into Court by Joseph RIDDICK Esquire Exor on oath &c

The Sherriff having returned the Pannel of a Jury with the Verdict thereof for laying out a Road & Cornell to be cutt by James BAKER which runs in these words (to wit) Agreeable to an Order of Court hereunto annexed we the Subscribers have met for the purpose of laying of James BAKERs Cannel which Begins near the mouth of Bennetts Creek runing half a mile in the Percoson to his Swamp which is to be thirty feet wide it is our Opinion that the said BAKER give the Propriators of the Land through which it passes Ten Shillgs pr Acre for the Bounds within mentioned we also take it in consideration that the said BAKER is to build three Bridges of planks twelve feet wide three Sleepers under each bridge a Cross the said Cannell Moses HILL Daniel POWELL Miles ROUNTREE John HARE Ameriah BLANSHARD Henry HOBBS Demsey JONES James HODGES George BROOKS Jacob SPIVEY Thomas HOBBS Willis BROWN

Ordered that Willis WIGGINS James B SUMNER & Jethro BENTON pay to Ruth ELLIS the sum of Twelve pounds for on or before the first day of Septr next and in case of failure thereof Execution Issue for the that sum and that they pay that sum annually until a Child begotten on the Body of the said ELLIS by the said Willis WIGGINS becomes old enough to be bound to some Buisiness

(127) 17 Ordered that Law BAKER Clerk of this Court be alld the sum of one pound Seventeen Shillings & 6 for so much he paid the Printer at Edenton for inserting a Presentment of the Grand Jury of this County

Simon STALLINGS Esqr who was appointed to receive lists of Taxables in the Captainy of Captn James WALTON returned his proceedings &c

Ordered that Henry GOODMAN late Sheriff of this County be allowed in the settlement of his accounts for the Poll Tax on James BRISTOW for two White Poll & Henry TURLEY for 1 Pole

Ordered that Isaac MILLER senr. Humphry HUDGINS Christopher RIDDICK and Robert PARKER or any three of them make a Division of the Negroes belonging to the Estate of Kedar RIDDICK decd. agreeable to the Will

Ordered that John COWPER Levin DUER Kedar BALLARD and Jethro BALLARD or any three of them make a Division of the Estate of James NORFLEET decd, agreeable to the Will

Ordered that Lawrence BAKER Clerk of this Court be allowed the sum of Twenty pounds for making out a Transcript and returning it of the Entry takers Book in this County & sending them to the Secys office of this State

Ordered that John POWELL Keep in good repair the Road aCross the Orapeak swamp and that he be exempt from working on any other Roads

Ordered that David RICE & Thos HUNTER Esquires & Josiah GRANBERY & Job RIDDICK or any three of them to audite State and settle the accounts of Isaac COSTEN Admr of Timothy LASSITER decd &c

(128) 18 Ordered that Henry GOODMAN late Sheriff of Gates County be allowed the sum of Fifteen pounds for Extra Services by him performed for the year passed

Ordered that Moor CARTER pay only a Single Tax instead of a double Tax his list not having been returned by mistake

Ordered that George WILLIAMS pay only a Single Tax instead of a Double Tax, his list not having been returned by mistake

       James GREGORY
       David RICE
       Jo RIDDICK

(129) 19 State of North Carolina 21 Novr. 1796
   Gates County)
      At a County Court of Pleas and Quarter Sessions begun and held for the County of Gates at the Court House on the third monday in November in the Twenty first year of the Independence of the Said State and in the year of our Lord One thousand seven hundred and Ninety Six

    Present
    Christopher RIDDICK)
    Jethro SUMNER)
    David RICE   ) Esquires Justices
    Thomas HUNTER)
    William GOODMAN)
    Simon STALLINGS)

Nov. 1796

Isaac HUNTER appointed Guardian to Whitmill HILL orphan of Kedar HILL decd, Ordered that he give Bond & Security in the sum of One thousand pounds each at same time Thos HUNTER & Benjamin GORDON came into Court and offered themselves as Securitys &c

Isaac HUNTER appointed Guardian to Robert HILL orphan of Kedar HILL decd Ordered that he give Bond & Security in the sum of One thousand pounds at same time Thos HUNTER came into Court and offered themselves as Securitys &c

Deed of Sale of Land James FREEMAN &Uxr to Timothy FREEMAN proved by the oath of Seth ROUNTREE &c.

(130) 20 Francis SAUNDERS came into Court and mooved for Admr on the Estate of William SAUNDERS decd which was granted Ordered that he give Bond & Security in the sum of Five hundred pounds at same time David CROSS & Benjamin BARNES came into Court and offered themselves as Securitys who were approved of &c

Ordered that Joseph TAYLOR be appointed Overseer of the Road in the district and stead of James OUTLAW decd

Christo RIDDICK Esqr. came into Court and mooved for Admr on the Estate of William HALL decd, which was granted Ordered that he give Bond & Security in the Sum of One hundred pounds at same time, Simon STALLINGS came into Court and offered himself as security &c

John RUSSEL came into Court and mooved for Administr. on the Estate of Sarah RUSSEL decd which was accordingly granted Ordered that he give Bond & Security in the sum of Fifty Pounds at same time Jeremiah JORDAN & Henry HILL came into Court and offered themselves as his Securitys &c

Ordered that the County Trustee pay Samuel SMITH the sum of Thirty Seven pounds Nineteen Shillings Currt money for Building a Bridge aCross Coles Creek below L BAKERs Mill

Inventory of the Goods & Chattels Lands & Tenements of Sarah RUSSEL decd was exhibited into Court by John RUSSEL Admr on oath &c

Deed of Sale of Land Peter PARKER to Jesse SAVAGE proved by the oaths of Caleb SAVAGE & Daniel PARKER subscribing Witnesses &c

(131) 21 Bill of Sale for Negro PHILL Joseph JONES to John COWPER Ackd.

Bill of Sale Seth EASON & William RIDDICK to John COWPER for three Negroes CATE JACK & TONEY, ackd by Wm W RIDDICK & the Signature of Seth EASON proved by the oath of Christopher RIDDICK &c

Deed of Sale Benjamin CROWELL to James KNIGHT proved by the oath of Seth EASON &c

Deed of Sale of Land Jesse EASON to James GORDON provd by the oath of David RIDDICK &c.

Deed of Sale of Land Jacob GORDON & Uxr. to Kinchen NORFLEET proved by the oath of James GORDON &c

Deed of Sale of Land Jesse EASON to James GORDON proved by the oath of David RIDDICK &c

Nov. 1796

Deed of Sale of Land Jesse WARD to Timothy FREEMAN proved by the oath of Frederick BLANSHARD &c

Deed of Sale of Land Josiah LASSITER to Aaron LASSITER proved by the oath of David RICE Esqr.

Deed of Sale of Land Amos FREEMAN & Uxr. to Elisha HUNTER proved by the oath of Thomas HUNTER &c

The Last Will & Testament of George PILAND decd was exhibited into Court by Edward PILAND Exr. therein appointed and was proved by the oath of William BROOKS & James PILAND subscribing witnesses thereto and on motion was ordered to be Recorded at the same time the said Executor came into Court and quallified himself for that office &c

(132) 22 Inventory of the Goods & Chattels Rights & Credits which were of the Estate George PILAND decd was exhibited into Court by Edward PILAND Exr. &c

Last Will and Testament of William HINTON decd was exhibited into Court by Isaac HUNTER & Lewis THOMPSON two of the Exors therein appointed and was proved by the oath of Mourning SUMNER one of the Subscribing Witnesses thereto at the same the said Exors quallified themselves for that office &c

Inventory of the Goods & Chattels Rights & Credits which were of the Estate of William HINTON decd was exhibited into Court by Isaac HUNTER & Lewis THOMPSON Exrs on oath &c

Last Will and Testament of William Barnes BARCLIFT was exhibited into Court by James BARNES Exr. therein appointed and was proved by the oath of John RIDDICK one of the subscribing Witnesses thereto, which was ordered to be Recorded at the same time the said Exr. quallified himself for that office &c

Inventory of the Goods Chattels Rights & Credits which were of the Estate of William SAUNDERS decd was exhibited into Court by Francis SAUNDERS Admr on oath &c

Jethro BALLARD Kedar BALLARD & Benjamin GORDON, three of the Gentn. who were appointed to audite State and settle the accounts of James SMALL Admr of Daniel GWINN decd made report of there proceedings thereon &c

Jethro BALLARD Kedar BALLARD & Seth EASON who were appointed to make a Division of the Estate of Daniel GWINN decd made report of their proceedings thereon &c

Account of Sales of the Estate of Daniel GWINN decd was exhibited into Court by James SMALL admr on oath &c

(133) 23 David RICE, Job RIDDICK & Thomas HUNTER, three of the Gentn who were appointed to Audite State and settle the Accounts of Isaac COSTEN Admr of Timothy LASSITER decd made report of their proceedings thereon &c

    Then the Court adjourned until tomorrow morning 10 oClock

    Tuesday Morning the Court met
      Present
      Thomas HUNTER)
      Jethro BALLARD)

Simon STALLINGS) Esquires Justices
William GOODMAN)

Deed of Sale of Land Michael PAYNE Esquire Marshall of the State to James GRANBERY of the Town of Edenton proved by the oath of William BLAIR Esq &c

Deed of Sale of Land Stephen PILAND Thomas PILAND & Willis PILAND to William BAKER proved by the oath of Anthony WILLIAMS &c

Bill of Sale for a Negro Man BOSON John LANG to Henry LEE, proved by the oath of William GOODMAN &c

Ordered that Thomas MARSHALL George WILLIAMS Charles EURE and Robert PARKER or any three of them make a Division of the Estate of Thomas PILAND decd agreeable to Law &c

Ordered that Timothy WALTON be appointed Guardian to David OUTLAW orphan of James OUTLAW and that he Give Bond & Security in the sum of Four thousand pounds at same time Willis BROWN & William VOLENTINE came into Court and offered themselves as Secys

(134) 24 James GORDON appointed Guardian to Mary NORFLEET Elizabeth NORFLEET & Philissia NORFLEET orphans of James NORFLEET decd. Ordered that he give Bond & Security in the sum of Three thousand (blank) pounds at same time John COWPER & Benjamin GORDON came into Court and offered themselves as Securitys &c

Jethro BALLARD appointed Guardian to Sarah NORFLEET orphan of James NORFLEET decd, Ordered that he give Bond and Security in the sum of Three thousand pounds At same time Jethro SUMNER & Timothy WALTON came into Court and offered themselves as Securitys &c

Ordered that William GOODMAN, Henry GOODMAN Philip LEWIS & William GATLING senr. or any three of them lay off to Joseph FREEMAN his part of a Certain Estate given to him and others by their Grand Father Joseph SPEIGHTs estate

James COSTEN appointed Guardian to James LASSITER Henry LASSITER, & Peggy LASSITER Orphans of Timothy LASSITER decd. Ordered that he give Bond & Security in the Sum of Three thousand pounds at same time Isaac COSTEN & Timothy WALTON came into Court and offered themselves as Securitys &c

Burwell GRIFFITH came into Court and mooved for Administration on the Estate of Demsey BARNES decd which was Granted Ordered that he give Bond and Security in the sum of Three thousand five hundred pounds, at same time Cyprian CROSS & John VANN came into Court and offered themselves as Securitys &c

Bill of Sale for a Negro Boy named BACCUS Jethro BENTON and Miles BENTON to Joseph ROOKS proved by the oaths of William BAKER and Lewis SPARKMAN Witnesses thereto &c

(135) 25 Inventory of the Goods & Chattels rights & Credits which were of the Estate of Demsey BARNES decd was exhibited into Court by Burwell GRIFFITH Admr on oath &c

Ordered that the Sheriff Summons a Jury and lay off to Leah LEWIS relict of William LEWIS decd, agreeable to her Petition filed her Dower, out of certain Lands which the said William LEWIS died seized & possessed &c

Ordered that Kedar BALLARD, James SMALL, Miles BENTON & Jethro BALLARD or any three of them make a Division of the Estate (Personal) of William ELLIS decd.

Ordered that Jonathan ROBERTS be appointed Guardian to Sarah LEWIS, Mary LEWIS, Elizabeth LEWIS & John LEWIS Orphans of William LEWIS decd Ordered that he give Bond & Security in the sum of one thousand pounds for each of them at same time Willis BROWN & Kedar HINTON came into Court and offered themselves as his Securitys &c.

Ordered that James PARKER orphan of William PARKER about Sixteen years of age be bound an Apprentice to Thomas PARKER to learn the Buisiness of Cooper &c

Ordered that William BLANSHARD orphan of Absolom BLANSHARD decd be bound as an Apprentice to Richard RAWLS, to Learn the Buisiness of a Mill Wright & House Carpenter &c orpn about 16 years old

Bill of Sale for Negro Boy named PHIL Levin DUER to Robert RIDDICK proved by the oath of Jethro BALLARD &c

Orderdered that Elisha CROSS be appointed Overseer of the Road instead of Mills ODOM resigned &c

(136) 26 Ordered that Thomas BARNES be appointed Overseer of the Road in the District and Stead of Isaac PIPKIN resigned.

Ordered that Christopher RIDDICK Admr of Wm HALL decd sell so much of the Estate of the Decedent as will pay his just Debts &c

Ordered that Christo RIDDICK, Humphry HUDGINS Robert PARKER and Isaac MILLER or any three of them make a Division of the Estate left by James RIDDICK in his last Will and Testament to the Orphans of Kedar RIDDICK decd

William HAYSE appointed Guardian to Hance HAYS & Howell HAYSE orphans of Wright HAYSE decd Ordered that he give Bond & Security in the sum of one hundred pounds for each of them, at same time Bond MINSHEW & Richard BOND came into Court and offered themselves as Securitys &c

Ordered that the Sheriff of this County Summon the following persons to attend this Court at next Term as Petit & Grand Jurys. to wit Aaron HOBBS, Thomas HOBBS, Jacob EASON, Richard MITCHELL, David HARRELL senr Moses HILL Miles ROUNTREE Isaac COSTEN John HOFFLER, Henry WALTON Ezekiel TROTMAN Miles BENTON James JONES of David, Amos PARKER, William ARNOLD John SMALL Moses SPEIGHT James FIGG Michael LAWRENCE, James BARNES, Richard BRIGGS Wm DOUGHTIE, Philip ROGERS, Jonathan ROGERS Francis SAUNDERS, William KING, David CROSS Charles EURE Isaac LANGSTON & Moses DAVIS

David LEWIS Benjamin BARNES, Isaac LANGSTON & Abraham BEEMAN with Patrick HEGERTY the Surveyor of this County who were appointed to make a Division of the real Estate of Lemuel HARRELL decd made report of their proceedings thereon &c

(137) 27 Ordered that, Jethro BALLARD Jethro SUMNER Kedar BALLARD & Levin DUER or any three of them Audite State and Settle the Accounts of Luke SUMNER Admr of John Randolph WILKINSON decd in right of his Wife who was relict of the Decedent

Ordered that Jethro BALLARD, Jethro SUMNER Kedar BALLARD & Levin DURE make a Division of the Estate of John Randolph WILKINSON

Ordered that James H KEYS Esquire Attorney at Law be appointed Attorney for the

State in this County instead of William CUMMING Esqr who has failed to give his Attendance &c

On Motion of William BAKER Ordered that he have a License to keep a Public House at Gates Court House and ih? same time Ordered that he give Bond & Security agreeable to Law, Saml SMITH came into Court and offered himself as Security &c

By order of the Court
Test Law BAKER C.

(138) 28 State of North Carolina   Feby 20th 1797

At a Court of Pleas and Quarter Sessions begun and held for the County of Gates at the Court House on the third Monday in February in the year of our Lord one thousd. seven hundred & Ninety Seven and twenty first year of the Independence of the said State.

Present
Joseph RIDDICK   )
Christopher RIDDICK   ) Esquires Justices
Henry GOODMAN   )

Grand Jury impannelled & sworn (to wit) Richard MITCHELL Jacob EASON Thomas HOBBS, Aaron HOBBS Philip ROGERS, Isaac LANGSTON Jonathan ROGERS, Michael LAWRENCE, James FIGG, John HOFFLER, Charles EURE, Moses SPEIGHT, James BARNES, Henry WALTON & William DOUGHTIE,

Ordered that John PILAND be appointed Overseer of the Road in the District and stead of Elijah HARRELL resigned &c

James CHERRY Sheriff of Hertford County having returned the Verdict of a Jury with the pannel thereof agreeable to a Writ of Dower to him directed, (to wit) Hertford County Feby 14th 1797 In obediance to Summons by the Sheriff of the County aforesaid We James BAKER, Elisha SCULL, James MOOR, John BARROW? Thos SMITH, William DOWNING, Abraham WALERIDGE Matthias DEANS, Blake BAKER William H BOYCE Francis EVINS and Joshua SIMONS, being quallified as the Law directs for the purpose of alotting to Leah LEWIS Relict of William LEWIS decd her right of Dower in the Lands of said deceased that

(139) 29 lyeth in the County aforesaid, after viewing the Premises do agree and allot to sd Leah LEWIS one part of sd Land that lyeth on the river Pocoson containing as appears by Plott of Survey one hundred and thirty Nine Acres, and also one third of the Saw and Grist Mill, reserving the Fishery for the benefit of the Orphans of the deceased, In Witness where of we have hereunto set our hands and fixed our seals Abraham WALERIDGE (seal) Matt DEANS (seal) Blake BAKER (seal) W H BOYCE (seal) Francis EVINS (seal) Joshua SIMONS (seal) James BAKER (seal) Elisha SCULL (seal) James MOORE (seal) John BARROW (seal) Thomas SMITH (seal) William DOWNING (seal)

Deed of Sale Isaac POWELL to Micajah RIDDICK proved by the oath of Noah FELTON &c

Bill of Sale for five Negroes Stock Plantation Utensils Household furniture Isaac POWELL to Micajah RIDDICK proved by the oath of Noah FELTON

Deed of Sale of Land with a receipt on the back thereof Reubin HOBBS to Ezekieel TROTMAN proved by the oath of Noah TROTMAN &c

Ezekiel TROTMAN Guardian to Christian SCOTT orphan of William SCOTT decd exhibited his account current with said Orphan wherein there appears to be a Balance due said Orpn. ₤49..19.0

Then the Court adjourned until tomorrow morning 10 oClock

(140) 30 Tuesday Morning the Court met
Present
William GOODMAN)
David RICE) Esquires Justices
Simon STALLINGS)

Bill of Sale for a Negro DANIEL William FREEMAN to John BRIDGER acknowledged &c

Inventory of the Goods & Chattels rights and Credits which were of the Estate of William Barnes BARCLIFT decd was exhibited into Court by James BARNES on oath &c

Bill of Sale Moses DAVIS to Isau?c HARRELL Junr proved by the oath of Henry MERONEY &c

Frederick BLANSHARD Guardian to William BLANSHARD orpn of Absolam BLANSHARD decd exhibited his account with said Orpn wherein there appears to be a Balance due said Orphan L108.10.11.

William James NUTTALL Guardian to Mary BLANSHARD exhibited his account with said Orphan wherein there appears to be a Balance due said Orpn the sum of ₤111.14 0

Christian BROWN & Robt PARKER Junr came into Court and mooved for Administration on the Estate of James BROWN decd which was accordingly granted Ordered that they give Bond and Security in the sum of One thousand Pounds at same time (Remainder of line is blank.) came into Court and offered themselves as Security who were approved off &c

Deed of Sale of Land David RIDDICK to Moses BRIGGS proved by the oath of Jacob GORDON &c

(141) 31 Deed of Sale of Land Lemuel TAYLOR to Nathaniel TAYLOR proved by the oath of Richard FREEMAN &c

Noncupative Will of Robert Foster BENTON was exhibited into Court by Jesse BENTON and was proved by the oath of Abel SAVAGE & William BENSON two of the Subscribing Witnesses thereto, at same time Jesse BENTON came into Court and mooved for Administration on the Estate of the said Robt. Foster BENTON with the will annexed which was accordingly Granted Ordered that he give Bond & Security in the sum of One thousand pounds at same time Jesse BENTON Jethro SUMNER & Joseph RIDDICK came into Court and offered themselves as Securitys &c

Last Will and Testament of William WARREN was exhibited into Court by John PARKER Exr therein appointed and was proved by the oaths of Thomas BARNES Henry SPEIGHT & Isaac CARTER witnesses thereto at same time the said Exr. came into Court and qualified himself for that office and prayed an order for Letters Testamentory thereon &c

Inventory of the Goods & Chattels Lands & Tenements of William WARREN decd was exhibited into Court by John PARKER Admr. &c

Deed of Sale of Land Joseph DAVIS to William HAYSE proved by the oath of Samuel HARRELL &c

Deed of Sale of Land Jacob HAYSE & William HAYSE to Mills FIELD ackd.

Deed of Sale of Land Demsey JONES jr to John SIMONS Ackd

Bill of Sale for a Negro Girl J B SUMNER & Jethro SUMNER to Cyprian CROSS Ackd.

(142) 32 David KILLY Guardian to Seth SPIVEY exhibited his account with said Guardn. wherein there appears to be a Balance due the Orphan 34..17.9 3/4

Elisha HARE Guardian to Mourning NORFLEET exhibited his account with the said Orphan wherein there appears to be a ballance due the said Orphan L32.0.0

Susanna BAKER Guardian to Peggy BAKER Orpn (End of entry.)

Ordered that John PARKER Exr of William WARREN decd sell so much of the Estate of the decedint as will pay his Just Debts &c

Deed of Sale of Land John LANDING to Abraham CURL proved by the oath of John VANN &c

Ordered that Jesse BENTON Admr of Robert F BENTON decd sell the Perishable part of the Estate of the decd &c

Samuel HARRELL Guardian to John Thos Millisen & William WALTON orphans of Thomas WALTON exhibited his account with said Orpns. wherein there appears to be a Balance due the Orphans as follows (to wit) to Thomas WALTON £98..7..3 John WALTON £95 3..10½ Millisen WALTON £87.4.3 to William WALTON £92.8..9 to Amelea WALTON £86..14.5

Isaac HUNTER Guardian to Whitmill HILL & Robert HILL orphans of Kedar HILL & to John H RIDDICK & Elizabeth RIDDICK orphans of Seth RIDDICK decd exhibited his accounts with said Orphans as follows (to wit) to Whitmill HILL £100..8 5½ to Robert HILL L90.003 to John H RIDDICK £52.3.3. to Eliza RIDDICK £83.19.8?

Deed of Sale of Land Lemuel TAYLOR to Joseph TAYLOR proved by the oath of Miles WALTON &c

(143) 33 Ordered that James GREGORY Thomas HUNTER David RICE, & Humphry HUDGINS or any three of them audit state and settle the accounts of Isaac HUNTER Exr of Sarah LASSITER decd &c

Martha Patsey WILKINSON orphan of John Randelph WILKINSON came into Court and made choice of Miles BENTON as her Guardian Ordered that he give Bond and Security in the sum of Five hundred pounds at same time Reube?n RIDDICK & Jethro BENTON came into Court and offered themselves as Securitys &c

Mary Reanalds WILKINSON orphan of John R WILKINSON came into Court and made choice of Jethro BENTON as her Guardn Ordered that he give Bond and Security in the sum of Five hundred pounds at same time Miles BENTON & James JONES came into Court and offered themselves as securitys &c

Ordered that Hardy HOWARD orphan of Hardy HOWARD decd about fourteen years of age be bound as an Apprentice to Isaac MILLER senr to learn the Buisness of a Farmer

Deed of Sale of Land John POWELL of Jacob to Isaac HARRELL junr. proved by the oath of Joseph RIDDICK &c

Deed of Sale of Land Francis SAUNDERS to Jethro SUMNER proved by the oath of Henry GOODMAN &c

Deed of Sale of Land John ODOM to Jethro SUMNER Ackd &c

Deed of Sale for Land David RIDDICK & Nathl RIDDICK to Samuel HARRELL proved by the oath of Levin DUER

(144) 34 Riddick TROTMAN came into Court and mooved for Admn on the Estate of Moses HILL decd which was granted Ordered that he give Bond & Security in the sum of Three thousand pounds at same time John HOFFLER and Jacob EASO__ (blot) came into Court and offered themselves as Securitys &c

Inventory of the Goods and Chattels rights and Credits which were of the Estate of Moses HILL deceased was exhibited into Court by Riddick TROTMAN Admr &c

Last Will and Testament of James BETHEY decd was exhibited into Court by John BETHEY Exr. and was proved by the oath of (Remainder of line left blank.) at same time the said Exr came into Court and quallified himself for that office and prayed an order for Letters Testamentary thereon &c

Inventory of the Goods and Chattels Rights and Credits which were of the Estate of James BETHEY was exhibited into Court by John BETHEY Exr.

Bill of Sale for a Negro Girl HETTY Mills RIDDICK to Levin DUER proved by the oath of David RIDDICK &c

Deed of Sale of Land James B SUMNER to James FIGG proved by the oath of Christoph RIDDICK &c

Inventory of the Goods & Chattels rights and Credits which were of the Estate of William HALL decd was exhibited into Court by Christo RIDDICK Admr on oath &c

Inventory of the Estate of James BROWN was exhibited into Court by Christian BROWN & Robert PARKER junr Admrs. &c

Bill of Sale for a Negro Boy BENJAMIN Jesse EASON to Levin DUER proved by the oath of Christopher GAYLE

Agreeable to the Petition of Ann HILL Relict of Abraham HILL for Dower Ordered that the Sheriff summons a Jury and allott and lay off the Dower of the said Ann agreeable to her Petition &c

(145) 35 William FREEMAN jr Guardian to Charles ROUNTREE and John ROUNTREE, orphans of John ROUNTREE decd exhibited his accounts with said Orphans wherein their appears to be a balance due the said Orphans as follow (to wit) to Charles £5.1.4¼ to Jno. £60.15.6½

William VOLENTINE Guardian to Henry BAGLEY Trotman BAGLEY & Miles HILL exhibited his accounts with them as Orphans wherein there appears to be Balances due said Orphans as follows (to Wit) to Henry BAGLEY £2.4.0 to Trotman BAGLEY £146.1..1 & to Miles HILL £80..10.9

Thomas HUNTER Joseph RIDDICK & James GREGORY three of the Gentlemen who were appointed to Audit State & settle the accounts of Ezekiel TROTMAN Exr of Demsey TROT-

MAN, made report of their proceedings thereon &c

Thomas HUNTER Joseph RIDDICK & James GREGORY three of the Gentn who were appointed to make a Division of the Estate of Demsey TROTMAN decd agreeable to his Will made report of their proceedings thereon &c

William GOODMAN Henry GOODMAN Philip LEWIS & William GATLING the Gentlemen who were appointed to make a Division of Certain property (or allot to Joseph FREEMAN his part given by Joseph SPEIGHT to his Grand Children &c made report of their proceedings thereon &c

Deed of Gift Nathl RIDDICK to William CARTER & Uxr proved by the oath of Joseph RIDDICK &c

Account of Sales of the Estate of William SAUNDERS decd was exhibited into Court on oath by Benjamin BARNES &c

Agreeable to the Petition of Thamor HILL, Ordered that the Sheriff of this County lay off to the said Thamor her right of Dower out of certain Lands Moses HILL her Husband Died possessed with.

(146) 36 Account of Sales of the Estate of Sarah RUSSEL decd was exhibited into Court by John RUSSEL Admr

Joseph RIDDICK Guardian to Joseph TROTMAN Love TROTMAN and Willis TROTMAN Orphans of Thomas TROTMAN & his account with Joseph Love & Willis TROTMAN exhibited on oath wherein there appears to be Balances due said Orpns as follows (to wit) to Joseph TROTMAN £89..9..6 3/4 to Love TROTMAN £74.7..11 & to Willis TROTMAN £329..1.0 and to Joseph Love & Willis TROTMAN jointly £192.5.2.

Joseph TAYLOR Guardian to Sally SPIVEY orphan of Thomas SPIVEY decd exhibited his account with said Orphan on oath wherein there appears to be a Ballance due the Orphan £49..14.11

Abraham HURDLE Guardian to Jacob SUMNER son of Abraham SUMNER exhibited his accot with said Jacob wherein there appears to be a Bale due said Jacob L95 3.11.

Law BAKER Guardian to Jacob ODOM & Jesse ODOM orphans of Elisha ODOM wherein there appears to be a Bale due the said Orpns as follows to Jacob 154.7.8½ to Jesse ODOM 8.13.2

Agreeable to a Writ of Dower for the Purpose of laying off to Leah LEWIS her Dower out of Certain Lands which William LEWIS died seized & possessed with (to wit) Agreeable to an order of Court hereunto annexed we the subscribers have met this 11th Feby 1797 and laid of the dower of Leah LEWIS Relict of William LEWIS Decd which is bounded as follows vizt Begining at a small Ditch on the North side of the Public Road, thence along the said Ditch to a Branch thence down the Branch to Mill Swamp then down the Swamp to Bennetts Creek thence down Bennetts Creek to Wm BOOTHs line thence along BOOTHs line to Bennetts Creek Road thence along the Road to a Poplar on the South side of said Road then along by a line of marked Trees to the first Station.

(147) 37 Robert RIDDICK, Jno B WALTON, Richard BOND Jonathan NICHOLS, John HARE, Daniel POWELL, Thomas HOFFLER William HINTON X Jacob OUTLAW Josiah X PARKER Danil X EURE Elisha Hance BOND

Then the Court adjourned until tomorrow morning 10 oClock

Wednesday morning the Court met
Present Joseph RIDDICK   )
         Jethro BALLARD   )
         James GREGORY   ) Esquires
         David RICE   ) Justices
         Simon STALLINGS   )
         Wm GOODMAN   )
         Thomas HUNTER   )

Aaron HOBBS Admr of Jacob HOBBS decd exhibited an account of Sales of part of the Estate of the Decedent on oath &c

Present Christopher RIDDICK Esquire
Peggy PARNEL who was delivered of a Bastard Child gave Bond with Thomas HURDLE and Jacob EASON her Securitys to Jos RIDDICK & Simon STALLINGS Esqrs Justices for maintenance of said Child &c fine paid to Jos. RIDDICK Esqr

The Sate against Thomas ELLEN Jury empannelled and Sworn (to wit) Isaac COSTEN Miles ROUNTREE, David HARRELL John SMALL Richard BRIGGS, William KING David CROSS, Moses DAVIS, Levin DUER James SMALL James B SUMNER, & William CLEAVES, say (End of entry.)

Thomas MARSHALL Guardian to John HILL, orphan of Guy HILL decd exhibited his account with said Orphan wherein there Appears to be a Balance due said Orphan the sum of 35.0.8

(148) 38 Additional Inventory of the Goods and Chattels rights and Credits which were of the Estate of Solomon KING decd, was exhibited into Court by Henry GOODMAN Exr. &c

Accounts of Sales of the Estate of Solomon KING decd was exhibited into Court by Henry GOODMAN Exr &c

Ordered that James SMALL be appointed Constable instead of Daniel DUKE resigned ordered that he give Bond and Security agreeable to Law at same time Humphry HUDGINS & Levin DURE came into Court & offered themselves Securitys &c

Demsey WILLIAMS Guardian to Saml BAKER Orpn of Sam BAKER decd exhibited his account with said Orphan where in there appears to be a Balance due said Orphan the sum of £65.8 5½

John B WALTON Guardn. to Guy HILL orpn. of Kedar HILL decd exhibited his accot with sd Orpn wherein there appears to be a balance due said Orphan £98.9..7

George WILLIAMS Thomas MARSHALL & Charles EURE three of the Gentn who were appointed to make a Division of the Estate of Thomas PILAND decd made report of their proceedings &c

James PILAND appointed Guardian to James PILAND orphan of Thomas PILAND decd Ordered that he give Bond & Secy in the sum of Two hundred & fifty pounds at same time Humphry HUDGINS & Willis PILAND came into Court and offered themselves as Securitys &c

Agreeable to the Petition of Jonathan ROBERTS Guardian to the Orphans of William

LEWIS decd. Ordered that the said Jonathan ROBERTS Guardian as aforesaid sell the Lands of the decd in Hertford County with the Grist & Saw Mill agreeable to Law including the Dower of Leah LEWIS Relict of sd William LEWIS Right of Dower in the said Mill after her Decease but not to sell the Lands Laid off to said Widow as her Dower but that the said Land laid off as the Dower aforesaid shall remain to the Heirs of said Wm LEWIS after (Remainder of line left blank.)

(149) 39 Ordered that the Exrs.. of William HINTON decd sell all the Perishable part of the Estate of said Decedent agreeable to Law &c

Ordered that the Sheriff of this County summon Cyprian CROSS David HARRELL son of Isaac James BAKER & James COSTEN as Jurors for the Supr Court in Apl next

Ordered that the Sheriff of this County summons Wm CLEAVES, Thomas SMITH, Jeremiah SPEIGHT William BROOKS Miles GATLING Israel BEEMAN Lewis SPARKMAN David LEWIS, William CRAFFORD John PARKER (Gatling) Abel CROSS Francis SPEIGHT Philip LEWIS Mills LEWIS James JONES Demsey WILLIAMS Elisha CROSS, Kedar HINTON, Joseph PARKER, Bond MINSHEW, John HUNTER, Seth ROUNTREE, John HAYSE Seth ROUNTREE Timothy FREEMAN James WALTON Seth EASON Abraham HURDLE Hardy EASON Miles WALTON & William HUNTER as Jurors for the next Court of this County &c

Ordered that Richard BOND pay to Absilla LASSITER by whom he had a Bastard Child the sum of Seven pounds ten Shillings immediately and five pounds pr year for seven years to commence from this time and also that Demsey JONES (Odom) pay the same sum and at the same periods to Mary RUSSEL and that Jno ELLIS pay to Mary SLAVIN the same sums at the same periods to Rachel SLAVIN

Ordered that John ELLIS Admr of William ELLIS decd sell as much of the Personal Estate of the deceased as will be sufficient for making a division of said Estate

Ordered that the hands belonging to John COWPER Esqr. that Work in the Shingle Swamps in this County Work on the road Contiguius to the Place or Read where the hands are employed

(150) 40 Ordered that Lawrence BAKER Clerk of this Court be allowed the sum of Twenty pounds for Extra Services by him performed the year passed &c

Ordered that Wm CUMMING Esqr who acted as Atto for the State in this County the sum of Nine pounds for his Services &c

Ordered that there be Levied on each Poll in this County one Shilling & Six pence & Six pence on each hundred Acres Land as a County Tax for the year passed

Ordered that Riddick TROTMAN Admr of Moses HILL, decd sell as much of the Personal Estate of the decedent as will pay his just debts

Ordered that Seth EASON turn the main road that leads through his Plantation as it is now staked

Ordered that Wm BAKER turn the main Road through the Plantation to run along by the Garden and into the Main Road through the Orchard

Ordered that Henry SMITH be appointed Constable in the room and stead of Isaac MILIER resigned Ordered that he give Bond and Security agreeable to Law

Ordered that Jonathan ROBERTS be appointed Treasurer of of Public Building, in this

Feb. 1797

County and that he give Bond & Security agreeable to Law at same time Joseph RIDDICK & Simon STALLINGS came into Court and offered themselves as Securitys &c

Ordered that Thomas MARSHALL & George WILLIAMS act with the ~~said~~ Treasurer of Public Buildings as Commissioners to act with him on the Building a Jail, and that the said Jail be Built on the same plan that the former one, only that there shall be a Room -- Built in the second Story of a Single Wall well grated with Glass Windows &c

   B o___ (blot) of ther? Court Test Law BAKER CC

(151) 41 State of No.. Carolina May 15 1797

     At a Court of Pleas and Quarter Sessions begun and held for the County of Gates at the Court House on the third Monday in May in the XXI year of the Independence of the said State and in the year of our Lord One thousand seven hundred & Ninety Seven

    Present.
    Christopher RIDDICK)
    Jethro SUMNER   )
    William GOODMAN) Esquires Justices
    Henry GOODMAN   )

Bill of Sale for two Negroe women PHILLIS CLOE & her Child HARRY Jesse BENTON to William DOUGHTIE proved by the oath of Jethro SUMNER &c

Deed of Gift for a Negro Boy ISAAC, Jesse BENTON to Charlotte NORFLEET proved by the oath of Jethro SUMNER &c

Deed of Gift for a Negro Boy ABRAM Jesse BENTON to Polly NORFLEET proved by the oath of Jethro SUMNER &c

Ordered that Simon STALLINGS, James WALTON Timothy WALTON & John HOFFLER or any three of them Audite & state the accounts of Wm VOLENTINE Admr of Henry HILL decd

Deed of Sale of Land David HARRELL to Demsey HARRELL Ackd &c

(152) 42 Ordered that Simon STALLINGS, James WALTON Timothy WALTON, & John HOFFLER or any three of them make a Division of the Estate of Henry HILL decd

Grand Jury empannelled & Sworn at this Term James WALTON Foreman, Hardy EASON, John HAYSE Seth ROUNTREE, Abel CROSS, James JONES (of Jesse) Jeremiah SPEIGHT, David LEWIS, Abraham HURDLE, Bond MINSHEW Elisha CROSS, Demsey WILLIAMS Miles GATLING, Seth EASON Kedar HINTON Lewis SPARKMAN & Timothy FREEMAN

Ordered that Cyprian ROOKS orphan of Thomas ROOKS about thirteen years of age be bound as an Apprentice to James TUGWELL to learn the Buisness of a Taylor &c

William BERRIMAN Guardian to James FREEMAN orphan of Richard FREEMAN decd exhibited his account current with said Orphan wherein there appears to be a Balance due said Orphan the sum of 108..15.1.

Deed of Sale of Land George LASSITER to Abner LASSITER proved by the oath of James HODGES &c

Deed of Sale of Land Demsey JONES of Hardy to Charles SMITH Ackd &c

Lease for Land Demsey JONES O to Winnefred LASSITER proved by the oath of James HODGES &c

Bill of Sale for a Negro named CLOAK Easther PARKER to Moses HINES proved by the oath of John PARKER &c

Bill of Sale for a Negro Girl named SENEY, Thomas BILLUPS & Jonathan ROBERTS to Noah HARRELL proved by the oath of James HODGES &c

Deed of Sale of Land William WILLIAMS Jethro SLAVIN Christian WILLIAMS & Dorothy WILLIAMS to William CLEAVES proved by the oath of Humphry HUDGINS &c.

(153) 43 Deed of Sale of Land Job FELTON & Sarah FELTON to Willis PILAND proved by the oath of Stephen HARRELL &c

Deed of Sale of Land with a Receipt thereon Luke SUMNER to Daniel FRANKLIN proved by the oath of William KNIGHT &c

Deed of Sale of Land Demsey JONES to Frederick LASSITER proved by the oath of Abner LASSITER &c

Deed of Sale of Land George LASSITER to Jonathan LASSITER, proved by the oath of James HODGES &c

Deed of Gift Aaron HARRELL to Willis SPARKMAN proved by oath of Easther GREEN &c

Ordered that John ARNOLD be appointed Overseer of the Road instead of Lewis WALTARS resigned

Christopher RIDDICK, Humphry HUDGINS & Isaac MILLER three of the Gentlemen who were appointed to make a Division of the Estate of a Certain Estate left by James RIDDICK decd bequeathed in his last Will & Testament to the Orphans of Kedar RIDDICK decd made report of their proceedings thereon &c

Deed of Sale of Land John ARNOLD to Micajah REID Ackd &c

Deed of Sale of Land Stephen ROGERS to James JONES Proved by the oath of James PARKER &c

Robert PARKER Admr of James BROWN decd returned an Account Sales of part of the Estate of the decd on oath &c

Ordered that the hands of William GATLING sen & William GATLING Junr and Amos DILDAY work on the Road under Thomas BARNES Overseer &c

(154) 44 Jethro SUMNER, Miles BENTON, & William HARRISS three of the Gentlemen who were appointed to make a Division of the Real Estate of Abraham MORGAN decd made report of their proceedings thereon &c

The Sheriff having returned the Pannel of a Jury with the Verdict Agreeable to an order of Court for laying off the dower of Ann HILL Relict of Abraham HILL decd out of certain Lands the said Abraham died seized & possessed of (which is as follows to wit)
Agreeable to an order of Court & hereunto annexed we the Subscribers have met this 10th May 1797 and laid off the dower of Ann HILL relict of Abraham HILL decd out of

the Lands the said HILL died seized and possessed with, which is bounded as follows Vizt. Begining at a Maple standing on the side of Catherine Creek Swamp then a streight Course through the Plantation to a Stake standing in the old Field, thence a line of marked Trees, to an old Field in Kedar HILLs line thence along the said HILLs line to the Swamp thence down the Swamp to the first Station. She is also to have a small piece including the House where she now lives which begins at the Corner of a Corn Cribb runing along the side of the Apple Orchard to the Kitchen then to the first Station including the house where she now lives & said Cribb William VOLENTINE Mills HURDLE, Wm FREEMAN Abraham HURDLE Jacob SPIVEY John SIMONS, Isaiah RIDDICK, William HAYS Thos HURDLE Bond MINSHEW William GOODMAN, John HUNTER.

The Sheriff having returned the Pannel of a Jury with the Verdict thereof to lay off to Thamar HILL Relict of Moses HILL decd out of Lands said HILL died seized & possessed with which which is bounded as follows vizt Begining at a Pine in Catherine Creek swamp thence to a Peach Tree thence a streight Course to a Stake standing in a Ditch then by a line of marked Trees to Kedar HILL decd

(155) 45 line she is to have all the Land on the west side of said Line belonging to that Tract, We have also laid off her Dower on a nother Tract of Land which is bounded as follows begining in the lane at Joseph BRINKLEY's line runing a streight Course by the smoke House to the fork of a Ditch in Ezekiel TROTMANs line, thence along the said TROTMANs line to Amos TROTMAN decd line thence to the first Station Abraham HURDLE Isaiah RIDDICK Mills HURDLE Jacob SPIVEY William FREEMAN, William HAYS John SIMONS Bond MINSHEW Thos HURDLE John HUNTER William GOODMAN Wm VOLENTINE

Then the Court adjourned until tomorrow morning 10 oClock

Tuesday morning the Court met
Present
James GREGORY
Christo. RIDDICK
David RICE
William GOODMAN
Thomas HUNTER

Deed of Sale of Land Lemuel COTTEN to Elisha FELTON proved by the oath of Moses HARE &c

In the Action Wm VOLENTINE against Thomas BILLUPS John B WALTON & Thomas MARSHALL Jury Impannelld & Sworn (to wit) Philip LEWIS, Wm HUNTER Miles WALTON John HUNTER, Mills LEWIS, William CRAFFORD, Wm CLEAVES, Joseph PARKER, John Parker GATLING Thomas SMITH Francis SPEIGHT William BROOKS, being Impannelled & Sworn say. (End of entry.)

(156) 46 In suit James SUMNER Exr of Seth SUMNER against Jas B SUMNER Jury impannelled & Sworn to wit Philip LEWIS William HUNTER, Miles WALTON, John HUNTER, Mills LEWIS Wm CRAFFORD, William CLEAVES, Joseph PARKER, John Parker GATLING Thos SMITH Francis SPEIGHT & William BROOKS Jury impannelled & Sworn say the Obligation declared on is the act & Deed of the Deft that there are no payments or set off & assess the Plffs Damage by way of Int to £16 & 6 Costs & 6

Last Will and Testament of Mary BROWN decd was exhibited into Court by Isaac COSTEN one of the Executors therein appointed and was proved by the oath of John CRAIPER one of the Subscribing witnesses thereto at the same time the said Isaac COSTEN came into Court and quallified thimself for that office &c

May 1797

Riddick TROTMAN exhibited an account of Sales of part of the Estate of Moses HILL decd on oath &c

In the suit Saml DONALDSON survg Partner of GIBSON GRANBERY & Co. against Miles Jethro & Josiah BENTON Heirs of Jethro BENTON, Jury impannelled & Sworn to wit) Philip LEWIS, William HUNTER, Miles WALTON, John HUNTER, Mills LEWIS, William CRAFFORD William CLEAVES, Joseph PARKER John Parker GATLING Thomas SMITH Francis SPEIGHT & William BROOKS say the Obligation declared on is the Act and Deed of the Defendants, that there are no payments or set offs & assess Six pence Intt by way of Damage & no more or other sum, & Six pence Costs

Ordered that David SMALL & Christian SMALL who were summoned as a Witness as in a Suit brought by David RIDDICK against Seth EASON be fined Ni Si &c

On a Warrant Henry HARE against Thomas RITTER Execution was Issd. for the sum of two pounds & two pence & costs return being made by Luten LEWIS Constable, Not satisfied there is no property but Land I levied the with Exn. on said Thos RUTTERs Land March 21. 1797 Ordered that Execution be ~~Levied on the~~ Issd against the Lands of the said Thos RUTTER

            constables Costs paid

(157) 47 Deed of Sale of Land Thomas YOUNG Norfleet HARRIS Bethal BELL to Elisha BENTON proved by the oath of Miles BENTON

Inventory of the Goods & Chattels rights & Credits which were of the Estate of Robert Foster BENTON decd was exhibited into Court by Jesse BENTON Admr on oath &c

Account of Sales of the Estate of Robert Foster BENTON was exhibited into Court by Jesse BENTON Admr on oath &c.

Deed of Sale of Land Luke SUMNER to William MATTHIAS ackd.

On a Warrant John ODOM son of Wm against Thomas RITTER Execution was Issd for the sum of Five pounds & __,, __,, __,, __,, --- (blank) return being made by Luten LEWIS two pounds nine Shillings 2d of the within Execution paid. the balance of it not satisfied because there is no property to be found but Land I levied the within Execution on sd Thos RITTERs Land March 21 1797 Ordered that Exn be Issued against the Lands of said RITTER to pay the Bale of Exn.

            constables fees paid

An Attachment Thos BARNES against Thomas RITTER the Land Attached Ordered that Execution be Issd against the Lands of said Tho RITTER to pay & satisfiy said Tho BARNES the sum of fourteen Shillings & two pence (Constables fees paid)

Ordered that William HAYS be appointed Guardian to Herman HAYS Henry HAYSE Hosey HAYSE and Mary HAYSE orphans of Wright HAYSE decd Ordered that he give Bond & Security in the sum of Five hundred pounds for each of them at same time Jacob HAYSE & (blank) came into Court and offered themselves as Securtys

(158) 48 Ordered that Thomas HUNTER John B WALTON Simon STALLINGS & Joseph RIDDICK Esquires or any three of them make a Division of the Personal Estate of Moses HILL decd.

Deed of Gift Luke SUMNER to Milicent Hunter SUMNER ackd.

The Worshipfull Court Taking into Consideration the Act of Assembly for the appointment of a Sheriff on Consideration Samuel SMITH was appointed Sheriff for the present year Ordered that he give Bond & Security agreeable to Law at same William HARRISS Humpy HUDGINS and Thomas SMITH came into Court and offered themselves as Securitys at same time the said Saml SMITH took the oaths of Government Justices of the peace on the Bench Thomas HUNTER Joseph RIDDICK William GOODMAN Simon STALLINGS, William BAKER James GREGORY & David RICE Esqr

Ordered that William HARRISS be appointed Coroner in this County Ordered that he give Bond & Security agreeable to Law, at Same time Humphy HUDGINS & Samuel SMITH came into Court and offered themselves as Securitys &c

Whereas it hath been represented to this Court that graet injustice hath been done Jemima ODOM relict of William ODOM decd in laying out her Dower in certain lands that her deceased Husband died seized & possessed with it is therefore Ordered that the Sheriff Summons a Jury and proceed to lay off her dower in said Lands &c

Whereas graet complaints was made of the riots and Disturbance made in consequence of the Taverns and Tipling Tables held in the Neighbourhood of the Court & Court House yard it is therefore Ordered that all such Taverns and Tipling Tables be altogether suppressed and that the Sheriff do suppress all such taverns & tipling Tables on sight

Then the Court adjourned until tomorrow morning 10 OClock

(159) 49 Wednesday morning the Court met
Present
Thomas HUNTER)
David RICE   ) Esquires
Jos RIDDICK   )

Ordered that the following Gentlemen receive Lists of Taxables and Taxable property from the citizens of this County (to wit) Simon STALLINGS in the District of Captain James WALTON James GREGORY in the District of Captain Isaac HUNTER David RICE in the District of Captain Jethro SUMNER Jethro SUMNER in Jesse BENTONs Captaincy Christo RIDDICK in the District of Captain William HARRISS William GOODMAN in the District of Captain Francis SPEIGHT William BAKER in the District of Captain David LEWIS

Ordered that the Sheriff of this County summons the following persons as Jurymen for this Court at next Term (to wit) James BAKER Samuel GREEN, Thomas TROTMAN William VOLENTINE, Jacob SPIVEY, Joseph TAYLOR, Charles POWELL, James FREEMAN, James BARNES Levin DUER John SMALL, Jacob GORDON, Robert POWELL, John ARNOLD John POWELL senr. William ARNOLD, David BENTON Moses DAVIS Noah FELTON, William DOUGHTIE Jesse BENTON, Willis BROWN, Jonathan SMITH Hillory WILLEY Charles EURE Henry SPEIGHT Ebron SEARS Joseph BRADY Robert RIDDICK & James PRUDEN

Ordered that Jethro MELTEAR Constable be allowed the sum of One pound four Shillings for summoning the Citizens of Captain James WALTONs District to return lists of their Taxables & Taxable property &c

(160) 50 Lawrence BAKER came into Court and mooved for Administration on the Estate of Jesse ODOM decd Ordered that he give Bond & Security in the sum of One thousand pounds at same time William BAKER & Saml SMITH came into Court and offered themselves as Securitys who were approved of a't &c

May 1797

Account of Sales of part of the personal Estate of William LEWIS decd was exhibited into Court by Jonathan ROBERTS one of the Executors on oath &c and Also an account of Sales of Lands and Mill in Hertford County sold agreeable to an order of Court was exhibited into Court by Jonathan ROBERTS Guardian to the Orphans of William LEWIS decd on oath &c

Ordered that Joseph RIDDICK Esq William VALINTINE James WALTON & Richard MITCHELL or any three of them audite & State the accounts of George OUTLAW junr Seth ROUNTREE & Isaac COSTEN Exrs of James OUTLAW decd &c

William BAKER County Trustee exhibited his Accounts current with this County wherein there appears to be a balance due the County the sum of One hundred & one pound five Shillings & three pence accounts filed

An __we? Exns. being issued by Henry GOODMAN Esqr from a Warrant Owin FLINN against James B SUMNER for L6.14.5.. each the Constable having returned on the said Exns that no property was to be found but Land and that he had Levied an Exn on the Land &c

Executions having been issued and? in favor of Patrick HEGERTY against James B SUMNER for 2.12 0 the Constable having returned not satisfied no property but Land and that he levied on the Land of the deft &c

William WALTERS & Luten LEWIS Constables exhibited their accounts against the County for their attendance on this Court & for summoning the citizens in their respective Districts ordered that the sum of five pounds four Shillings be paid by the County Trustee to each of them

(161) 51 Ordered that Isaac PIPKIN senr Isaac PIPKIN junr William GOODMAN & Henry GOODMAN or any three of them make a division of the Estate of Jesse ODOM decd who was orphan of Elisha ODOM decd. agreeable to Law

Ordered that William BAKER James GREGORY Lawrence BAKER & Thomas MARSHALL or any three of them Audite & State the accounts of Josiah COLLINS Admr of Samuel H JAMESON decd &c

By Order of the Court
Test Law BAKER CC

(162) 52 State of No Carolina.   August 21: 1797.

At a Court of Pleas and Quarter Sessions begun and held for the County of Gates at the Court House on the third Monday in August in the XXii year of the Independence of the said State Anno Dom MCDCCXCVII.

Present
Christopher RIDDICK)
David RICE)
William GOODMAN) Esquires Justices
Henry GOODMAN)

Deed of Gift Stephen COPELAND to Henry COPELAND proved by the oath of William GOODMAN &c

Grand Jury impannelled & Sworn for this Term (to wit) Jacob GORDON Foreman, James PRUDEN, Levin DUER Robert POWELL, Jonathan SMITH, Willis BROWN Noah FELTON, Moses DAVIS, Charles EURE William ARNOLD, James BAKER, Charles POWELL Samuel GREEN, William DOUGHTIE.

Deed of Sale Henry GOODMAN to Jethro SUMNER Ackd

Ordered that Richard CURL a Base born Child Son of Milicent CURL about Seven years of age be bound as an Apprentice to Winborn JENKINS to learn the Buisiness of a Glover & Leather Breechis maker &c

Ordered that James WALTON, Jacob SPIVEY, Simon STALLINGS James B WALTON & John HOFFLAR with Jos RIDDICK Esquire for Surveyor make a Division of the Estate Real of Moses HILL deceased &c

(163) 53 Bill of Sale Francis SPEIGHT to Susanna SPEIGHT provd by the oath of Luten LEWIS &c

Ordered that Isaac HUNTER Job RIDDICK Isaac COSTEN & James HODGES or any three of them Audite & State the accots of Moses LASSITER Exr of George LASSITER decd and make report &c

Ordered that Jonathan ROBERTS John B WALTON Miles ROUNTREE & Kedar HINTON or any three of them Audite the accounts of Aaron BLANSHARD Admr of Demsey BLANSHARD decd. &c

William GOODMAN Esquire came into Court and mooved for Administration on the Estate of Francis SPEIGHT deceased which was considered of and granted Ordered that he give Bond & Security in the sum of Five thousand pounds at same time William BAKER & Henry GOODMAN came into Court and offered themselves as security who were approved off &c

Inventory of the Goods & Chattels rights and Credits which were of the Estate of Francis SPEIGHT decd was exhibited into Court by William GOODMAN Admr &c

Guy HILL orphan of Kedar HILL decd came into Court and made choice of Jacob SPIVEY as his Guardian Ordered that he give Bond and Security in the sum of Five hundred pounds at same time James FREEMAN & Joseph RIDDICK came into Court and offered themselves &c

(Entire entry crossed out.) Bill of Sale Francis SPEIGHT to Susanna SPEIGHT for a Negro Girl named MARY proved by the oath of Luten LEWIS &c

Account of Sales of Part of the Estate of William WARREN decd was exhibited into Court by John PARKER on oath &c

Agreeable to the Peto of Frederick Hardy & Solomon EASON Ordered that Abraham HURDLE, William KING, William BERRYMAN Samuel HARRELL & Isaac HUNTER together with the surveyor of this County make a division of the real Estate of William EASON agreeable to the Will of William EASON decd agreeable to his Will

(164) 54 Deed of Sale James FREEMAN & Uxr to Thomas FREEMAN acknowledgd by James FREEMAN &c

Deed of Sale James FREEMAN & Uxr to William FREEMAN ackd by James FREEMAN &c

Deed of Sale Samuel SMITH Sheriff of Gates County to Abraham RIDDICK proved by the oath of John PARKER &c

Deed of Sale Ezekiel TROTMAN Executor of Demsey TROTMAN decd to Joseph RIDDICK Ackd &c

Deed of Sale with a receipt thereon Reuben LASSITER & Uxr to Willis WOODLEY proved by the oath of Richard BOND Junr &c

Deed of Sale with a recept thereon James HODGES & Uxr to Willis WOODLEY proved by the oath of James SMALL &c

Bill of Sale for a Negro Girl named DINAH Peggy RICE to Willis WOODLEY with a receipt thereon proved by the oath of Robert RIDDICK &c

Deed of Gift Richard BOND to Willis WOODLEY for Negroes JACK, ABRAHAM, CHERRY & BOBB proved by the oath of James COSTEN &c

Deed of Sale William BOND & Uxr to Willis WOODLEY proved by the oath of John SMALL &c with a receipt on the back thereof

Deed of Sale of Land William BAKER to Joseph BRADY proved by the oath of Reuben WILLIAMS &c

Deed of Sale Edward BRISCO to Ebron SEARS proved by the oath of Joseph PARKER &c

Deed of Sale William BAKER to Ebron SEARS proved by the oath of Reuben WILLIAMS &c

Ordered that Reuben RIDDICK Constable be allowed the sum of Twenty Shillings for two days warning the Citizens in Capt HUNTERs Capty to return Lists of their Taxables &c

(165) 55 Ordered that James SMALL Constable be allowed forty Shillings for his services warning the citizins of Capt SUMNERs Capty to return lists of their Taxables &c

Account of Sales of the Estate of George LASSITER decd was exhibited into Court by Moses LASSITER Exr on oath &c

Account of Sales of the Estate of Demsey BLANSHARD decd was exhibited into Court by Aaron BLANSHARD decd on oath &c

Inventory of the Estate of Mary BROWN decd was exhibited into Court by Isaac COSTEN Exr on oath &c

Philip LEWIS appointed Guardian to Joseph & Susanna SPEIGHT orphans of Francis SPEIGHT decd Ordered that he give Bond with security in the sum of three thousand pounds for each of them at same time James GATLING & David LEWIS came into Court and offered themselves as securitys &c

Jesse SAUNDERS appointed Guardian to William ODOM & Polly ODOM Orphans of William ODOM decd Ordered that he give Bond with security in the sum of one thousand pounds for William & five hundred pounds for Polly ODOM at same time Demsey ODOM & Law SAUNDERS came into Court and offered themselves as securitys &c

Isaac PIPKIN Junr William GOODMAN Isaac PIPKIN senr & Henry GOODMAN the Gentn appointed to make a division of the Estate of Jesse ODOM made report of their proceedings thereon &c

Deed of Sale of Land Nathl RIDDICK to Samuel HARRELL proved by the oath of Patrick HEGIRTY &c

Account of Sales of the Estate of James BETHEY decd was exhibited into Court by John

BETHEY Exr on oath &c

Bill of Sale for four Negroes DINAH, CATE, SARAH & HANNAH James B. SUMNER & Jethro SUMNER to Isaac PIPKIN proved by the oath of David RIDDICK &c.

(166) 56 Agreeable to a Writ of dower for the purpose of setting apart the dower of Jimmima ODOM relict of William ODOM decd the Sheriff made the following report (to wit) State of No Carolina Gates County ss We the Subscribers Freehoulders being summoned by the Sheriff of Gates County for the purpose of laying out alloting and setting apart the dower of Jemmima ODOM relict of William ODOM decd. out of certain Lands which the said William died seized & possessed with whereon Uriah ODOM lately lived after meeting on the premises & viewing the same have layed off the dower of the said Jimmima ODOM in the following manner (to wit) begining at a pine and runing near a Northwest course along a line of sliped Trees to the old line of John ODOMs thence the said line to a sliped pine thence along a line of sliped trees near an east Course to a sliped Water Oak standing in the Bee tree Branch, thence the said branch to the first Station Given under our hands and seals this 3 day of August 1797 James GATLING (seal) John LEWIS L. S. John PARKER LS Thomas BARNES LS James his + mark JONES LS James his I mark BRADY LS Mills LANDING LS H Ebron SEARS LS Thomas HEALL (HIATT?) his + mark LS. Henry SPEIGHT LS Amos DILDAY LS Jonathan ROGERS LS Henry SMITH D Shff

Then the Court adjourned until tomorrow morning 10 oClock

Tuesday morning the Court met
Present
Joseph RIDDICK)
David RICE   ) Esquires Justices
Jethro BALLARD)

Bill of Sale for four Negroes DINAH, CATE, SARAH, & HANNAH, Isaac PIPKIN Junr to Cyprian CROSS Ackd &c

(167) 57 David RIDDICK who prayed for and obtained an Appeal in a suit brought by him against Seth EASON at this Court at last term came into Court and dismised the Appeal by him taken &c

James GREGORY Esquire who was appointed to take a list of the Taxables in Captn Isaac HUNTERs Capy &c

David RICE Esqr. who was appointed to take a list of the Taxables in Captn Jethro SUMNERs Capty (End of entry.)

In a suit Barsheba SUMNER against Miles PARKER Jury impannelled & sworn (to wit) William VOLENTINE Jacob SPIVEY, John ARNOLD, John POWELL senr Henry SPEIGHT, James FREEMAN, David BENTON, Henry E SEARS Jesse BENTON, John SMALL, Joseph TAYLOR & Thomas SMITH jr, say the Defendant is Guilty and assess for the Plaintiffs Damage Two pounds one Shilling & Six penc Costs

Deed of Sale of Land Samuel SMITH Sheriff of this County to Isaac HUNTER ackd.

Bill of Sale for a Negro Woman PATT which was the property of Joseph John SUMNER, Samuel SMITH Sheriff to Anthony MATTHEWS Ackd. &c

James GREGORY David RICE & Humphry HUDGINS Esquires three of the Gentn who were appointed to Audite & State the accounts of Isaac HUNTER Executor of Sarah LASSITER decd made report of their proceedings thereon &c

Ordered that David HARRELL son of Abraham be appointed Overseer of the Road instead of Jacob GORDON resigned &c

Ordered that Lawrence SAUNDERS be appointed Overseer of the Road in the District and stead of Francis SAUNDERS, remooved

(168) 58 Ordered that Isaac COSTEN Exr to Mary BROWN sell the Perishable part of the Estate of the decedent

Deed of Gift for Six Negroes (to wit) PHILLIS, SEAR? BURRIL NELSON LUCY & JACK William BENNETT to Barsheba SPEIGHT Ackd &c

Deed of Sale of Land James JONES & Uxr to Jonathan ROGERS Ackd. &c

Ordered that Micajah RIDDICK Humphry HUDGINS John RIDDICK and James BARNES or any three of them Audite & State (written over) Settle the accounts of Jeremiah SPEIGHT Administrator of the Estate of William SPEIGHT decd. &c

Jethro SUMNER Esquire who was appointed to take a List of Taxables in Captn BENTONs Capty made report of his proceedings &c

Deed of Sale of Land Joseph TAYLOR to Nathl TAYLOR Ackd &c

Bill of Sale Joseph TAYLOR to Nathl TAYLOR for Goods & Chattels ackd &c

Frederick BLANSHARD appointed Guardian to Mary BLANSHARD orphan to Absalom BLANSHARD Ordered that he give Security in the sum of Five hundred pounds at same time Amerias BLANSHARD & Miles ROUNTREE came into Court and offered themselves as securitys &c

Ordered that William GOODMAN Henry GOODMAN Richard BARNES & Elisha CROSS or any three of them Audite & State the accounts of Jonathan ROGERS Exor of Zelpha ROGERS decd. with the Estate of the decedent &c And that the same Persons divide the Estate of the decedent agreeable to the Will &c

Agreeable to the Peto. of Ann SPEIGHT relict of William SPEIGHT decd Ordered that the Sheriff of this County summons a Jury and allot to the said Ann SPEIGHT her dower out of certain Lands which her deceased Husbd died seized and possessed with &c

(169) 59 Ordered that Wm BAKER Lawrence BAKER Miles GATLING & James GATLING or any three of them make a Division of the Estate of William FRYOR decd which was in the possession of Sarah HUGHS decd who was relict of Said? (written over) The said William &c

Ordered that Nathaniel BURGESS orphan of Thomas BURGESS decd about the age of (blank) years be Bound as an Apprentice to Cordel NORFLEET to learn the Buisness of House Carpenter & Joyner

Ordered that James COWPLAND a Bastard Child of Hester COPELAND about the age of (blank) years be bound as an Apprentice to Henry LEE to learn the Buisness of a House Carpenter &c

Ordered that the Ameriah BLANSHARD Exr of Jesse SPIVEY decd, sell as much of the personal Estate of the decedent as will pay the just Debts of the deceased

Bill of Sale for two Negroes AGGY & CEASRE? Pasco TURNER to Robt PARKER proved by the oath of Jethro SUMNER &c

Ordered that William GOODMAN Admr of Francis SPEIGHT sell as much of the Estate of the decedent as will pay his Debts

    Then the Court adjourned until tomorrow morning 10 OClock

(170) 60 Wednesday morning the Court met
    Present the Worshipfull Justices to wit
    Joseph RIDDICK)
    David RICE   ) Esquires
    William GOODMAN)

Robert PARKER came into Court and mooved for Administration on the Estate of Robert PARKER decd. Ordered that he give Bond & Security in the sum of One thousand five hundred pounds at same time James FREEMAN and Henry Ebron SEARS came into Court and offered themselves as Securitys &c

Inventory of the Goods and Chattels rights & Credits which were of the Estate of Robert PARKER decd was exhibited into Court by Robert PARKER Admr. &c

Ordered that John RIDDICK Humphry HUDGINS, Isaac MILLER and James PRUDEN or any three of them make a Division of the Estate of William SPEIGHT decd agreeable to Law.

Ordered that the Sheriff of this County summons Abraham HURDLE, John ODOM, Miles BENTON & Isaac BENTON COSTEN to attend at Edenton as Jurymen to the Supr Court to be held for the district of Edenton on the Sixth day of October next

Inventory of the Goods and Chattels rights & Credits which were of the Estate of Jesse ODOM decd was exhibited into Court by Lawrence BAKER Admr

Ordered that the Sheriff summons Abraham GREEN Moses BRIGGS Samuel BROWN Mills BENTON, James KNIGHT, Simeon BRINKLEY Willis WOODLEY James JONES of David, William HUNTER, Willm HUNTER William BERRIMAN Thomas HOBBS, John B WALTON Kedar HINTON, Timothy WALTON Philip ROGERS, Elisha CROSS Jonathan ROGERS, Jesse Benton PARKER Robert RIDDICK Demsey WILLIAMS Henry LEE Abel CROSS, William GATLING junr Bray SAUNDERS Isaac LANGSTO Demsey LANGSTON Cyprian CROSS Asa HARRELL James JONES son of Jesse Moor CARTER & Wm Wright RIDDICK as Jurymen next Term &c

(171) 61 Henry SMITH Constable made return ____ (blot) Execution against James B SUMNER on behalf of Bond MINSHEW that he had executed the said same on Land there being no property but land to be found, Ordered that the said Land be sold by Exn. to pay £7.16 3
        Constable Costs 0 11 0

Ordered that John B WALTON, Timothy WALTON Thomas MARSHALL and Simon STALLINGS or any three of them Audite & State and settle the accounts of Amerias BLANSHARD Exr. of Jesse SPIVEY decd &c

Ordered that Robt PARKER Admr. of Robert PARKER decd sell as much of the Perishable estate of the decedent as will pay his just Debts.

Aug. 1797

Bill of Sale for two Negroes MINGO & REUBEN Jesse EASON to David RIDDICK proved by the oath of James H KEYS &c

Ordered that George WILLIAMS be exempt from the payment of a double Tax, there being a mistake in the return against him &c

Ordered that Isaac PIPKIN late Sheriff of this County be allowed in the settlement of his accounts with the Public Treasurer and County Trustee for the Tax on the following Persons to wit Joseph PLATT 5/6 Uriah ODOM 11/ John ODOM 22/. Francis SAUNDERS 11/ and on Benjamin EURE 5/6.

Ordered that Robert PARKER senr be exempt from the payment of a ---- double Tax &c

By order
Test Law BAKER
CC

(172) 62 State of No.. Carolina   Novr. 20 1797
Gates County) ss

At a Court of Pleas and Quarter Sessions begun and held for the County of Gates at the Court House on the third Monday in November in the XXii year of the Independence of the said State Anno Domini MDCCXCVii.

Present
Christopher RIDDICK
William GOODMAN
Henry GOODMAN

Ordered that Henry GOODMAN Esquire Cyprian CROSS John ODOM & Jesse VANN or any three of them Audite State the? Accounts of John PARKER Executor of Francis SAUNDERS decd &c

Ordered that ~~Bathsheba SPEIGHT~~ the Sheriff of this County Summons a Jury and lay off the dower of Bathesha SPEIGHT Relict of Francis SPEIGHT (agreeable to her Peto).

Ordered that Henry GOODMAN Esquire Isaac PIPKIN Senr. Isaac PIPKIN jr. & Wm GATLING senr. lay off to Bathsha SPEIGHT so much of the property of her decd Husband as will be sufficient for hers and her Familys support during one year

Ordered that Joseph RIDDICK & Simon STALLINGS Esqrs John B WALTON & Abraham HURDLE or any three of them Audite & State the accounts of Aaron HOBBS Admr of the Estate of Jacob HOBBS decd.

Ordered that Ann SIMONS Administratrix of John SIMONS decd sell so much of the Personal Estate of the decedent as will pay his just Debts &c

(173) 63 Grand Jury impannelled & Sworn for Novr Term 1797 (to wit John B WALTON Foreman, Isaac LANGSTON, Asa HARRELL, William HUNTER, James KNIGHT, Jonathan ROGERS Kedar HINTON, William BERRYMAN, Abraham GREEN, Wm W RIDDICK Timothy WALTON, Henry LEE, Cyprian CROSS Moor CARTER Simeon BRINKLEY

Ordered that the Perishable part of the Estate of the Orpns of Moses HILL decd be sold by Riddick TROTMAN their Guardian &c

Ann SIMONS came into Court and mooved for Administration on the Estate of John SIMONS decd which was accordingly granted Ordered that she give Bond & Security in the sum of Five hundred pounds, at the same time Abraham RIDDICK & John HUNTER came into Court and offered themselves as Securitys &c

Inventory of the Goods and Chattels Rights and Credits which were of the estate of John SIMONS decd was exhibited into Court by Ann SIMONS Administratrix on oath &c

Mills LEWIS came into court and mooved for Administration on the estate of John BURGES decd which was accordingly granted Ordered that he give Bond & Security in the sum of five hundred pounds, at the same time Miles GATLING & William GATLING senr. came into Court and offered themselves as Securitys &c

The Last Will and Testament of James DAVIS was exhibited into Court by Keziah DAVIS Executrix therein appointed and was proved by the Oath of Jonathan LASSITER one of the subscribing Witnesses, at the Same time the said Executrix came into Court and quallified herself for that office and prayed an Order for Letters Testamentory thereon &c

(174) 64 Inventory of the Goods and Chattels rights and Credits which were of the Estate of James DAVIS decd was exhibited into Court by Keziah DAVIS on oath &c

Bill (written over) Deed of Sale of Land James GRANBERY to Jethro SUMNER and Demsey ODOM proved by the oath of Isaac PIPKIN junr &c

Deed of Sale of Land James JONES to Isaac PIPKIN proved by the oath of Isaac PIPKIN Junr.

Deed of Sale of Land Levi OWNLY to Edward OWNLY proved by the oath of Norman KING &c

William GOODMAN Henry GOODMAN Richard BARNES & Elisha CROSS the Gentn who were appointed to make a division of the Estate of Robert ROGERS decd made report of their proceedings &c

William GOODMAN Henry GOODMAN Richard BARNES & Elisha CROSS the Gentlemen who were appointed to Audite & State the Accots. of Jonathan ROGERS Executor of Zilpha ROGERS decd and also to make a Division of the Estate of the Decedent made report of their proceedings &c

Deed of Sale of Land Isaac HUNTER to William CARTER proved by the oath of James COSTEN &c

Deed of Sale of Land Halen WILLIAMS to David RAWLS acknowledged &c

Deed of Sale of Land James KNIGHT to Ambroose WIGGINS Acknowledged &c

Account of Sales of part of the Estate of Robert PARKER senr deceased was exhibited into Court by Robert PARKER his Admr on oath &c

Humphry HUDGINS John RIDDICK & James BARNES three of the Gentn Who were appointed to Audite & State the Accots of Jeremiah SPEIGHT Admr of William SPEIGHT decd made report of their proceedings &c

(175) 65 Luten LEWIS Constable having returned an Execution from Henry GOODMAN Esquire on behalf of Thomas MARSHALL against Samuel GREEN for £8.14.9 & 9s. Costs

return being made thereon that there could be found no Property but Land and that the said Exn was levied on it Ordered that Exn Issue from this Court to sell the same &c

Bill of Sale for a Negro Girl named LIDDEY Seth EASON to James KNIGHT proved by the oath of Demsey KNIGHT &c

John RIDDICK James PRUDEN & Isaac MILLER senr. three of the Gentn. who were appointed to make a Division of the Estate of William SPEIGHT decd made report of their proceedings &c

Ordered that Simon STALLINGS Esqr. John Bunbery WALTON John HOFFLER Riddick TROTMAN James WALTON Patrick HEGERTY the Surveyor of this County make a Division of the Real Estate of Kedar HILL decd agreeabl to Law &c

Riddick TROTMAN appointed Guardian to Christian HILL and Mary HILL orphans of Moses HILL Ordered that he give Bond & Security in the sum of One thousand Pounds for each of them at same time Charles POWELL & Seth TROTMAN came into Court and offered themselves as Secys &c

John FREEMAN David FREEMAN & Anna FREEMAN Orpns of Solomon FREEMAN came into Court and made choice of their Brother Joseph FREEMAN as their Guardian Ordered that he give Bond and Security in the sum of One thousand pounds for each of them At same time Henry SPEIGHT and William GATLING came into Court and offered themselves as Securitys &c

(176) 66 Inventory of the Goods and Chattels Rights & Credits which were of the Estate of John BURGESS deceased was exhibited into Court by Mills LEWIS Admr &c

Then the Court adjourned until tomorrow morning 10 oClock

Tuesday morning the Court met
Present   James GREGORY, William GOODMAN
Christopher RIDDICK) Esqrs.

Samuel SMITH came into Court and mooved for Administration on the Estate of Thomas SMITH junr deceased, which was considered of and granted, Ordered that he give Bond & Security in the sum of Three hundred pounds at same time James BARNES & Henry SMITH came into Court and offered themselves as Securitys &c

Inventory of the Goods & Chattels Rights and Credits of the Estate of Thos SMITH deceased was exhibited into Court by Saml SMITH Admr on oath &c

Ordered that William HAYSE Admr of Wright HAYSE decd sell all the Negroes belonging to the Estate of the decedent in order that a division be made &c

James BARNES came into Court and mooved for Administrato ixed?, Debonus Non on the Estate of John SUMNER decd which was accordingly granted Ordered that he give Bond & Security in the sum of One thousand pounds at same time William HARRISS & Robert RIDDICK came into Court and offered themselves as Securitys &c

Deed of Sale of Land Samuel SMITH Sheriff to Isaac HUNTER Ackd &c

(177) 67 Deed of Sale of Land Cyprian CROSS to Jesse VANN Ackd &c

Deed of Sale of Land Jesse VANN to Cyprian CROSS Ackd. &c

Isaac HUNTER Job RIDDICK, & James HODGES the Persons appointed to Audite & State the accounts of Moses LASSITER Exr with the Estate of George LASSITER decd made report of their proceedings &c

Agreeable to the Peto of Abigal HOBBS relict of Jacob HOBBS decd Ordered that the Sheriff of this County summons a Jury and lay off allot and set apart unto the said Abigal HOBBS her dower out of certain Lands her deceased Husband died seized and possessed with &c

Ordered that William VOLENTINE, John HOFFLER, James WALTON Thomas BRICKELL and Jacob SPIVEY with Patrick HEGERTY the Surveyor of this County make a division of the real Estate of Jacob HOBBS decd. agreeable to Law &c

Ordered that Miles GATLING be appointed Overseer of the Road in the district and stead of Abraham BEEMAN resigned.

Bill of Sale for a Negro PAUL Jethro SUMNER to John ODOM proved by the oath of Wm HARRISS. &c

Deed of Sale of Land William BAKER to Danie_ SOUTHALL proved by the oath of Isaac HUNTER &c

Deed of Sale of Land James RIDDICK to John SHEPHERD proved by the oath of Patrick HEGERTY &c

Accot Sales of part of the Estate of Francis SAUNDERS decd was exhibited into Court by John PARKER his Exr on oath &c

(178) 68 Ordered that John B WALTON Thomas MARSHALL Richard BOND Senr. & William VOLENTINE or any three of them Audite the Accounts of Jonathan ROBERTS Admr of Henry FORREST decd &c

Ordered that the Sheriff of this County summons a Jury and lay off the dower of Abigal PARKER relict of Robert PARKER decd out of certain Lands her Husband died seized and possessed with &c

Then the court adjourned until tomorrow morning 10 oClock

Wednesday morning the Court met
Present
Christopher RIDDICK)
James GREGORY) Esquires
Simon STALLINGS)

Joseph PARKER came into Court and mooved for Administration on the Estate of Kedar PARKER minor Orphan of Joseph PARKER decd Ordered that he give Bond & Security in the sum of One hundred pounds at same time Elisha CROSS & Demsey ODOM came into Court and offered themselves as Securitys &c

Joseph PARKER came into Court and mooved for Administration on the Estate of James PARKER minor Orphan of Joseph PARKER decd Ordered that he give Bond & Security in the sum of One hundred pounds at same time Elisha CROSS & Demsey ODOM came into Court and offered themselves as Securitys &c

William HARRISS Coroner returned an Inquisition taken on the Body of TOM a Negro Man the Property of Henry GOODMAN Esquire &c

Nov. 1797

Ordered that the Sheriff of this County Summons the following Gentn: Petit & Grand Jurors to serve? at this Court at next Term to wit Aaron HOBBS, Richard MITCHELL Jacob EASON, James FREEMAN David HARRELL Senr William VOLENTINE John HOFFLER, George BROOKS James WALTON

(179) 69 Amos LASSITER Miles WALTON, William CARTER James COSTEN Michael LAWRENCE, William CLEAVES, Thomas SMITH Micajah RIDDICK Jr.. James PILAND, William BROOKS Richard BARNES, Philip LEWIS William KING Wm GOODMAN Junr. Thomas BARNES, Miles BENTON James JONES of Davd. Benjamin GORDON James GORDON Levin DEUR & Kedar BALLARD &c

Samuel HOBBS appointed Guardian to John HOBBS orphan of Jacob HOBBS Ordered that he give Bond and Security in the sum of One hundred & fifty pounds at same time William BERRYMAN & Abraham GREEN came into Court and offered themselves as securitys &c

William BAKER Esquire appointed Guardian to Noah HINTON & William HINTON Orphans of William HINTON deceased Ordered that he give Bond and Security for each of them in the sum of Seven thousand five hundred pounds at same time William HARRISS Timothy WALTON and Lawrence BAKER came into Court and offered themselves as Securitys &c

Ordered that James GREGORY David RICE Josiah GRANBERY & Jethro BALLARD Esquires or any three of them Audite & State the Accounts of Isaac HUNTER and Lewis THOMPSON Executors of William HINTON decd. with the Estate of the decedent

Isaac HUNTER William BERRYMAN William KING & Samuel HARRELL with Patrick HEGERTY the Surveyor of this County who were appointed to make a division of the Real Estate of William EASON decd. made report of their proceedings thereon &c

Ordered that the Admr of Robert PARKER decd sell the Negroes belonging to the Estate of the decedent in order to make a Division

(180) 70 --- --- --- Joseph PARKER Admr to Kedar PARKER & James PARKER Orphans of Joseph PARKER decd mooved the Court to have persons appointed to make a division of the Estate of the decedents which was accordingly granted, at same time John B WALTON Timothy WALTON Jonathan ROBERTS & Jethro MELTEAR a----- were appointed &c

On a Motion of Daniel SOUTHALL it was ordered that he be licensed to keep a Public House at the Court in this County and that he give Bond and Security agreeable to Law at same time Samuel SMITH and William GATLING Junr. came into Court and offered themselves as Securitys &c

On motion Ordered that Samuel SMITH Admr of Thomas SMITH sell as much of the Estate of the decedent as will pay his Debts &c

By Courts order   Test Law BAKER CC

(181) 71 State of No Carolina.
At a Court of Pleas and Quarter Sessions begun and held at the Court House for of? County of Gates on the IIIrd Monday in February in the XXIInd year of the Independence of the said State Anno Domini MDCCXCVIII.

Present. Joseph RIDDICK Esquire

The Court adjourned, until tomorrow morning 10 oClock

Tuesday morning the Court met

Present
Joseph RIDDICK)
James GREGORY) Esquires
David RICE)

Deed of Sale of Land Thomas SMITH to George ALLEN acknowledged &c Jethro SUMNER Esquire present

Marriage Contract Thos PARKER & Leah RIDDICK proved by the oath of John MILLER &c

Deed of Sale of Land James JONES to William BAKER acknowledged &c

Grand Jury impannelled & Sworn to wit Richard MITCHELL Foreman, Aron HOBBS James WALTON Amos LASSITER James JONES of David, Miles WALTON, William CLEAVES James PILAND William BROOKS Wm CARTER James FREEMAN, Thomas SMITH, John HOFFLER & David HARRELL.

Deed of Sale of Land James HODGES & Uxr to Willis WOODLEY proved by the oath of John BLUNT With a Receipt thereon the signaturre of James HODGES proved by Jno BLUNT &c

Deed of Sale of Land Wm FREEMAN & James FREEMAN to Riddick TROTMAN proved by the oath Joseph RIDDICK Esquire &c

Deed of Sale of Land Samuel HARRELL to Willis WOODLEY ackd

Bill of Sale Henry SPEIGHT to Thomas BARNES for a Negro Man ABRAM ackd &c

(182) 72 Joseph RIDDICK Esquire Guardian to Joseph TROTMAN Love TROTMAN Willis TROTMAN & to Joseph Love & Willis TROTMAN Orphans of Thomas TROTMAN decd Wherein there appears to be the following balances due said Orphans to wit To Joseph TROTMAN £89..9..6 To Love TROTMAN £74..7..11, to Willis TROTMAN £329..1.0 & to Joseph Love & Willis TROTMAN the sum of £199..3..7½

Joseph RIDDICK, Simon STALLINGS & John B WALTON who were appointed to Audite State and settle the accounts of Riddick TROTMAN Administrator to the Estate of Moses HILL decd, made report of their proceedings thereon &c

The Last Will and Testament of Bridget WIGGINS decd was exhibited into Court by David RICE Esquire Executor therein appointed and was proved by the oath of Hezekiah JONES one of the subscribing witnesses thereto, which was ordered to be recorded at the same time the said Exor came into Court and quallified himself for that office &c

Sarah PHELPS relict of Demsey PHELPS decd came into Court & mooved for Administration on the Estate of her deceased Husband which was accordingly granted ordered that she give Bond & Secy in the sum of One hundred & fifty pounds at same time Jonathan ROBERTS & Jethro MELTEAR came into Court and offered themselves as Securitys &c

Inventory of the Goods and Chattels Rights & Credits which were of the estate of Demsey PHELPS decd was exhibited into Court by Sarah PHELPS on oath &c

Joseph RIDDICK Simon STALLINGS, John B WALTON & Abraham HURDLE the Gentlemen who were appointed to Audite the accounts of Aaron HOBBS Admr of Jacob HOBBS decd made report of their proceedings thereon &c

Feb. 1798

Robt PARKER Admr of James BROWN decd exhibited an account of the Sales of the Estate of the deceased on oath &c

James COSTEN Guardian to ~~Timothy~~ James LASSITER Henry LASSITER & Margaret LASSITER Orphans of Timothy LASSITER decd exhibited his accot with said Orphans wherein there appears to be balances due said orphans as follows (to wit) To James LASSITER 368..18.5 to Henry LASSITER 422.18.7, to Margaret LASSITER 372.11.1 3/4 &c

(183) 73 Jacob SPIVEY Guardian to Guy HILL orphan of Kedar HILL decd exhibited his accot with said Orphan wherein there appears to be a Balance due said orphan 117.6.11 &c

Abraham HURDLE Guardian to Jacob SUMNER Son of Abraham SUMNER wherein there appears to be a Balance due said Jacob the sum of 95 3..11. &c

Bill of Sale Thomas HUNTER and Thomas HOFFLER to Moor CARTER for a Negro Boy called JEREMIAH proved by the oath of Lawrence BAKER &c

Isaac PIPKIN jr. William GATLING Henry GOODMAN & Isaac PIKEN senr who were appointed to allot and point out such part of the Crop & Stock of Provisions as they may conceive necessary for the support of Basheba SPEIGHT relict of Francis SPEIGHT decd made report of their proceedings &c

Ordered that Joseph RIDDICK Simon STALLINGS John B WALTON and Abraham HURDLE or any three of them make a division of the Personal estate of Jacob HOBBS decd agreeable to Law.

Deed of Sale of Land Amos DILDAY to H Ebron SEARS proved by the oath of James HODGES &c

Deed of Sale of Land Isaac HUNTER to James FIGG proved by the oath of Thomas RIDDICK &c

Deed of Sale of Land William WILLIAMS to Halen WILLIAMS proved by the oath of Jonathan WILLIAMS &c

Deed of Sale of Land Jethro SUMNER & Demsey ODOM to Winborn JENKINS proved by the oath of Isaac WALTERS Junr.

Account of Sales of the Property of Christian HILL orphan of Moses HILL and also the Property of Polly HILL orphan of the said Moses HILL was exhibited into Court by Samuel SMITH Sheriff &c

Bill of Sale George GATLING to David HARRELL for a Negro Woman and two Children called EASTER SUKY & NED proved by the oath of Wm GATLING jr &c

Bill of Sale ofor a Negro man named CARY George GATLING to David HARRELL proved by the oath of William GATLING Junr

(184) 74 Jethro SUMNER Esquire came into Court and mooved for Administration on the Estate of John DARDEN decd which was granted Ordered that he give Bond & Security in the sum of two thousand pounds at same time William WALTERS & Willis WOODLEY came into Court and offered themselves as Security &c

Inventory of the Goods & Chattels Rights & Credits which were of the Estate of John

DARDEN decd was exhibited into Court by Jethro SUMNER Esquire on oath &c

Deed of Sale of Land Bryant WALTERS to William GATLING Junr proved by the oath of William GATLING Senr.

Deed of Sale of Land Robert TAYLOR & Hillory TAYLOR to Elisha Hance BOND proved by the oath of Richard BOND &c

Ordered that the Sheriff of this County Summons a Jury & and allot to Mary DARDEN relict of John DARDEN decd her dower in certain Lands which her Husband died seized and possessed with &c

Ordered that Jethro SUMNER Esquire Thomas PARKER William WALTERS & Jesse BENTON Freehoulders and Allot and lay off to Mary DARDEN relict of John DARDEN decd Such part of the Provisions &c on hand as will be sufficient for hers and familys support, agreeable to Law &c

Joseph RIDDICK Richard MITCHELL & James WALTON three of the Gentn who were appointed to Audite the Accots Seth ROUNTREE Isaac COSTEN & George OUTLAW Junr Exrs of James OUTLAW decd exhibited their proceedings thereon &c

Deed of Sale of Land Simon STALLINGS Sheriff of this County to James BARNES proved by the oath of Luten LEWIS &c

(185) 75 Ordered that David RICE Esquire Kedar BALLARD Thomas PARKER, Jesse BENTON & William WALTERS make a Division of the real estate of John DARDEN decd &c

Ordered that David RICE Esquire Kedar BALLARD Jesse BENTON & Thomas PARKER or any three of them make a division of the personal estate of John DARDEN decd &c

   Then the Court adjourned until tomorrow morning 10 oClock

   Wednesday the Court met agreeable to adjournment
    Present
    William BAKER)
    David RICE) Esquires Justices
    Joseph RIDDICK)

Ordered that Joseph RIDDICK Esquire Simon STALLINGS Esquire, Thomas MARSHALL, & William VOLENTINE or any three of them audite the accounts of William WILLIAMS Administrator of Abner BLANSHARD decd &c

Deed of Sale Jesse EASON to James GORDON acknowledged &c

Account of Sales of the Estate of Thomas SMITH decd was exhibited into Court by Samuel SMITH Admr on oath &c

Ordered that John COWPER Isaac HUNTER Levin DEUR & James SMALL or any three of them audite the accounts of Sarah HUNTER Extrix of James NORFLEET decd &c

Account of Sales of Negroes belonging to the Estate of Wright HAYSE decd was exhibited into Court by William HAYSE Administrator &c

Inventory of the Goods and Chattels rights and Credits which were of the estate of Kedar PARKER decd orphan of Joseph PARKER decd was exhibited into Court by Joseph

PARKER Admr on oath &c

Inventory of the Goods and Chattels rights and Credits which were of the Estate of James PARKER decd who was orphan of Joseph PARKER Admr on decd was exhibited into Court by Jos PARKER Adm on oath &c

(186) (Page not numbered.) Ordered that Christopher RIDDICK Wm W RIDDICK Robert PARKER James B SUMNER or any three of them make a division of the Personal estate of Wright HAYSE &c

Frederick BLANSHARD Guardian to William BLANSHARD orphan of Absolom BLANSHARD decd exhibited his account with said Orphan wherein there appeared to be a balance due said Orphan the sum of £115.10.1

Inventory of the Goods and Chattels rights & Credits which were of the Estate of Bridgit WIGGINS decd was exhibited into Court by David RICE Esqr Exr on oath

Deed of Sale of Land Jacob Parker JONES to Isaac HARRELL junr proved by the oath of David RICE

Deed of Sale Gift of Land John POWELL to John POWELL junr proved by the oath of James JONES &c

James PILAND Guardian to James PILAND Orphan of Thos PILAND decd. exhibited his account with said Orphan wherein there appeared to be a Balance due said Orphan the sum 45.0.0½

Contract of Marriage between Thomas HUNTER & Sarah NORFLEET was exhibited into Court for probate the witnesses not appearing ordered that a Subpona be Issd

Simon STALLINGS Jno B WALTON & Joseph RIDDICK Esquires who were appointed to make a division of the Estate of Moses HILL decd exhibited their proceedings thereon &c

Jacob SPIVEY, James WALTON John B WALTON Simon STALLINGS John HOFFLER with Joseph RIDDICK Surveyor who were appointed to make a division of the Real estate of Moses HILL decd made a report of their proceedings &c

Ordered that Sarah PHELPS Admr of the Estate of Demsey PHELPS decd sell as much of the perishable estate of the decd as will pay his Debts &c

Ordered that John WALTON Orphan of Thomas WALTON decd Abus? Seven Eighteen years of age be bound as an Apprentice to Joseph TAYLOR to learn the Buisness of a Cooper

(187) 77-A Ordered that the hands of Jeremiah SPEIGHT work on the Road (and also Joseph GARRETT) under Humphry HUDGIS Overseer

Ordered that the Sheriff Summons Henry LEE Kedar BALLARD Thomas PARKER & Micajah RIDDICK to Appear as Jurymen at the Superior Court at Edenton in Apl next &c

The Last Will and Testament of Thomas HUNTER was exhibited into Court by Joseph RIDDICK & Elisha HUNTER Executors therein appointed and was proved by the oath of William CARTER & George OUTLAW two of the Witnesses thereto and on motion was ordered to be recorded at the same time the said Exrs came into Court and quallifyed themselves for that office &c

Feb. 1798

Deed of Sale of Land Jacob THOMAS to Seth ROUNTRE_ proved by the oath of Joseph RIDDICK &c

Ordered that Joseph RIDDICK & Elisha HUNTER Exors of Thos HUNTER decd sell the Perishable part of the Estate of the decedent &c

William WALTERS Guardian to Bray BAKER Orphan of Samuel BAKER deceased exhibited his account with said orphan wherein there appears to be a balance due said Orphan £107.7.2

Ordered that Jethro BALLARD Kedar BALLARD, Levin DUER & James SMALL or any three of them Audite the accounts of Robert POWELL Admr of James POWELL decd &c

Ordered that the County Trustee pay Henry SMITH Thirty two Shillings for summoning the citizens in Captn Wm HARRISS's Capty to return lists of their Taxables & Taxable property &c

(188) 76 Ordered that Miles ROUNTREE be appointed Guardian to Charles ROUNTREE & John ROUNTREE Orphans of John ROUNTREE decd and that he give Bond and Security in the sum of One thousand pounds each at same time John HOFFLER & Miles WALTON came into Court and offered themselves as Securitys &c

Deed of Sale of Land Miles WALTON to Miles ROUNTREE Ackd &c

George WILLIAMS Guardian to Willis FIGG Orphan of Joseph FIGG decd exhibited his account with said Orphan wherein there appears to be a Balance due said Orphan the sum of 116..7..0..

Ordered that Benjamin BARNES James GATLING Philip LEWIS and Elisha CROSS or any three of them Audite & State the accounts of Henry GOODMAN Exr of Solomon KING decd &c

Ordered that Samuel HOBBS Guardian to John HOBBS ophan of Jacob HOBBS deceased sell the Personal property of the said Orphan &c

Ordered that Henry GOODMAN Wm GOODMAN Isaac PIPKIN & James GATLING or any three of them Audite & State the accounts of John ODOM Exr of Wm ODOM decd

Ordered that the Sheriff of this County Summons the following persons to serve at this Court next term as Jurymen (to wit) William HINTON Junr Jno B WALTON Timothy FREEMAN Abraham HURDLE, William HUNTER Isaac COSTEN, Noah HARRELL John RIDDICK, Richard BRIGGS Moses DAVIS, Moses SPEIGHT, John SMALL Simion BRINKLEY William MATTHIAS William GATLING jr. Henry SPEIGHT Isaac PIPKIN Junr. Hillory WILLEY Elisha CROSS Cyprian CROSS David CROSS Stephen EURE Mills EURE Moor CARTER Noah FELTON, John ARNOLD Jesse BENTON David BENTON Wm W RIDDICK & Willis BROWN

Protest by the Sheriff generally against the Jaoil and County &c

(189) 77-B Ordered that the sum of Eight pence on each hundred Acres of Land & two Shillings on each Poll be levied for a County Tax &c

Ordered that Lawrence BAKER Clerk of this Court be allowed the sum of Twenty pounds for extra services for the year passed &c

Ordered that Joseph RIDDICK Esquire be appointed Specially for processioning the

Feb. 1798

Lands of Richard MICHELL &c

Ordered that the real Estate which was given by Thomas TROTMAN to his Daughter Mary ROUNTREE who intermarried with John ROUNTREE and afterwards intermarried with William FREEMAN be equally divided between her Heirs & that the real Estate of John ROUNTREE decd. be divided equally between his Heirs, Soseph RIDDICK Simon STALLINGS James WALTON Seth ROUNTREE & John HOFFLER be appointed to make a division agreeable to Law &c

                              By order of the Court
                                  Law BAKER CC

(190) 78 State of No Carolina   May 21 1798
         At a Court of Pleas and Quarter Sessions begun and held for the County of P Gates at the Court House on the third Monday in May in the XXIInd year of the Independence of the said State Anno Domini MDCCXCVIII.

              Present
              Jethro SUMNER   )
              David RICE   ) Esquires Justices
              Henry GOODMAN   )
              Simon STALLINGS)

Ordered that John BEST orphan of Lewis BEST decd be bound as an Apprentice to John SHEPHERD to learn the buisiness of a Shoemaker orphan about (blank) years of age

William BOND appointed Guardian to John HILL orphan of Guy HILL decd. Ordered that he give Bond & Security in the sum of Five hundred pounds at same time Timothy FREEMAN & Richard BOND came into court and offered themselves as securitys &c

Deed of Sale Richard BOND to Noah HARRELL proved by the oath of Lassiter RIDDICK &c

Deed of Sale of Land with a receipt thereon William SPEIGHT to John RIDDICK proved by the oath of Wm HARRISS &c

Amos DILDAY and Thomas HIATT who entered into Recognizince for the personal Appearance of Hamilton WINBORN came into Court and surrendered the defendant WINBORN in discharge of themselves &c

Deed of Sale of Land Stephen EURE to Mills EURE ackd &c

(191) 79 Hamilton WINBORN who was surrendered up by Amos DILDAY & Thos HIATT his securitys produced further security for his personal appearance (to wit) Henry Ebron SEARS & Joseph BRADY &c until Wednesday next.

Selah VOLINTINE came into Court and mooved for Admn. on the Estate of William VOLINTINE decd which was granted Ordered that she give Bond with Security in the sum of Four thousand pounds at same time John HOFFLER and James BAKER came into Court and offered themselves as securitys who were approved of &c

Account of Sales of the Estate of John SIMONS deceased was exhibited into Court by Ann SIMONS & Abraham RIDDICK on oath &c

Ordered that Christian BROWN Relict of James BROWN decd only pay a single Tax on her Taxable property in stead of a double Tax demanded by the Sheriff

Account of Sales of part of the Estate of Francis SPEIGHT decd was exhibited into Court by Wm GOODMAN Admr on oath &c

Bill of Sale Burwell GRIFFITH to Jesse VANN acknowledged

Deed of Land John ELLIS Charity ELLIS & Edith ELLIS to Benjamin BARNES proved by the oath of Cyprian CROSS &c

Bill of Sale for a Negro Girl named PATT and her increase Abel CROSS to William VANN proved by the oath of David CROSS &c

Deed of Sale of Land Clement HILL to Joseph RIDDICK provd by the oath of Simon STALLINGS &c

(192) 80 Deed of Sale of Land Aaron HARRELL to John HARRELL proved by the oath of Asa HARRELL &c

On motion ordered that William GOODMAN & Henry GOODMAN Isaac PIPKIN junr and Philip LEWIS or any three of them Audite & State the accots. of John BETHEY Executor of James BETHEY &c

Deed of Sale of Land Moses DAVIS to Isaac HARRELL Junr. proved by the oath of Samuel HARRELL &c

Ordered that John SAUNDERS an Illegitimate Child about thirteen years old be bound as an Apprentice to Richard RAWLS to learn the Business of a House Carpenter & Millwright.

Ordered that Jethro ROBBINS son of Mary ROBBINS about twelve years of age be bound as an Apprentice to Richard RAWLS to learn the Business of a House Carpenter & Millwright

Ordered that Bray SAUNDERS pay Edith WALTERS the sum of three pounds for one month after the Birth of an Illegitimate Child born of the said Mary Edith, the said Bray the reputed Father and five pounds pr year for seven years afterwards for the maintenance of the said Child

Bill of Sale for Land a Negro Man named JOHN James RANSOM to Jonathan ROGERS proved by the oath of Wm KING &c

Deed of Sale of Land John BRINKLEY to Elisha BRINKLEY Ackd.

Deed of Sale of Land John BRINKLEY to William BRINKLEY ackd.

Deed of Sale of Land Luke SUMNER to Lewis JONES proved by the oath of John BRINKLEY &c

(193) 81 Bill of Sale William HARRISS to Jesse BENTON proved by the oath of Jethro SUMNER &c

Deed of Sale of Land Luke SUMNER to John BRINKLEY proved by the oath of Miles BENTON &c

Deed of Sale of Land Timothy FREEMAN to James BAKER proved by the oath of Ezekiel TROTMAN &c

Deed of Sale of Land William BOYCE to Miles BOYCE proved by the oath of Abraham RIDDICK &c

Deed of Sale of Land with a Receipt thereon Richard BOND to Willis WOODLEY proved by the oath of Wm BOND

Deed of Sale of Land William SPEIGHT senr. to Humphry HUDGINS Ackd.

Deed of Sale of Land Luke SUMNER to John BRINKLEY proved by the oath of Thomas BRINKLEY &c

Deed of Sale of Land Robert POWELL to William POWELL Ackd.   X

Deed of Sale of Land Cyprian GOODMAN to James GOODMAN proved by the oath of William GOODMAN jr

Deed of Sale of Land Luke SUMNER to Miles BENTON proved by the oath of Simion BRINKLEY &c

Bill of Sale for a Negro Man named CARRY Miles BENTON to Jesse BENTON Proved by the oath of Jethro SUMNER. &c

Bill of Sale Christopher GALE for a Negro Man HARRY to Isaac PIPKIN Senr proved by the oath of Isaac PIPKIN Junr

Bill of Sale for a Negro Girl named SUIAH? Lawrence BAKER Attorney for Ebenezer GRAHAM to Mills LANDING ackd.

(194) 82 Account of Sales of part of the Estate of William ELLIS decd was exhibited into Court by John ELLIS Admr on oath &c

Bill of Sale for a Negro Woman & three Children William SPEIGHT to Isaac COSTEN ackd &c

Deed of Sale of Land Thos HUNTER to Timothy FREEMAN proved by the oath of John B WALTON &c

The Last Will of David JONES decd was exhibited into Court and was proved by the oaths of Thomas PARKER & Elisha HARE and on motion was ordered to be Recorded

The Last Will of Christopher RIDDICK decd was exhibited into Court by William Wright RIDDICK & Miles GATLING two of the Executors therein appointed and was proved by the oath of Mary CLEAVES & Lawrence BAKER witnesses thereto and on motion ordered to be Recorded.

Eliza KITTRELL Guardian to Charity KITTRELL Elizabeth KITTRELL & George KITTRELL orphans of Moses KITTRELL deceased exhibited her accounts with said orphans on oath &c

William BERRYMAN Guardian to James FREEMAN Orpn. of Richard FREEMAN decd exhibited his account with said Orphan on oath &c

Ezekial TROTMAN Guardian to Christian SCOTT orpn of William SCOTT decd exhibited his accot with said Orpn on oath &c

Bill of Sale Thomas HIATT to William FROST for Lands &c ackd &c

Bond Peter MARBLE to William WALTERS & Elisha CROSS proved by the oath of Elijah LEWIS &c

Kedar BALLARD Thos PARKER Jesse BENTON & William WALTERS who were appointed to make a division of the real Estate of John DARDEN decd made report of their proceedings thereon &c

Then the Court adjourned until tomorrow morning 10 oClock

(195) 83 Tuesday morning the Court met
        Present
        Jethro SUMNER   )
        Joseph RIDDICK   ) Esquires Justices
        William GOODMAN)

Deed of Gift for Lands and Personal Estate Mary DARDEN to Peggy HARE proved by the oath of Demsey KNIGHT

Jethro SUMNER Jesse BENTON William WALTERS & Thomas PARKER the Gentn who were appd to allot & lay off to Mary DARDEN her Provision &c made report of their proceedings &c.

Deed of Sale of Land Samuel SMITH Sheriff of this County to Levin DEUR proved by the oath of Humphry HUDGINS &c at same time the relinquishment of the right & title of the said Levin DEUR was proved by the oath of Luke SUMNER.

Deed of Sale of Land Seth EASON to William HARRISS proved by the oath of Kedar BALLARD &c

Deed of Sale of Land Mills RIDDICK Nathaniel RIDDICK & David RIDDICK to Jacob GORDON proved by the oath of James GORDON &c

Ordered that John SMALL be appointed Overseer of the road from the Folly to the Orapeak Swamp instead of James SMALL resigned

Deed of Sale of Land Joseph BRADY to William BAKER proved by the oath of Robert WIGGINS &c

Ordered that Willis BROWN be appointed Overseer of the Road from Bennetts Creek Bridge to Knotty pine Swamp instead of Stephen HARRELL mooved away &c

Deed of Sale of Land Nathaniel Taylor to Joseph TAYLOR proved by the oath of Docton BAGLEY &c

Deed of Sale of Land Henry SPEIGHT to Jesse SAUNDERS ackd &c

Deed of Sale of Land Thomas TRAVIS to David HARRELL proved by the oath of Jonathan ROBERTS &c

(196) 84 Mrs. Sarah HUNTER relict of Thomas HUNTER decd comes into Court and decents to her deceased Husbands Will &c

Bill of Sale Jeremiah SPEIGHT to James COSTEN proved by the oath of Humphry HUDGINS &c

May 1798

Deed of Sale Thos HUNTER to John B WALTON proved by the oath of Timothy FREEMAN &c

Samuel EURE Guardian to Nancy EURE Orphan of Enos EURE decd exhibited his account with said orphan on oath &c

Inventory of the Goods & Chattels rights & Credits which were of the Estate of Thomas HUNTER deceased was exhibited into Court by Elisha HUNTER & Joseph RIDDICK Executors on oath &c

Account of Sales of the Estate of Thomas HUNTER deceased was exhibited into Court by Elisha HUNTER & Joseph RIDDICK Executors on oath

Account of Sales of the Estate of Robert PARKER decd was exhibited into Court by Robert PARKER on oath &c

Ordered that Richard BOND junr be appointed Overseer of the Road in the room and stead of Noah HARRELL resigned

Ordered that Moses LASSITER be exempt from the payment of a Tax on a black Poll for the year 1797 one being listed to him by mistake

Deed of Sale of Land Jesse VANN & Benjamin BARNES to William REA proved by the oath of Thomas WYNNS &c

Deed of Sale of Land Thomas FITT to William REA (or RICE) the Acknowledgement proved by Anthony WILLIAMS &c

Deed of Sale of Land John COWPER & William COWPER to Wm REA proved by the oath of James GORDON &c

Contract of Marriage between Thomas HUNTER & Sarah NORFLEET proved by the oath of John COWPER & Thomas W BALLARD the witnesses thereto &c

Deed of Sale of Land Miles BOYCE to Moses DAVIS proved by the oath of Richard BRIGGS &c

(197) 85 Isaac PIPKIN, James GATLING & William GOODMAN three of the Gentn who were appointed to Audite & State the accounts of John ODOM Exr of Wm ODOM deceased made report of their proceedings &c

Account of Sales of the Estate of James DAVIS decd was exhibited into Court by James HODGES for Keziah DAVIS on oath &c

Deed of Sale of Land Isaac PIPKIN Sheriff of this County to James GATLING acknowledged

Deed of Sale of Land Alexander EASON to Jesse EASON proved by the oath of Richard FOSTER a subscribing witness before William RANEY Esquire one of the Justices of the peace of Orange County at same time Morgan HART Clerk of the County Court of Orange certified that William RANEY Esquire who attested the Certificate that he was an acting Justice of the Peace for the County of Orange under the seal of said County

Deed of Sale for Land Alexander EASON to Jesse EASON proved by the oath of Richard FOSTER a Subscribing witness before William RANEY Esquire one of the Justices of the peace of Orange County, at same time Morgan HART Clerk of the County Court of Orange certified under his hand & Seal of said County that William RANEY Esquire who attested the Probate was an acting Justice of the peace for said County &c

Deed of Sale of Land Alexander EASON to Jesse EASON proved by the oath of Richard FOSTER a subscribing Witness before Wm RANEY Esquire one of the Justices of the peace of Orang_ County at same time Morgan HART Clerk of the County Court of Orange certified under his hand and Seal of said County that William RANEY Esquire who attested the probate of said Deed was an acting Justice of the peace for said County &c

(198) 86 On motion Ordered that David RICE John COWPER Samuel HARRELL, and Josiah GRANBERY allot and set apart to Sarah HUNTER Relict of Thomas HUNTER deceased such part of the Provisions on hand &c as will be sufficient for hers and her familys support agreeable to Law As if the said Thos HUNTER had died intestate

Ordered that James FREEMAN be appointed Guardian to (blank) son of William FREEMAN junr. and that he give Bond & Security in the sum of (blank) pounds at same time (blank) came into Court and offered themselves as Sec_s.

The Court taking into consideration the act of Assembly for the appointment of Sheriff after mature Con__deration (blot) Samuel SMITH was unanimously elected Sheriff of this County at the same time the said Samuel SMITH came into Court and quallified himself for that Office and offered Miles BENTON Humphry HUDGINS & Levin DEUR as Secys who were approved of &c with P----- Bond given in the presence of James GREGORY Joseph RIDDICK Wm GOODMAN Henry GOODMAN Jethro BALLARD & William BAKER & David RICE Justices

Isaac PIPKIN Junr appointed unanimously Public Register of this County instead of Christopher RIDDICK Esquire resigned Ordered that he give Bond and Security agreeable to Law at same time Henry GOODMAN & Lawrence BAKER came into Court and offered themselves as security who were approved of &c

Agreeable to a Writ f--- D---- for the purpose of laying off the dower of Mary DARDEN relict of John DARDEN deceased the Sheriff having returned the Pannel of a Jury with the Verdict thereof &c

~~Ordered~~
Joseph RIDDICK & Simon STALLINGS Esqrs Abram HURDLE & John B WALTON the Gentn who were appointed to make a Division of the Estate of Jacob HOBBS decd made report of their proceedings &c

(199) 87 Thomas BRICKELL James WALTON John HOFFLER Wm VOLINTINE & Jacob SPIVEY with Patrick HEGERTY the surveyor who were appointed to make a Division of the real Estate of Jacob HOBBS deceased, made report of their proceedings thereon &c

Simon STALLINGS, John HOFFLER, James WALTON John B WALTON & Riddick TROTMAN with Patrick HEGERTY the surveyor, who were appointed to make a Division of the Real Estate of Kedar HILL decd made report of their proceedings thereon &c

    Then the Court adjourned until tomorrow morning 10 oClock

    Wednesday morning the Court met agreeable to adjournment
    Present
    Joseph RIDDICK)
    William GOODMAN) Esquires Justices
    Henry GOODMAN)

May 1798

Kedar BALLARD Levin DEUR & Jethro BALLARD three of of the Gentn. who were appointed to audite the accounts of Robt POWELL Admr of James POWELL made report of their proceedings thereon &c

Jury impannelled and sworn The State against John LANG & Joshua LANG Willis BROWN Simion BRINKLEY, Moses DAVIS, Wm HUNTER Hillory WILLEY, Wm. GATLING Junr. Elisha CROSS Noah FELTON David CROSS, Mills EURE, William W RIDDICK & Patrick HEGARTY say the defendants are Guilty Judgment by the Court that John LANG and Joshua LANG both receive at the Public Whiping post thirty nine lashes each on their Bare backs

Thomas MARSHALL Guardian to John HILL orphan of Guy HILL deceased exhibited his account with said Orphan wherein there appears to be a balance due the sad orphan the sum of £35.0.8.

(200) 88 Ordered that Jethro MELTEAR Constable be allowed the sum of one pound four Shillings for warning the citizens in the Captaincy of Captn James WALTON to return lists of their Taxable Property

Jesse SAUNDERS came into Court and mooved for Administration on the Estate of Philip DUNFORD decd which was granted at same time David CROSS & William GATLING came into Court and offered themselves as security who were approved off &c

Deed of Sale of Land Joseph John SUMNER to Jethro SUMNER Ackd.

Ordered that the Sheriff of Gates County Summons the following persons to serve as Grand & Petit Jury for August Term next (to wit) Thomas SMITH Thomas RIDDICK, Jonathan ROGERS, William DOUGHTIE Demsey WILLIAMS Carpenter, Jonathan WILLIAMS Lewis WALTERS Charles EURE, Blake EURE, Israel BEEMAN Stephen EURE, James GORDON Robert POWELL, Elisha BRINKLEY John POWELL Mills BENTON Levin DEUR, William KING Abel CROSS, William GOODMAN, Richard BARNES John LEWIS, William CLEAVES, William BROOKS, James COSTEN George BROOKS Miles WALTON, Reuben LASSITER Jacob HAYSE Bond MINSHEW, &c

Ordered that the following Gentn take lists of Taxables and Taxable property from the citizens in the different Captaincys in this County (to wit) in Captain Mills LEWIS's Captaincy Major William GOODMAN, Henry GOODMAN in Captain David LEWIS's, William BAKER, in Captn William HARRISS's Captaincy, Jethro SUMNER in Captn Jesser? BENTON Captaincy, Joseph RIDDICK in Captain Isaac HUNTERs Captaincy Simon STALLINGS in Captain James WALTONs Capty &c

(201) 89 Ordered that Jethro BALLARD Kedar BALLARD, James SMALL, & John SMALL or any three of them make Division of the Personal Estate of William ELLIS agreeable to Law

Ordered that Miles BENTON Jethro BENTON Kedar BALLARD, James SMALL & Levin DEUR together with the surveyor (of required) make a division of the real Estate of William ELLIS decd & make report &c

Ordered that Henry SMITH Constable be allowed the sum of ~~Twenty~~ forty Shillings for attendance on this Court & that the County Trustee pay the same &c

Ordered that the Executors of Christopher RIDDICK sell so much of the estate personal of the decd. as will pay his Debts

Ordered that Selah VOLINTINE Relict of William VOLINTIN and Administratrix sell so much of the personal Estate of the decedent to pay his Debts &c

May 1798

Then the Court adjourned until tomorrow morning 10 oClock

        Thursday morning the Court met
        Present
        William BAKER   )
        Joseph RIDDICK) Esquirs Justices
        Henry GOODMAN   )

Ordered that the Sheriff of this County Summons a Jury to view the ground where Thomas MARSHALL moovs the Court to have ~~turned~~ the Publick road turned near his Plantation & make report &c

(202) 90 Ordered that Benjamin PRICE about Eleven years of age & Robert PRICE about Nine years of age be bound as Apprentices to Willis BROWN to learn the business of -- a Farmer.

Ordered that Seven hands of William BAKER Esquire Work on THOMPSONs Bridge and be exempt from Working on all other Roads and the Balance of his hands at Buckland and Knotty pine work on the road under Willis BROWN Overseer.

Ordered that William WALTERS Constable be allowed the sum of Five pounds twelve for his Services warning the citizens in Captain Jesse BENTONs Captaincy to return lists of their Taxable property and attending on this Court in the y___ (blot) 1797 and that the County Trustee pay the same

Ordered that Luten LEWIS Constable be allowed the sum of two pounds Sixteen Shillings for his services warning the Citizens in the Captaincy of Captain Francis SPEIGHTs to return lists of their Taxables & Taxable property and for his attendance on this Court for the year passed &c

Ordered that Samuel SMITH Sheriff of this County be allowed the sum of Fifteen pounds for Extra Services by him performed the year passed &c

                By order of the Court
                Test Law BAKER CC

(203) 91 State of North Carolina   August 20th 1798
        At a Court of Pleas and Quarter Sessions begun and held at the Court House for the County of Gates on the IIIrd Monday in August in the XXIII year of the Independence of the above said State and in the year of our Lord MDCCXCVIII.

        Present
        William BAKER   )
        William GOODMAN) Esquires Justices
        Henry GOODMAN   )

Ordered that William Wright RIDDICK be appointed Overseer of the Road instead of Michael LAWRENCE resigned

Deed of Sale of Land with a receipt thereon Richard BRIGGS to Willis WOODLEY proved by the oath of Robert RIDDICK &c

Ordered that John B. WALTON Timothy WALTON Jonathan ROBERTS & Jethro MELTEAR or any three of them Audite & State the accounts of Joseph PARKER Admr of the Estates of Kedar PARKER and James PARKER orphans of Joseph PARKER decd with the decedents Estates, and that the same Gentlemen make a division of the Estates of the decedents &c

Deed of Sale of Land David RIDDICK & Nathaniel RIDDICK to Samuel HARRELL proved by the oath of Henry MERONEY &c

Deed of Sale of Land Luke SUMNER to Henry BRINKLEY proved by the oath of Eliza BROTHERS &c

Inventory of the Goods and Chattels Rights and Credits which were of the Estate of William VALENTINE decd was exhibited into Court by Selah VOLENTINE Admtx &c

Bill of Sale for a Negro Man KEDAR Lemuel POWELL & John POWELL to Abraham RIDDICK proved by the oath of William HURDLE

(204) 92 Miles BENTON Jethro BENTON & James KNIGHT three of the Gentlemen who were appointed to audite the accounts of Amos PARKER surviving Exr of William PARKER decd made report of their proceedings thereon &c

Bill of Sale for a Negro Boy GEORGE William TAYLOR & Elizabeth POWELL to James BENTON proved by the oath of Abraham BENTON &c

Sarah PHELPS Admrx of Demsey PHELPS exhibited an account of Sales of part of the Estate of the decedent on oath &c

Joseph RIDDICK Simon STALLINGS & Thos MARSHALL three of the Gentn who were appointed to Audite the accots of William WILLIAMS Admr (in Right of his Wife) of Abner BLANSHARD made report of their proceedings thereon &c

Account of Sales of part of the Estate of William HINTON decd was exhibited into Court by Isaac HUNTER & Lewis THOMPSON Exrs on oath &c

Josiah GRANBERY David RICE & James GREGORY three of the Gentn who were appointed to Audite the Accounts of Isaac HUNTER & Lewis THOMPSON Exrs of William HINTON decd made report of their proceedings &c

Inventory of the Goods & Chattels rights and Credits which were of the Estate of Christopher RIDDICK decd was exhi (Remainder of word omitted.) into Court by Wm W RIDDICK & Miles GATLING Exrs on oath

Account of Sales of part of the Estate of Christopher RIDDICK decd was exhibited into Court by Wm W RIDDICK & Miles GATLING on oath &c

Deed of Sale of Land William REA to Benjamin BARNES proved by the oath of Jesse VANN &c

(205) 93 Ordered that Mills LEWIS Admr of John BURGESS decd sell all the personal poperty of the decedent &c

Ordered that Wm GOODMAN Henry GOODMAN Isaac PIPKIN & Henry COPELAND or any three of them make a Division of the Estate of John BURGESS decd &c

Execution having been issued by Jethro BALLARD Esquire in favor of Elisha CROSS against Joseph John SUMNER for One? pound one Shilling & five pence and Twelve Shillings costs & the Deputy Shff Henry SMITH having returned the said Execution that there was no personal property to be found and that, it was levied on the Land of the defendant. It is therefore ordered that Execution be issued out of this Court against the Land of the sd defendant for the said debt and Costs

Aug. 1798

Execution having been issued by Jethro BALLARD Esquire in favor of John VANN against Joseph John SUMNER for four pounds twelve Shillings & Eight pence & eight Shillings Costs, & Henry SMITH deputy Sheriff having returned the same thereon that there was no personal property to be found and that he had levied on the land of the defendant, It is therefore Ordered that Execution be issued out of this Court against the Lands & Tenements of the said defendant for said debt and Costs

Then the Court adjourned until tomorrow morning 10 oClock.

    Tuesday morning the Court met
  Present William BAKER)
      James GREGORY) Esquires
      William GOODMAN) Justices
      Joseph RIDDICK)

(206) 94 Lease Daniel SOUTHALL to Seasbrook WILSON acknowledged &c

Demsey JONES who was Security for the Personal Appearance of Miles BOYCE at the instance of Isaac PARKER came into Court and delivered him to this Court in discharge of himself at same time Moses DAVIS came into Court and offered himself as Special Bond for the said BOYCE &c

Account of Sales of the estate of William VOLINTINE decd was exhibited into Court by Joseph RIDDICK Esquire in behalf of Selah VOLINTINE Administratrix and was proved before the said Joseph RIDDICK Esquire.

Deed of Gift for Land Joseph RIDDICK Esqr to Solomon EASON Acknowledged &c

Deed of Sale of Land Samuel SMITH Sheriff of this County to Joseph RIDDICK Esquire ackd. &c

(207) 95 Miles BENTON came into Court and mooved for Administration on the Estate of Luke SUMNER decd which was accordingly granted at the same James SMALL & Humphry HUDGINS came into Court and offered themselves as security &c

Levin DEUR who was security for the personal appearance of Jesse EASON came into Court and delivered up the said Jesse EASON, at the same time Patrick HEGERTY came into Court and acknowledged himself as Security at the instance of Jethro SUMNER Esqr. &c

Ordered that John COWPER Kedar BALLARD William HARRISS & James GREGORY or any three of them audite & State the accounts of Seth EASON Admr of Seth Elisha SUMNER decd with the Estate of the decedent

In the following actions Judgments were entered upon Warrants and executions issued against Joseph John SUMNER the Constable made return thereon that no personal property to be found and Execution levied on the Lands of the said Joseph John SUMNER (to wit) Charles WHITLOCK against Joseph John SUMNER Judgmt for 4..9.2 & 8s. Costs: Willis WOODLEY against ditto........ for 13..3..9 & 8s Costs John POWELL Junr against ditto for £17..10.0 & 8s. Costs William SEVILS....against ditto for 2.15,0 & 8s Costs Moses DAVIS.... against ditto for 20..0..0 & 8s Costs Moses DAVIS....against ditto for 5..10..0 & 8s. Costs Moses DAVIS....against ditto for 5..0..0 & 8s Costs Moses DAVIS....against ditto for 17..0..6. & 8s. Costs it was ordered that Execution be issued against the above said Joseph John SUMNER for the above Judgments &c

Aug. 1798

Then the Court adjourned until tomorrow 10 oClock

(208) 96 Wednesday morning, the Court met
        Present
        William BAKER   )
        William GOODMAN) Esquires Justices
        Henry GOODMAN   )

Deed of Sale of Land Sarah DANIEL to Lawrence BAKER proved by the oath of Whitmel EURE &c

Ordered that William HAYSE be appointed Overseer of the Road instead of Bond MINSHEW &c

Ordered that William W RIDDICK William BROOKS, Miles GATLING Michael LAWRENCE & Thomas MARSHALL with the surveyor of this County, make a Division of the real Estate of Robert PARKER decd

Ordered that the Sheriff of this County Summons the following Citizens of this County to serve at this Court as Petit & Grand ef? Jurors at Novr Term next vizt William HURDLE, Aaron HOBBS Charles POWELL, Hardy EASON, Moses BRIGGS, William HUNTER Kedar HINTON, Colo Robert RIDDICK Abel CROSS, Henry LEE Mills LEWIS James BRADY, John VANN, Jesse BENTON Philip ROGERS Richard BRIGGS Micajah RIDDICK jr Mills EURE Lewis SPARKMAN, Asa HARRELL Benjn BARNES William W RIDDICK, Jonathan SMITH Miles GATLING Michael LAWRENCE John SMALL Robert RIDDICK Junr Elisha HARE Simeon BRINKLEY & Wm MATTHIAS.

Ordered that Thomas PARKER Micajah RIDDICK, ~~John B WALTON~~, Cyprian CROSS Kedar BALLARD be summonsed to attend at the Superior Court at October Term next as Jurymen

Ordered that Miles BENTON Admr of Luke SUMNER sell so much of the Estate of the decedent as will pay his Debts &c

(209) 97 Account of Sales of the Estate of Philip DUNFORD decd was exhibited into Court by Jesse SAUNDERS Admr of the decedent on oath &c

On an Indictment the State against Bryant WALTERS. Jury impanelled and sworn to wit Levin DEUR George BROOKS Israel BEEMAN Thomas SMITH Jonathan ROGERS William DOUGHTY James GORDON Robert POWELL Elisha BRINKLEY Bond MINSHEW Miles BENTON & William GOODman say the defendant is Guilty of the charge contained in the Indictment. Ordered by the Court that he receive forty Lashes on his bare back

Jonathan ROBERTS came into Court and mooved for Administration on the Estate of Susana FORREST which was granted at same time John B WALTON and William Wright RIDDICK came into Court and offered themselves as Securitys wh_ (torn) are to enter into Bond in the sum of Five hundred pounds

On an Indictment the State against Mary WALTERS Jury impannelled and sworn to wit Levin DEUR George BROOKS Israel BEEMAN Thomas SMITH Jonathan ROGERS Wm DOUGHTIE James GORDON Robert POWELL Elisha BRINKLEY Bond MINSHEW Miles BENTON & William GOODMAN say the defendant is Guilty, on motion new trial granted and gives Henry Ebron SEARS & James HODGES as her Securitys the Defendant in the sum of Fifty pounds and the Securitys in Twenty five pounds each

The Gentn who were appointed to make a division of the Estate of Henry FORREST decd (to wit) Thos MARSHALL John B WALTON & Richard BOND made report of their proceedings thereon &c

Aug. 1798   106

Thomas MARSHALL, John B. WALTON & Richard BOND three of the Gentlemen who were appointed to Audite the accounts of Jonathan ROBERTS ~~of Jonathan ROBERTS~~ Admr of Henry FORREST decd with the Estate of the decedent made report of their proceedings &c

(210) 98 Jonathan ROBERTS appointed Guardian to Anna FORREST Orphan of Jonathan ROBERTS decd. which was granted Ordered that he give Bond & Security in the sum of Five hundred pounds at same time John B WALTON & Miles GATLING came into Court and offered themselves as Security &c

On an Indictment the State against Joseph ALPHIN for Petit Larceny the Defendant Joseph came into Court and entered into Recognizence In the sum of Fifty pounds & at same time Aaron LASSITER and Miles ROUNTREE came into Court and offered themselves as Secy in the sum of £25 each

Ordered that the hands that have worked on the ---- Fort Island Road that lives out of the Island shall for the future work on the Road under the Overseer of the ~~Sarum Creek~~ Road, that leads from the Winton Road to the Bennitts Creek Road

Ordered that Uriah EURE be appointed Overseer of the Sarum Creek Road instead of John PILAND resigned

Ordered that Isaac GREEN John FELTON & James EUREs hands work on the Sarum Creek Road under Uriah EURE Overseer

   Then the Court adjourned until tomorrow morning 10 oClock

  Thursday morning the Court met
  Present William BAKER)
       Henry GOODMAN) Esquires Justices
       David RICE   )
       Joseph RIDDICK)

Ordered that Thomas TROTMAN be exempt from the payment of a Tax on four hundred & Twenty Acres Land & and two black Tithables it being entered by mistake

(211) 99 Ordered that Willis BROWN be allowed the sum of Fifteen Shillings for repairing Bennetts Creek Bridge and that the County trustee pay the same

Ordered that James Henry KEYS be allowed the sum of Twenty four pounds for his Services as Attorney for the State two years passed and that the County trustee pay the same

Ordered that Samuel SMITH Sheriff of this County be allowed in the settlement of his accounts with the Public Treasurer and County Trustee the Tax on the following Persons to wit Benjamin REID William TAYLOR Benton JONES Edward KELLY John LAMB & William FREEMAN jr four blk & one white Poll

   Then the Court adjourned until Court in Course
     By order of the Court
       Law BAKER CC

(212) 100 State of North Carolina Monday Novr 19 1798
      At a Court of Pleas and Quarter Sessions begun and held for the County of Gates at the Court on the third Monday in November in the XXIIIrd year of the Independence of the above State and in the year of our Lord MDCCXCVIII.

Nov. 1798

Present
William GOODMAN)
Henry GOODMAN) Esquires Justices
David RICE)
)

Ordered that Jethro SUMNER Jethro BALLARD Kedar BALLARD & William ARNOLD or any three of them Audite & State the Accounts of Thos PARKER Admr of Elizabeth NORFLEET decd

Ordered that Isaac PIPKIN Senr Isaac PIPKIN Junr. Philip LEWIS & William GATLING senr or any three of them make a division of Property given to John David & Anna FREEMAN by Jos SPEIGHT their Grandfather

Grand Jury Impannelled and swon for this term to wit Benjamin BARNES Foreman Mills EURE, John SMALL William W RIDDICK, Elisha HARE, Charles POWELL Hardy EASON Simeon BRINKLEY Richard BRIGGS, William MATTHIAS, Abel CROSS Mills LEWIS Aaron HOBBS, & John VANN

Deed of Sale of Land Thos. GRANBERY to John CAMPBELL proved by the oath of John ASKEW &c

Deed of Sale of Land David RAWLS & Uxr to John LANGSTON Ackd. private examination of Pennina RAWLS taken before William GOODMAN Esquire whereon he reported that she Ackd. her right &c

On Motion of John BROWN Esquire Attorney at Law Ordered that James GATLING Esquire be Administrator of of the Estate of Henry SPEIGHT decd and that he enter into Bond with Security in the sum of Ten thousand pounds at the same time William GOODMAN & Jesse SAUNDERS came into Court and offered themselves as Secys &c

(213) 101 Ordered that James GORDON be appointed Guardian to Reuben ELLIS orphan of William ELLIS decd it is also Ordered that he give Bond and security in the sum of Five hundred pounds at same time David RICE and Simon STALLINGS came into Court and offered themselves as Secys &c

Ordered that James GATLING Admr of Henry SPEIGHT decd sell so much of the Estate of the Decedent as will pay his Just Debts &c

Ordered that Isaac PIPKIN Senr. Isaac PIPKIN Junr, & Henry GOODMAN allot and set apart unto Ann SPEIGHT Relict of Henry SPEIGHT Provisions &c under the Act of Assembly &c

Deed of Sale of Land Elisha BRINKLEY Elizabeth BRINKLEY & Martha BRINKLEY to Cyprian CROSS proved by the oath of Joseph SMITH &c

Bill of Sale William MARCH to John MARCH proved by the oath of Bray SAUNDERS &c

Inventory of the Goods and Chattels, Rights, & Credits which were of the Estate of Henry SPEIGHT decd was exhibited into Court by James GATLING Admr on oath &c

~~Bill of Sale for Deed of Gift~~ ---- Goods & Chattels Ann HILL to Abraham SPIVEY proved by the oath of Simon STALLINGS &c

Deed of Gift Ann HILL to Abraham SPIVEY proved by the oath of Simon STALLINGS &c

Deed of Gift for Negroes & Stock & houshold furniture Elisha NORFLEET to Kinchen NORFLEET proved by the oath of Elisha HARE &c

Deed of Sale of Land Solomon HOBBS to Levi EASON proved by the oath of Samuel HOBBS (son of John)

(214) 102 Account of Sale of part of the perishable estate of William WARREN decd exhibited into Court by John PARKER Admr on oath &c

Deed of Sale of Land Barnaby BLANSHARD to Samuel BROWN proved by Moses LASSITER &c

Bill of Sale for a Negro Man SAML Jacob SPIVEY to Ezekiel TROTMAN ackd &c

Bill of Sale for two Negroes ROSE SILLER Joseph John SUMNER to Patty MIRONEY proved by the oath of Thomas PARKER

Deed of Sale of Land Elisha NORFLEET to Kinchen NORFLEET proved by the oath of Jethro BALLARD &c

Deed of Sale of Land Elisha BRINKLEY Elizabeth BRINKLY & Martha BRINKLEY proved by the oath of Joseph SMITH

Agreeable to the Petition of Mary ELLIS Relict of William ELLIS decd Ordered that the Sheriff of this County Summons a Jury and allot and lay off to the said Mary ELLIS her Dower in certain Lands her deceased Husband died seized and possessed of &c

Then the Court adjourned until tomorrow morning 10 oClock

Tuesday morning the Court Met
Present
William BAKER   )
William GOODMAN) Esquires Justices
David RICE   )

Inventory of the Goods and Chattels Rights and Credits which were of the estate of Susanna FORREST Minor orphan of Henry FORREST decd Was exhibited into Court by Jonathan ROBERTS &c

(215) 103 James RANSOM who was surrendered by Jos. BRADY his security at same time Luten LEWIS & William GATLING Junr came into Court and entered themselves as his Bail &c

Bill of Sale for two Negroes Luke SUMNER to Jethro BALLARD proved by the oath of Thos W BALLARD &c

Deed of Sale of Land John ROBBINS to Kedar HINTON proved by the oath of Jethro MILTEAR &c

Deed of Sale of Land Samuel HARRELL to Jonathan ROBERTS proved by the oath of David HARRELL &c

Ordered that the Sheriff of Pitt County to wit Wm EASTWOOD be sighted to appear at this Court at next Term to shew cause why he did not make a return of a Subpona to summons Uriah ODOM in a suit Francis SAUNDERS Admr of Wm SAUNDERS agains HY GOODMA

Deed of Sale of Land Jethro SUMNER & Demsey ODOM to Isaac WALTERS ackd. by Isaac Demsey ODOM & and proved as to Jethro SUMNER by the oath of John BABB &c

Inventory of the Goods and Chattels Rights & Credits which were of the Estate of Luke SUMNER decd was exhibited into Court by Miles BENTON Admr on oath &c

Deed of Sale of Land Isaac WALTERS to John BABB ackd &c

Deed of Sale of Land Isaac HUNTER Executor of William HINTON to Amos LASSITER Ackd. &c

Uriah ODOM fined Nesi? for not appearing at this Court as a Witness in a suit brought by Francis SAUNDERS Admr of William SAUNDERS against Henry GOODMAN &c (Issue Sure Facies)

Then the Court adjourned until tomorrow morning 10 oClock   P

(216) 104 Wednesday morning the Court met
     Present
     James GREGORY   )
     David RICE   ) Esquires Justices
     William GOODMAN)

Deed of Sale of Land Samuel SMITH, Thomas SMITH, Jonathan SMITH to Henry SMITH proved by the oath of Patrick HEGERTY &c

Ordered that the Sheriff Summons James WALTON Timothy WALTON Riddick TROTMAN, David HARRELL Senr Noah HARRELL William CARTER, James COSTEN, Abraham HURDLE Robert POWELL, Jethro BENTON David BENTON Thomas SMITH, William CLEAVES, John ARNOLD, William DOUGHTIE Elisha CROSS Jonathan ROGERS James TUGWELL David CROSS, John LEWIS, John ODOM William GOODMAN Junr David LEWIS Charles EURE William CRAFFORD, Isaac LANGSTON John PARKER (Gatling) William BROOKS Willis BROWN & Robt PARKER son of Robt. personally to be and appear at this Court at next term &c

Bill of Sale for two Negroes PENNY & AGATHA her Child John B WALTON to Richard FREEMAN Ackd &c

Bill of Sale for a Negro Woman LEWSY Richard FREEMAN to John B WALTON proved by the oath of George OUTLAW &c

William W RIDDICK the entry taker of this County came into Court and resigned his appointment to that office and delivered his Book of entrys &c

Ordered that ~~Lawrence BAKER~~ Lewis SPARKMAN, ~~J---- GATLING~~ Stephen EURE Miles GATLING & Michl LAWRENCE make a Division of the Estate of William FRYER deceased agreeable to his Will &c

(217) 105 In the Indictment the State against Mary WALTERS for Petty Larceny Jury impannelled and sworn to wit Henry LEE, William HURDLE, James BRADY William HUNTER Philip ROGERS, Jonathan SMITH Miles GATLING Robert RIDDICK Junr, Lewis SPARKMAN, Michael LAWRENCE Moses BRIGGS & Asa HARRELL say the said Mary WALTERS is not guilty of the charge contained in the Indictment

Then the Court adjourned untill tomorrow morning 10 oClock

Thursday Novr. 22 1798 the Court met
   Present William BAKER   )
          William GOODMAN) Esquires
          Henry GOODMAN   )
          James GREGORY   )

Ordered that the Sheriff of this County pay to William GATLING Senr. the amount of a Judgment by him received from an Execution issued against William GATLING Junr in behalf of Peter MARBLE.

In Suit William GATLING Senr. against William WALTERS & Elisha CROSS William WALTERS as a Garnishee maketh oath that as a Constable & Garnish_? in that case made a return to the Court & which he believes is now on the Execution Dockett of £16..18.½ & which sum he paid to the Sheriff on the Execution and has a Receipt for the same on the 21st May 1798 since that time he hath received the sum of 4..19.2 from Richard FRYER and E MARTIN on two Executions against the said two persons, and he hath the Judgments & Execution in his hands now to deliver up in the above cases, and one other Exn againt Bryan WALTERS on which he hath received nothing and he hath also a List of the Judgments at the Instance of MARBLE which he now also returns to this Court and the above statement is a full and to the best of his knowledge Just amount of the Debts and Judgments due to Peter MARBLE in his hands as Garna?shar & Cunstable that he oweth nothing himself to the said MARBLE & he knoweth of no other persons that are actually indebted to the said MARBLE he hath a List of Debts but knoweth not whether any thing is due or not

(218) 106 Elisha CROSS as Garnishee maketh oath that he knoweth not that he is indebted to Peter MARBLE, he once thought that he was indebted but on examining the Book of Peter MARBLE in the presence of the said MARBLE the account of the said MARBLE against the defendant amounted to the sum of £33.3.4 as far as he recollecteth that the Rects. of the Deponent, on examination amounted to £36..8.0 from whence he const?er?deth himself not to be indebted to the said MARBLE. That since the time of the deponant being summoned as a Garnashee on New and fra?sh contract with the said MARBLE he became indebted to him the said MARBLE to the amount of £29.0.0 or thereabouts, which Debt the Deponant soon after the debt was contracted did discharge to the said MARBLE, by taking up his note for the same. The Deponant knoweth not of any other person being indebted to the said MARBLE.

Memo. the Garnishment of the above Garnashees being omitted inadvertantly to be taken on the return of the Suir? Facies the same was directed by the Court to be now taken Nemi Pro tune.

It appearing to this Court that Rachel VANN the Testamentory Guardian of William VANNs Children, and the Childrens not agreeing, and that the Children are not educated and the Estate perishing and it appearing that the Widow desirous of relinquishing the trust and accepting the share of the moovables stated in the Will. It is therefore ordered that the Exor Jesse VANN do sell the estate under the act of assembly and that Wm BAKER Esqr. Jonathan WILLIAMS Mills LEWIS Hillory WILLEY and James BRADY be appointed to divide and distribute the whole of the said Estate and make report thereof to this Court at next sitting; and that in particular such a division to the Widow as is allowed in the Will of the said Wm VANN provided that she is inclined to accept of the same

Deed of Sale of Land John GRANBERY, James GRANBERY & Josiah GRANBERY Junr to James GREGORY proved by (blank) as to John GRANBERY by Wm SLADE as to James GRANBERY &? by Wm HARRISS as to Josiah GRANBERY Junr &c.

(219) 107 Ordered that Etheldred BRADY alias SEARS about the age of (blank) years be bound as an Apprentice to Richard RAWLS to learn the business of a House Carpenter and Mill Right

William BROOKS William Wright RIDDICK Michael LAWRENCE & Miles GATLING with the surveyor of this County who was appointed to make a division of the real Estate of

Robert PARKER deceased made report of their proceedings thereon

Ordered that the Bounds of Prisoners extend as follows to wit Begining at Bennetts Creek Bridge and up the road to a Mulberry tree on the side of the Road thence a westwardly course to the upper part of the Orchard thence a Southward course to the edge of the Plantation thence along the edge of Said Plantation to the begining

Ordered that the four Commissioners who made a division of the Real Estate of Robert PARKER decd amongst the Heirs be paid the sum of Ten Shillings pr day and the Surveyor the sum of Twenty Shillings pr day for their Services fiv_ days each & Six days to the Survr

        Then the Court adjourned until Court in Course
          By order of the Court
            Test Law BAKER CC

(220) 108   State of No.. Carolina.   February 18th 1799
                            At a Court of Pleas and Quarter Sessions begun and held for the County of Gates at the Court House on the third Monday in February in the XXIIIrd year of the Independence of the said State and in the year of our Lord MDCCXCIX.
        Present Joseph RIDDICK)
                  David RICE   ) Esquires Justices
                  Henry GOODMAN)

Grand Jury Impannelled & Sworn to wit John ODOM Foreman John ARNOLD, David BENTON, Elisha CROSS, Charles EURE John LEWIS, Jethro BENTON, John PARKER (Gatling) David HARRELL senr Robert POWELL, William CRAFFORD, David CROSS, Riddick TROTMAN & Timothy WALTON.

Ordered that a Commission be issued to the County of Nansemond Virginia to Robert RIDDICK Archibald RICHARDSON & John CAHOON Esquires Or any two of them to take the private examination of Elizabeth ALLEN Wife of Edward ALLEN relative to a Deed executed by the said Edward & Eliza. to Micajah RIDDICK junr

Lassiter RIDDICK who was bale for the personal appearance of John HUDGINS at the suit of Fanny MILLER surrendered him up to this Court at same time Jonathan ROBERTS came into Court and acknowledged himself to be Special Bail &c

David HARRELL junr. came into Court and mooved for Administration on the Estate of Shadrah ELLIS decd which was granted Ordered that he give Bond & Security in the sum of Five hundred pounds at same time Mills EURE & Levi EURE came into Court and offered themselves as Securitys &c

Ordered that James BARNES John RIDDICK Micajah RIDDICK jr & Noah FELTON or any three of them Audite & State the accounts of Humphry HUDGINS Exor of James PHELPS decd

Ordered that Thomas MARSHALL John B WALTON John HOFFLER & Joseph RIDDICK Esquire Audite & State the accounts of Sealah VOLENTINE Admtx. of William VOLENTINE decd &c

(221) 109 Ordered that Thos MARSHALL, John B WALTON, John HOFFLER & Jos RIDDICK Esquire or any three of them make a division of the Estate of William VOLENTINE agreeable to Law &c

Micajah RIDDICK junr came into Court and mooved for Administration on the Estate of

James PARKER deceased which was granted Ordered that he give Bond and Security in the sum of One thousand pounds at same time Humphry HUDGINS & Kedar BALLARD came into Court and offered themselves as Secys. &c

Account of Sales of part of the Estate of James BROWN decd was exhibited into Court by Robert PARKER Admr on oath &c

Isaac PIPKIN junr Isaac PIPKIN Senr Philip LEWIS & William GATLING senr. the Gentn who were appointed to make a Division of Negroes between given by Joseph SPEIGHT to John FREEMAN David FREEMAN & Ann FREEMAN, made report of their proceedings &c

Ordered that Cyprian CROSS, Mills LEWIS Philip LEWIS & Jesse VANN or any three of them audite & State the accounts of Francis SAUNDERS Admr of William SAUNDERS decd &c

Isaac PIPKIN Junr. William GATLING, Henry GOODMAN & Isaac PIPKIN senr Gentlemen who were appointed to allot and point out such part of the Crop, Stock and provisions for the support of Ann SPEIGHT widow of Henry SPEIGHT, made report of their proceedings &c

Deed of Sale of Land Isaac WALTERS Senr to Isaac WALTERS Junr Ackd

Deed of Sale of Land James FREEMAN to Jethro LASSITER Ackd

Samuel HARRELL Guardian to John WALTON, Milicen WALTON Emilia & William WALTON Orphans of Thomas WALTON decd, exhibited his account with said Orphans on oath &c

Deed of Sale of Land Luke SUMNER to John POWELL proved by the oath of Kedar ~~BALLARD~~ POWELL

(222) 110 Deed of Sale of Land Henry HILL to Daniel POWELL proved by Mills R FIELD &c

Deed of Sale of Land Abraham RIDDICK to Humphry HUDGINS Ackd

Deed of Sale of Land James BRISTOW & Mary his Wife to Lawrence BAKER proved as to James BRISTOW by William BROOKS and as to Mary BRISTOW by Warner BRISTOW &c

Deed of Sale of Land John SHEPHERD to William SHEPHERD provd by the oath of James HODGES &c

Deed of Sale of Land Demsey JONES senr to Sarah JONES proved by the oath of Demsey JONES Junr &c

Deed of Sale of Land James JONES to William BAKER ackd &c

Deed of Sale of Land Joseph John SUMNER to Kedar BALLARD provd by the oath of Ambroose WIGGINS &c

Deed of Sale of Land Noah TROTMAN to Seth TROTMAN proved by the oath of Miles WALTON

Deed of Sale of Land Lewis SUMNER to Joseph SUMNER proved by the oath of Joseph SAUNDERS &c

Ordered that George WILLIAMS William CLEAVES Charles EURE & William W RIDDICK or any three of them make a Division of the Personal Estate of Robert PARKER deceased agreeable to Law

Ordered that William WALTON Orphan of Thomas WALTON decd about the age of thirteen years be bound as an Apprentice to to Thos WALTON to learn the business of a Cooper &c

Bill of Sale of Land for a Negro Boy SILAS William HAYSE to Jonathan LASSITER proved by the oath of Saml SMITH &c

Deed of Sale of Land Seth TROTMAN & Uxr to Noah TROTMAN proved by the oath of Miles WALTON &c

Deed of Sale of Land Timothy FREEMAN to Josiah PARKER Acknowledged

(223) 111 Deed of Sale of Land William SPEIGHT to John DUKE proved by the oath of J Miles BENTON &c

Deed of Sale of Land Hugh KING & Purnell KING to Mills EURE acknowledged by Hugh KING and proved as to Hugh Purnell KING by the oath of Willis PILAND &c

Deed of Sale of Land Edward ALLEN & Uxr & Katey REED to Micajah RIDDICK proved by the oath of Jethro SUMNER

Deed of Sale of Land William REA to Benjamin ROBERTS, the acknowledgment of said Deed by Wm REA proved by John VANN &c

Deed of Sale of Land William CRAFFORD to Benjamin ROBERTS Ackd

Last Will and Testament of William MATTHIAS decd was exhibited into Court by Kedar BALLARD one of the Executors therein appointed and was proved by the oaths of Joseph John SUMNER and John DUKE the witnesses thereto at the same time the said Exr quallified himself for that office and prayed for Letters Testamentory thereon &c

Inventory of the Goods & Chattels rights & Credits which were of the Estate of William MATTHIAS decd was exhibited into Court by Kedar BALLARD Exr

James RAWLS Guardian to James & Eliza BOOTH exhibited his account with said Orphans on oath &c

William BERRYMAN Guardian to Jacob FREEMAN exhibited his Account with said Orphan on oath &c

Abraham HURDLE Guardian to Jacob SUMNER exhibited his Account with said orphan on oath &c

(224) 112 James COSTEN Guardian to James LASSITER Henry LASSITER & Margaret LASSITER Orphans of Timothy LASSITER decd exhibited his account with said Orphans on oath &c

William Frederick BLANSHARD Guardian to William BLANSHARD & Mary BLANSHARD orphans of Absolom BLANSHARD exhibited his account with said Orphans on oath &c

Jonathan WILLIAMS, Mills LEWIS, Hillory WILLEY & James BRADY the Men who were appointed to make a Division of the Estate of William VANN decd made report of their proceedings &c

Feb. 1799

Agreeable to the Peto of W SLADE Esqr Atto at Law it is Ordered that William GOOD-
MAN Henry GOODMAN John ODOM James GATLING and Lewis SPARKMAN make a Division of the
Real Estate of Demsey LANG?STON agreeable to Law &c

Then the Court adjourned until tomorrow morning 10 oClock

Tuesday morning the Court met
Present   Jethro SUMNER)
          Jethro BALLARD) Esquires Justices
          David RICE   )

Inventory of the Goods and Chattels rights and credits which were of the Estate of
Shadrach ELLIS decd was exhibited into Court by David HARRELL Admr on oath &c

Ordered that David HARRELL junr Admr of Shadrach ELLIS decd sell the perishable part
of the Estate of the decedent

Bond William HARRIS to Seth EASON proved by the oath of Kedar BALLARD &c

(225) 113 Last Will and Testament of Mary ELLIS decd was exhibited into Court by
James GORDON Executor therein appointed and was proved by the oath of Jethro BALLARD
Esquire one of the subscribing witnesses thereto and on motion was ordered to be recorded at same time the said Exr came into Court and quallified himself for that
office &c

Deed of Sale of Land Samuel SMITH Sheriff of this County to John COWPER Ackd &c

Ordered that John JONES and James JONES orphans of James JONES decd John about the
age of thirteen years & James about the age of ten years, be bound as apprentices
to Levi LEE to learn the business of House Carpenters &c

Ordered that Thomas JONES, & David JONES orphans of James JONES decd Thomas about
the age of Fifteen years and David about the age of Seven years be bound as apprentices to Willey LEE to learn the business of House CARPENTERS &c

Deed of Sale of Land Charles EURE to Levi EURE ackd

Inventory of the Goods and Chattels rights and Credits which were of the Estate of
James PARKER decd was exhibited into Court by Micajah RIDDICK Admr on oath &c

Jethro LASSITER came into court and mooved for Administration on the said Estate of
Jesse WARD decd which was accordingly granted Ordered that he give Bond and securi-
ty in the sum of Five hundred pounds at the same time Timothy FREEMAN & Thos FREE-
MAN came into Court and offered themselves as Secys &c

Inventory of the Goods and Chattels rights and Credits which were of the Estate of
Jesse WARD decd was exhibited into Court by Jethro LASSITER Admr &c

Agreeable to the Petition of Elizabeth PARKER Relict of Jas PARKER deceased it is
Ordered that Jethro SUMNER Esqr Jesse BENTON James PRUDEN & Miles BENTON allot set
apart and Lay off such part of the Crop Stock and Provisions for her support &c

(226) 114 Riddick TROTMAN Guardian to Polly HILL orphan of Moses HILL decd exhibited his accot. with said Orphan &c

Feb. 1799

Riddick TROTMAN Guardian to Christian HILL orphan of Moses HILL decd exhibited his accot with said Orphan &c

An Execution having been returned by David HARRELL Constable against Samuel GREEN from a judgment obtained by Lewis SPARKMAN before Henry GOODMAN Esquire for two pounds five Shillings & twelve Shillings Costs, the said Constable having Returned no personal property to be found and Executed on Land Ordered that Execution be issued against the Lands &c

An Execution having been returned by David HARRELL Constable against Saml GREEN from a Judgment obtained by Jesse TAYLOR before William BAKER Esquire for Ten Shillings & eight Shillings Costs the said Constable having returned no personal property executed on Land Joins Peter HARRELL, ordered that Exn Issue against the Lands &c

Ordered that Micajah RIDDICK junr Admr of James PARKER deceased sell all the Perishable Estate of the decedent to pay his Debts &c

Ordered that Jethro LASSITER Admr of Jesse WARD decd sell the perishable part of the estate of the decedent to pay his Debts &c

Ordered that James GORDON be appointed Guardian to Elizabeth ELLIS orphan of William ELLIS decd and that he give Bond & Security in the sum of five hundred pounds at the same time (blank) came into Court and offered themselves as Secys &c

Demsey WILLIAMS Guardian to Samuel BAKER orphan of Saml BAKER decd exhibited his account with said Orphan on oath &c

Ordered that Isaac LANGSTON Cyprian CROSS, John ODOM & Benj BARNES or any three of them Audite & State the accots of John (Gatling) PARKER with the Estate of William WARREN decd

(227) 115. Isaac LANGSTON came into court and mooved for Administration on the estate of Demsey LANGSTON decd which was granted Order'd that he give Bond & Security in the sum of one thousand pounds at same time William BAKER Esquire & John ODOM came into court and offered themselves as securitys &c

Ordered that Isaac LANGSTON Admr of Demsey LANGSTON decd sell the perishable estate of Demsey LANGSTON decd &c

Agreeable to the Petition of Ann SMITH it is ordered that Ordered that the Sheriff of this County summons a Jury and Allot set apart and lay off to the said Ann SMITH her dower in certain Lands her husband died seized and possessed

Henry K BENTON orphan of Henry BENTON decd came into Court and made choice of Miles BENTON as his Guardian at the same time it was Ordered that he give Bond and security in the sum of two thousand pounds at same time Jethro SUMNER & James GORDON came into court and offered themselves as as securitys &c

    Then the Court adjourned until tomorrow morning 10 oClock

    Wednesday morning the Court met
    Present William BAKER)
             Joseph RIDDICK) Esquires
             William GOODMAN)
             Henry GOODMAN)

Agreeable to the Petition of Eliza BURGES vs Jno VANN senr. isse? copy to John VANN senr

Ordered that Thos MARSHALL, John B WALTON Timothy WALTON & Simon STALLINGS or any three of them Audite & State the accounts of Jonathan ROBERTS Noah HARRELL & Joseph RIDDICK Executors of William LEWIS decd with Estate of the decedent &c

(228) 116 James GORDON came into Court and mooved for Administration on the Estate of William ELLIS decd orphan of William ELLIS decd which was granted at same time Ordered that he give Bond & Security in the sum of five hundred pounds at the same time Miles BENTON & Saml SMITH came into court and offered themselves as Securitys &c

Bill of Sale for two Negroes PATT & AGGY Luke SUMNER to Levin DEUR proved by the oath of Miles BENTON &c

The Sheriff having returned the Verdict of a Jury with the pannel thereof for the laying off the dower of Mary ELLIS relict of William ELLIS decd &c

Ordered that James GORDON Admr of Mary ELLIS decd sell the Estate of the decedent, agreeable to Law in order that a division be made

Ordered that James GORDON Admr on the Estate of William ELLIS minor Orphan of William ELLIS decd sell the Estate of the decedent in order that a Division of the same be made

Ordered that William GOODMAN & Henry GOODMAN Esquires & Isaac PIPKIN senr Isaac PIPKIN Junr & William GATLING senr lay off a Legacy given to Anna? SPEIGHT by her Husband Joseph SPEIGHT decd in his last Will and Testament &c

On motion ordered that the Sheriff of this County summons a Jury and lay off allott and set apart to Anna SPEIGHT her dower in certain Lands that her late Husband Henry SPEIGHT died seized & possessed &c

Agreeable to the petition of Judith SUMNER Relict of Luke SUMNER decd. it is Ordered that Jethro SUMNER one of the Justices of this County, James SMALL Thomas PARKER & John POWELL freehoulders Alot and lay off such part of the Crop, Stock, and provisions that were of the property of the decedent for the support of the said Judith & her family

Inventory of the Goods and chattels Rights and credits which were of the ___ te (blot) of Demsey LANGSTON was exhibited into Court by Isaac LANGSTON Admr on oath

(229) 117 Ordered that the Sheriff of this County summons Miles GATLING William KING David RIDDICK & David CROSS personally be and appear at the Supr. Court to be held at Edenton for the district of Edenton at Edenton on the third day of Apl next

Ordered that the Sheriff of this County summons Miles BENTON Thomas PARKER James GORDON Robert RIDDICK son of Micajah John RIDDICK Philip ROGERS Demsey WILLIAMS, Jonathan WILLIAMS Micajah RIDDICK Junr Wm W RIDDICK Thomas RIDDICK Moor CARTER, Asa HARRELL, Charles EURE Levi EURE, Jesse HARRELL Abel CROSS Henry LEE Richard BARNES, Thomas BARNES William HUNTER Miles WALTON, Hardy EASON, Moses BRIGGS, Aaron HOBBS William BERRYMAN, Abraham GREEN, James BAKER Josiah PARKER & William CARTER personally be and appear at this Court at next Term as Jurors

Bill of Sale for Negro SAM Joseph RIDDICK & Elisha HUNTER Exrs. of Thomas HUNTER decd & Thomas HOFFLER to William BAKER ackd.

Stephen EURE, Lewis SPARKMAN, & Miles GATLING three of Gentlemen who were appointed to make a Division of the Estate of William FRYER decd. made report of their proceedings thereon &c

James B SUMNER Wm.. W.. RIDDICK & Robert PARKER three of the Gentlemen who were appointed to make a Division of the personal Estate of Wright HAYSE decd ~~agreeable to law~~ made report of their proceedings thereon &c

Kedar BALLARD James SMALL & Miles BENTON three of the Freehoulders with Patrick HEGERTY the County Surveyor who were appointed to make a Division of the Real estate of William ELLIS decd. made report of their proceedings &c. Commissioners 10/ pr day Surveyor 20s

(230) 118 Ordered that William BROOKS be appointed Overseer of the Road instead of Willis BROWN resigned

Ordered that Isaac HARRELL jr be appointed Overseer of the road instead of David HARRELL resigned

Ordered that Lawrence BAKER Clerk of this Court be allowed the sum of Twenty pounds for extra Services by him performed for the year passed

             By order of Court
              Law BAKER CC

(231) 119 State of No.. Carolina   May 20th. 1799

   At a Court of Pleas and Quarter Sessions begun and held for the County of Gates at the Court House on the third Monday in May in the XXIII year of the Independence of the said State and in the year of our Lord MDCCXCIX.

      Present
      James GREGORY
      Simon STALLINGS
      Henry GOODMAN

Deed Edward ALLEN, Elizabeth ALLEN, & Catey REID to Micajah RIDDICK which was proved at this Court at last term by Jethro SUMNER a Subscribing witness thereto. And a Commission having been issued to Robert RIDDICK Archibald RICHARDSON & John COOHOON Esquires Justices assigned to keep the Peace in the County of Nansemond & State of Virginia to take the private examination of Elizabeth ALLEN wife of Edward ALLEN the said Robert RIDDICK and John COHOON Esquires made return under their hands & Seals that Elizabeth ALLEN was examined apart from her Husband and acknowledged the Deed that she did voluntaryly signed by herself

Deed of Gift of Land Thomas SMITH to Richard SMITH his Son proved by the oath of Henry SMITH &c

Deed of Sale of Land Willis PILAND to James PILAND proved by the oath of John PILAND &c

Deed of Sale of Land William POLSON to John POLSON proved by the oath of James WILLIAMS &c

Deed of Sale of Land Demsey JONES Senr. to Kedar HINTON proved with the Receipt thereon by Mills R. FIELD &c

Deed of Trust Jeremiah SPEIGHT to WATSON STOTT & Company proved by the oath of Wm FISHER &c

Deed of Sale of Land George OUTLAW to Nathaniel TAYLOR Ackd

(232) 120 Grand Jury impannelled & Sworn for this term to wit James GORDON Foreman William BERRYMAN Moor CARTER Levi EURE, Thomas BARNES Demsey WILLIAMS Asa HARRELL Richard BARNES, Miles WALTON Thomas RIDDICK, Henry LEE Aaron HOBBS William W RIDDICK Charles EURE Robert RIDDICK

Deed of Sale of Land Thomas HURDLE & Uxr to Simon STALLINGS Ackd. in open Court private examination of Judith? HURDLE taken by James GREGORY Esquire

Last Will of Elisha BENTON decd was exhibited into Court by Miles BENTON and Abraham BENTON Executors therein appointed and was proved by the oaths of Charity MORGAN & Christian BENTON the subscribing witnesses thereto which was ordered to be Recorded at the same time the said Exors came into Court and quallified themselves for that office &c

Ordered that Uriah MORRIS orphan of William MORRIS decd about twelve years old be bound as an Apprentice to Jesse HARRELL Junr to learn the Business of a Cooper &c

Deed of Sale of Land Henry GRIFFIN & Uxr. to Jonathan PARKER proved by the oath of Patrick HEGERTY &c

Bill of Sale for a Negro Man named BOBB Ann PILAND to David LEWIS &c

Deed of Sale of Land Micajah RIDDICK to Humphry HUDGINS Ackd &c

Nancy HINTON came into Court and mooved for Administration on the Estate of Leasbrook HINTON decd which was granted Ordered that she give Bond & Security in the sum of One thousand pounds at same time Jonathan ROBERTS & Kedar HINTON came into Court and offered themselves as Securitys &c the said Admtx.. quallified herself for that office &c

Inventory of the Goods & Chattels rights and Credits which were of the Estate of Seasbrook HINTON decd was exhibited into Court by Nancy HINTON Admr. &c

(233) 121 Ordered that Miles BENTON & Abraham BENTON Exors of Elisha BENTON decd sell the Perishable part of the Estate of the decedent in order to make a Division &c

Ordered that the Admx. of Seasbrook HINTON sell as much of the perishable ____? Estate of the decedent as will pay his Debts &c

Isaac HUNTER Guardian to John Hunter RIDDICK exhibited his Account with said Orphan wherein there appears to be a balance due the Orphan the sum of £62.10.5.

Isaac HUNTER Guardian to Robert HILL & Whitmill HILL orphans of Kedar HILL decd exhibited his accounts with said orphans wherein there appears to be Balances due said orphans as follows to wit to Kedar HILL £96.0.0½ to Whitmill HILL £100..1.6½.

May 1799

Contract of Marriage Thomas HILL & Moses BRIGGS proved by the oath of Frederick EASON &c

Deed of Sale of Land Isaac FRYER Judith HARRELL Hetty CRAFFORD & Rebecca ____? (written over) ELLIS? to David HARRELL proved by the oath of Josiah HARRELL &c

An additional Inventory which were of the Estate of Shadrach ELLIS decd was exhibited into Court by David HARRELL Admr on oath &c

John RIDDICK Micajah RIDDICK Junr & Noah FELTON three of the Gentlemen who were appointed to Audite & State the accounts of Humphry HUDGINS & James PRUDEN Executors of James PHELPS decd. made report of their proceedings &c

Ordered that Simon STALLINGS Esqr. William KING Abraham HURDLE & Joseph RIDDICK Esqr or any three of them make a Division of the Estate personal of Amos TROTMAN decd &c

Ordered that Geo WILLIAMS Thomas MARSHALL Charles EURE, & Wm CLEAVES or any three of them Audite & State the accounts of Robert PARKER Adm of James BROWN decd and they make a Division of the Perishables Estate of the (End of entry.)

(234) 122 Bill of Sale James B SUMNER & Jethro SUMNER to Micajah RIDDICK proved by the oath of Anthony MATTHEWS

Bill of Sale for a Negro Boy named GILBERT Joseph John SUMNER & Kedar BALLARD to Micajah RIDDICK provd by the oath of Isaac MILLER senr

Deed of Sale of Land Demsey JONES (Odom) to Demsey JONES Senr. proved by the oath of Mills FIELD &c

Timothy WALTON Guardian to David OUTLAW orphan of Jas OUTLAW decd exhibited his account with said Orphan wherein there appears to be a Balance due the orphan the sum of 693.8 3 3/4

Joseph RIDDICK Guardian to Joseph TROTMAN Love TROTMAN & Willis TROTMAN & to Joseph Love & Willis TROTMAN orphans of Thos TROTMAN exhibited his accounts with said orphans seperately and all together wherein there appears to be balances due said orphans as follows to wit To Joseph TROTMAN £98. 0 0? To Love TROTMAN £74 7..11. to Willis TROTMAN £329.1.0 and to Joseph Love & Willis TROTMAN £193.10.10 3/4

   Then the Court adjourned until tomorrow morning 10 oClock

    Tuesday the Court met
    Present James GREGORY)
        Jethro BALLARD)
        Joseph RIDDICK) Esquires Justices
        William BAKER)
        Simon STALLINGS)
        William GOODMAN)
        Henry GOODMAN)

(235) 123 Deed of Sale of Land Jethro SUMNER to William GOODMAN proved by the oath of Henry GOODMAN &c

In the action James BAKER against William FREEMAN Jury impannelled & Sworn (to wit) Miles BENTON, Philip ROGERS, William HUNTER Abel CROSS, William CARTER, Thomas PARKER

Moses BRIGGS Hardy EASON, Jonathan WILLIAMS Micajah RIDDICK Abraham GREEN & Abraham HURDLE say the Defendant did assume and assess the plaintiff damage to £51.10?..6 and 6 Costs

Ordered that Henry GOODMAN Esquire, John ODOM & Benjamin BARNES, Freehoulders allot and lay off such part of the Crop, Stock and provisions that were of the Estate of Shadrach ELLIS decd for the support of Rebeca ELLIS, Widow of the decedent

Ordered that Josiah BRIGG be appointed overseer of the Road instead of Isaac PEIRCE resigned &c

In the Action Timothy WALTON Asigne of Willis BROWN against David BENTON, Jury impannelled and sworn (to wit) Philip ROGERS William HUNTER Abel CROSS Josiah PARKER William CARTER Thomas PARKER Moses BRIGGS Hardy EASON Jonathan WILLIAMS Micajah RIDDICK, Abraham GREEN, & Abraham HURDLE say the defendant is not Guilty that he was detained by sickness

Power of Attorney Jeremiah JORDAN for himself & Sarah his Wife Hy HILL for himself and Eliza his Wife, Josiah LASSITER & Mary his Wife to John Armstead RUSSEL Acknowledged &c

Deed of Sale of Land Josiah PARKER to James BAKER proved by the oath of Patrick HEGERTY &c

Inventory of the Goods and Chattels rights and Credits which were of the Estate of Mary ELLIS decd was exhibited into Court by James GORDON Exor on oath &c

Inventory of the Goods and Chattels rights and Credits which were of the Estate of William ELLIS Admr decd was exhibited into Court by James GORDON Admr on oath &c

Account of Sales of the Estate of Mary ELLIS decd was exhibited into Court by James GORDON Executor &c

(236) 124 Jethro SUMNER Esqr. James SMALL John POWELL & Thomas PARKER Freehoulders who were appointed to allot and point out such part of the Crop Stock & provisions which were of the Estate of Luke SUMNER decd for the support of Judith SUMNER widow of the Decedent made report of their proceedings &c

Jethro SUMNER Esquire, Jesse BENTON, James PRUDEN & Miles BENTON, Freehoulders who were appointed to allot and point out such part of the Crop Stock & Provisions which were of the Estate of James PARKER decd for the support of Elizabeth PARKER widow of the decedent

Deed of sale of Land George LASSITER to Abner PEIRCE proved by the oath of Aaron LASSITER &c

Deed of Sale of Land George LASSITER to Abner PIERCE proved by the oath of Aaron LASSITER &c

Ordered that Benjamin GORDON be appointed Overseer of the Road instead of William HUNTER resigned

Aaccount of Sales of the Estate of Shadrach ELLIS decd was exhibited into Court by David HARRELL on oath &c

Ordered that the County TRUSTEE pay James SMALL Constable Forty Shillings for summoning the Inhabitants in Captain Jethro BENTONs Capy to return a list of their Taxables &c

James GORDON came into Court and mooved for Administration on the Estate of Sarah HUNTER decd who was Relict of Thos HUNTER decd which was accordingly granted Ordered the he give Bond & Security in the sum of One thousand two hundred & fifty pounds at same time James SMALL & James COSTEN came into Court and offered themselves as Securitys &c

Deed of Sale of Land John COWPER & William COWPER to William REA acknowledged by John COWPER and the Signature of William COWPER proved by the oath of James REA &c

Deed of Sale of Land John COWPER & William COWPER to Wm REA acknowledged by John COWPER and the Signature of Wm COWPER proved by the oath of Jas REA &c

(237) 125 Account of Sales of the Estate of James PARKER decd was exhibited into Court by Micajah RIDDICK Junr on oath &c

Additional Inventory of part of the Estate of James PARKER decd was exhibited into Court by Micajah RIDDICK Admr on oath &c

Ordered that William DUVAL of Virga only pay a single Tax on 3000 Acres of Land instead of a double tax which he is charged with &

        Then the Court adjourned until tomorrow morning 10 oClock

Wednesday morning the Court met
    Present the
    James GREGORY   )
    Jethro SUMNER   )
    David RICE   ) Esquires Justices
    William GOODMAN   )
    Simon STALLINGS   )
    Joseph RIDDICK   )

Ordered that Mills FIELD, Thomas RIDDICK, William W RIDDICK, James B SUMNER & Moses DAVIS, with the Surveyor of the County, make a Division of the real Estate of Wright HAYSE deceased agreeable to Law.

Ordered that the County Trustee pay Jethro MELTEAR the sum of one two pounds ten fourteen Shillings for summoning (three days) the Inhabitants in the Captain James WALTONs Captaincy to return lists of their Taxables

Ordered that David HARRELL Constable be allowed the sum of one pound ten Shillings for Three days summoning the Citizens in Captn David LEWIS Captaincy to give in Lists of their Taxables

(238) 126 James GATLING, Lewis SPARKMAN, & John ODOM, Freehoulders the Gentn who were appointed with Patrick HEGERTY survey to make a Division of the Estate of Demsey LANGSTON decd made report of their proceedings thereon &c

The Court taking into their consideration the Act of the General Assembly in respecting the Appointment of a Sheriff of this County after mature consideration Jethro SUMNER Esquire was appointed Sheriff of this County Ordered that he go?ive Bond and Security agreeable to Law, at the same time William HARRISS and Miles BENTON came into Court and offered themselves as Securitys who were approved off at the same time the said Jethro SUMNER qualified himself for that office &c when the Bonds were given William BAKER, Joseph RIDDICK Simon STALLINGS David RICE James GREGORY & Henry GOODMAN Esquires were on the Bench

Then the Court adjourned until tomorrow morning 10 oClock

        Thursday the Court met
   Present William BAKER)
                James GREGORY)
                Joseph RIDDICK)
                David RICE   ) Esquires Justices
                Simon STALLINGS)
                Henry GOODMAN)
                William GOODMAN)

Ordered that Henry SMITH Constable be allowed the sum of Four pounds for summoning the citizens in the Captaincy of Captain William HARRISS to return lists of their Taxables and for his attendance on this Court

Ordered that Humphry HUDGINS be appointed Guardian to Kinchin PHELPS orphan of James PHELPS decd, and that he give Bond and Security in the sum of two hundred pounds at same time Micajah RIDDICK & Levin DUER Came into Court and offered themselves as Securitys who were approved of

(239) 127 Ordered that the Sheriff of this County Summons Mills EURE William BROOKS, Blake EURE, John PARKER (Gatling) Abraham BEEMAN, William DOUGHTIE, Jonathan ROGERS, James TUGWELL Isaac PARKER junr, Mills LEWIS, James BRADY, Bray SAUNDERS John ODOM Michael LAWRENCE, Robert PARKER Abner ROUNTREE Thomas RIDDICK, David HARRELL senr, Kedar HINTON, Timothy WALTON Richard MITCHELL, George BROOKS, Thomas TROTMAN, Elisha HUNTER, Isaac HARRELL Junr. Richard BRIGGS, Lassiter RIDDICK Isaac COSTEN, John SMALL & Richard BOND personally to be & appear before the Justices of this Court at next term as Juriors &c

Deed of Sale of Land Henry GRIFFIN to Jno B WALTON proved by the oath of Guy HILL &c

It being suggested by Jno HAMILTON Esqr Atto at Law in behalf of Levin DUER that Jethro SUMNER Esquire has property in his hands which was conveyed to him by Joseph John SUMNER to evade the payment of a Debt due from sd Jos, Jno, to the said DUER. Ordered that a Sere Facies Issue to the said Jethro SUMNER to appear before this Court to shew if any conveyance hath been made to him as aforesaid

Ordered that the following Gentlemen secure? from the Citizens of this County the Inventory of their taxables and Taxable property (to wit) Simon STALLINGS Esquire in Captain ~~David LEWIS's~~ Jas WALTONs Captaincy James GREGORY Esquire in Captain Isaac HUNTERS - - - - - Do David RICE Esquire in Captain Jethro BENTONs Captaincy Jethro BALLARD Esquire in Captain ~~Capt~~--- Jesse BENTONs Capty William BAKER Esquire in Captain William HARRISS's Capty William GOODMAN Captain Mills LEWIS's Capty Henry GOODMAN in Captain David LEWIS's Captaincy

Agreeable to the Petition of Jonathan ROBERTS Guardian to the Orphans of William LEWIS deceased it is Ordered that the said Jonathan ROBERTS Guardian as aforesaid sell all the Real Estate of the Deceased lying and being in the County of Hertford and as much of the Real Estate of the Decedent whereon he formerly lived as will be sufficiant to pay and discharge all the Debts and demands that are due from the said Decd Estate

(240) 128 Ordered that one Shilling on each Poll be levied and four pence on each hundred Acres of Land be levied on the Citizens of this County for a County Tax for the year one thousand seven hundred & Ninety eight and that the same be collected by Samuel SMITH the late Sheriff of this County.

In the Action Ann PILAND against David LEWIS (to wit) Miles BENTON, Philip ROGERS William HUNTER Josiah PARKER, William CARTER Thomas PARKER Moses BRIGGS Hardy EASON, Jonathan WILLIAMS Micajah RIDDICK Abraham GREEN & James JONES Impannelled & Sworn say the Defendant does detain the Negro BOB named in the Pltfs Declaration at the price of £150. 0 0 that he detains within? 3? years & assess 6? damage & 6d Costs

Ordered that the County Trustee pay to William WALTERS the sum of Six pounds eight Shillings for his Services Summoning the Citizens in Captain Jesse BENTONs Capty to return lists of their Taxables and Taxable property and for his attendance on this Court

Ordered that the County Trustee pay Luten LEWIS Constable the sum of two pounds eight shillings for summoning the Citizens in Captain Mills LEWIS's Captaincy to return a list of their Taxables and Taxable property and for attending this Court.

Ordered that William James NAO?TALL be summoned to appear at this Court at next Term to shew in what manner he has kept the Estate of Jesse SPIVEY &c

                        Copy Test
                        Law BAKER

(241) 129 State of North Carolina   August 19th 1799
       Gates County) ss
At a Court of Pleas and Quarter Sessions begun and held for the County of Gates at the Court House on the third monday in August in the XXIVth year of the Independence of the said State Anno Domini MDCCXCIX.

            Present
            William GOODMAN)
            David RICE   ) Esquires Justices
            Simon STALLINGS)
            Henry GOODMAN   )

Luten BRADY & John BRADY orphans of John BRADY deceased came into Court and made choice of James BRADY to be their Guardian Ordered that he give Bond & Security in the sum of five hundred pounds each at same time Jonathan ROGERS & Thomas RIDDICK came into Court and offered themselves as Securitys &c

Deed of Sale of Land William FREEMAN & Uxor. to Daniel RIDDICK Acknowledged in open Court and on motion it was ordered that William GOODMAN Esquire take the private Examination of Sarah FREEMAN who made report of the Examination &c

Account of Sales of the Estate of William MATTHEWS deceased was exhibited into Court by Kedar BALLARD Exr. on oath.

Deed of Sale of Land Jesse BROWNE Samuel BROWNE Albridgton John BROWN Edward BROWNE James BROWNE & Anthoney BROWNE, proved as to Jesse BROWNE Samuel BROWNE Albridgton BROWNE & Anthony BROWNE by Benjamin BARNES and as to Edward BROWNE & James BROWNE by Robert WIGGINS &c

Jethro BALLARD Esquire who was appointed at this Court last Term to receive Lists of Taxables and Taxable Property from the Citizens of Captn Jesse BENTON's Captaincy made report of his proceedings &c

(242) 130 Ordered that Isaac HUNTER Samuel HARRELL, Benjamin GORDON, David DAVIS & Robert RIDDICK with the Surveyor of the County make a division of the Real Estate of Thomas FULLINGTON deceased agreeable to his Last Will & Testament &c

Ordered that Kedar BALLARD John DUKE junr Miles BENTON Thomas PARKER & Jethro BENTON with the surveyor of this County make a Division of the Real Estate which was of the Estate of Moses HARE decd agreeable to his Last Will &c

Agreement Jesse BROWNE Samuel BROWNE Albridgton BROWNE John BROWNE Edward BROWNE James BROWNE & Anthony BROWNE to Wm BAKER proved by the oath of Benjamin BARNES as to Jesse BROWNE Samuel BROWNE Albridgton BROWNE John BROWNE & Anthony BROWNE and by Robert WIGGINS as to Edward BROWNE & James BROWNE &c

Jethro BALLARD Kedar BALLARD & William ARNOLD three of the Gentlemen who were appointed audite & State the Accounts of Thomas PARKER Admr of the Estate of Eliza NORFLEET decd made report of their proceedings thereon &c

Inventory of the Estate of Elisha BENTON decd was exhibited into Court by Abraham BENTON Admr on oath &c

Deed of Gift Willis WIGGINS to his Sons Willis WIGGINS Kedar WIGGINS Thomas WIGGINS Pugh WIGGINS & Jacob WIGGINS proved by the oath of Ambroose WIGGINS &c

Deed of Sale Land Henry GOODMAN to Thomas & Richard BARNES Ackd &c

Deed of Sale of Land William FREEMAN & Uxr to Richard RAWLS proved by the oath of James FREEMAN &c

Deed of Sale of Land Willis BROWNE to Michael LAWRENCE Ackd

Bill of Sale for a Negro Girl named FANNY James SMALL to Theophulis HARRELL proved by the oath of John SMALL &c

Account of the Sales of the Estate of Demsey LANGSTON decd was exhibited into Court by Isaac LANGSTON Admr on oath &c

(243) 131 John ODOM Cyprian CROSS Benjamin BARNES & Isaac LANGSTON the Gentn who were appointed to Audite & State the accounts of John PARKER Admr of William WARREN decd exhibited their proceedings thereon &c

The Last Will of William ELLIS decd was exhibited into Court by David HARRELL one of the Executors therein appointed and was proved by the oath of James CARTER one of the subscribing witnesses thereto and on motion was ordered to be Recorded at the same time the said Exr. came into Court and Quallified himself for that office &c

Inventory of the Goods & Chattels rights and Credits which were of the Estate of William ELLIS decd was exhibited into Court by David HARRELL Exr on Oath &c

Deed of Sale of Land Levin DUER to David RIDDICK proved by the oath of Isaac HUNTER

Bill of Sale William HAYSE to Moses LASSITER proved by the oath of James HODGES &c

Aug. 1799

Last Will of Jonathan CULLINS decd was exhibited into Court by Thomas CULLINS Exr. therein appointed and was proved by the oath of Asa HARRELL one of the witnesses thereto and on motion was Ordered to be Recorded at the same time the Exr came into Court and quallified himself for that office &c

(Entire entry crossed out.) Ordered that Isaac COSTEN Mills LEWIS & Bray SAUNDERS be fined the sum of Twenty Shillings each for failing to attend this Court as Jurors at this Term &c

In the Action Josiah GRANBERY against (End of entry.)

Then the Court adjourned until tomorrow morning 10 oClock

(244) 132 Tuesday Morning 10 oClock the Court met
                Present   James GREGORY)
                          David RICE   ) Esquires Justices
                          Jethro BALLARD)

In the Action Josiah GRANBERY against Seth EASON Jury being impannelled & Sworn (to wit) David HARRELL, Michael LAWRENCE James BRADY, John PARKER (Gatling) Blake EURE, Kedar HINTON George BROOKS, Timothy WALTON, Jas B SUMNER David RIDDICK Jesse TAYLOR & Jesse SAVAGE say the Defendand did assume & assess for the Plaintiffs damage 40..6.6 --- --- --- & 6d Costs

James COLE who was summonsed to this Court as Guarnashee at the instance of James COTTEN & Henry Ebron SEARS, came into Court and made oath that there is a Small account unsettled between himself and William GATLING Junr. but does not know whither there will be a balance due to him as William GATLING that he had a Horse in his possession but that he had delivered him to GATLING the day before he was summoned as Guarnashee but that he was ou?t his House on the day, that he was summoned,

Bill of Sale for a Negro Man named KEDAR Abraham RIDDICK to John POWELL senr. proved by the oath of Jacob Sumner POWELL &c

Isaac PIPKIN Junr. William GOODMAN Henry GOODMAN Isaac PIPKIN Senr & William GATLING Senr. the Gentlemen who were appointed to Lay off to Anna SPEIGHT a Legacy given her by her deceased Husband Joseph SPEIGHT made report of their proceedings thereon &c

Henry GOODMAN John ODOM & Benjamin BARNES three of the Gentlemen who were appointed to allot and Lay off to Rebecca ELLIS Relict of Shadrach ELLIS decd made report of their proceedings &c

(245) 133 Inventory of the Goods and Chattels Rights & Credits which were of the Estate of Sarah HUNTER decd was exhibited into Court by James GORDON Admr. &c

Bill of Sale Sarah HUNTER to James GORDON for Goods & Chattles proved by the oath of Benjamin GORDON &c

Deed of Sale of Land Joseph RIDDICK Esquire to Solomon EASON Ackd

In the Action Amos RAYNOR against Katherine PILAND Jury impannelled and Sworn to wit Benjn GORDON, James COSTEN, John PARKER (Babtist) John HUNTER, James BARNES, John VANN Henry Ebron SEARS Mills LEWIS Isaac COSTEN Benjamin BARNES William WILLIAMS & Bray SAUNDERS, say the Defendant does not detain.

Aug. 1799

In the Action Levin DUER Assigne of Thos B LITTLEJOHN against James BAKER. Jury impannelled and sworn to wit, David HARRELL, Michael LAWRENCE James BRADY John PARKER (Gatling) Blake EURE Kedar HINTON George BROOKS Timothy WALTON James B SUMNER, David RIDDICK Jesse TAYLOR Jesse SAVAGE Plaintiff Nonsuit.

Joseph RIDDICK William KING & Simon STALLINGS three of the Gentn who were appointed to make a Division of the personal Estate of Amos TROTMAN decd made report of their poceedings &c

In the Action James JONES against James PARKER Jury impannelled and sworn (to wit) David HARRELL, Michael LAWRENCE James BRADY John PARKER (Gatling) Blake EURE, Kedar HINTON George BROOKS Timothy WALTON James B SUMNER David RIDDICK Jesse TAYLOR & Jesse SAVAGE say. (End of entry.)

Ordered that Jacob GORDON being exempt from the payment of a double Tax he having not given in his list for the year 1798 there appearing a mistake &c

Ordered that Thos MARSHALL be exempt from the payment of a double Tax for the year 1798 he being returned as not having given his Taxables &c

Account of Sales of part of the Estate of Seasbrook HINTON decd was exhibited into Court by Nancy HINTON Admtx on oath &c

(246) 134 Deed of Sale of Land Israel BEEMAN to Abraham BEEMAN Ackd

Power of Attorney Josiah COLLINS Junr to William SLADE proved by the oath of Alexander MILLEN &c

Deed of Sale of Land Benjamin BAKER to Henry Ebron SEARS proved by the oath of Joseph PARKER &c

James JONES who was Security for the personal appearance of Elisha CROSS on the suit Jas COTTEN & Henry Ebron SEARS against him delivered him up to the Court at same time Demsey ODOM & Patrick HEGERTY came into Court and entered themselves Special Bail

Deed of Sale of Land James FREEMAN & Uxr. to Charles POWELL Ackd by James FREEMAN in open Court &c

Agreeable to the Peto. of Rebecca WARD Ordered that the Sheriff Summon a Jury and Lay off to her, her Dower in Lands that her husband died seized and possessed with &c

        Then the Court adjourned until tomorrow morning 10 oClock

        Wednesday morning the Court met
            Present
              Joseph RIDDICK)
              Jethro BALLARD)
              William GOODMAN) Esquires Justices
              Henry GOODMAN)

Agreeable to a Writ of Dower for the purpose of setting apart the dower of Anna SPEIGHT relict of Henry SPEIGHT decd the Sheriff having made the following report (to wit) State of North Carolina Gates County Pursuant to a Writ of Dower hereunto annexed, We the subscribers Jurors after being duly quallified have proceeded to allot and set apart off to Anna SPEIGHT Widow of Henry SPEIGHT decd. her Dower of the Land & Plantation whereon the said Henry formerly lived in the following manner (to wit) Begining at the main Road where the land belonging to the Orphans of Francis SPEIGHT decd Joins thence along the Road to a path that Leads to John LANGs thence along said Path to a sliped Oak thence by a line of ---- sliped Trees to a marked Red oak then by a line of marked trees to Jesse SAUNDERS's line and along his line to the Orphans of Francis SPEIGHTs decd line and along

(247) 135 their line to the begining Including the Plantation Houses Orchards & Also we have alloted and set of to said Widow her Dower in one other tract of Land commonly called the Pocoson Begining at a sliped white oak in Thos BARNES's line then by a line of sliped Trees to DUNN's line and along his line to Thos. BARNES's line and then along his line to the begining, in witness our hands and seals this 6th day of August 1799 Philip LEWIS, Jesse B BENTON Miles GATLING, Hillory WILLEY, Jesse SAVAGE, Jesse VANN, David CROSS, John LEWIS, Halen WILLIAMS James BRADY Mills LEWIS Ebron SEARS (Seals) Jethro SUMNER Sheriff

Ordered that Lewis SPARKMAN be appointed Overseer of the Road instead of Miles GATLING resigned &c

Mortgage Bill of Sale Willis WOODLEY to Jethro SUMNER & Miles BENTON for three Negroes One Negro Man named TOBY one Negro Woman named LUCY & one Girl named KITTY proved by the oath of Jesse BENTON &c

Account of Sales of the Estate of Henry SPEIGHT decd were exhibited into Court by James GATLING Admr on oath &c

Ordered that Jethro SUMNER, Miles BENTON Kedar PARKER & Wm DOUGHTIE or any three of them Audite & State the accounts of Jesse BENTON Admr of Robert Foster BENTON decd

Ordered that Jack PRICE an Illegitimate Son of Rachel PRICE about two years old be bound as an Apprentice to George WILLIAMS to learn the Business of a Cooper

Ordered that the Sheriff of this County summons Thomas HOBBS Elisha TROTMAN, Isaiah RIDDICK, John HOFFLER, James COSTEN William HINTON (of Kedar) Richard BOND senr. Charles POWELL Seth ROUNTREE John ODOM Riddick CROSS John LEWIS David CROSS Asa HARRELL, Elisha HARRELL (son of Peter) William CRAFFORD Charles EURE, Philip ROGERS Jesse B BENTON Kedar PARKER, Hillory WILLEY Jeremiah SPEIGHT, Thomas SMITH William R RIDDICK Noah FELTON Abraham MORGAN John BRINKLEY, Elisha HARE & Amos PARKER personally to be and appear at this Court at next Term

(248) 136 Ordered that the Sheriff of this County summons Lewis WALTERS John RIDDICK Demsey ODOM & Abel CROSS personally to be and appear as Jurymen at the Supr Court to be held at Edenton for the District of Edenton in Octr. next &c

Simon STALLINGS Esquire who was appointed to receive Lists of the Taxables and Taxable property in the Capty of Capt. Jas WALTON to return lists of their Taxables and Taxable &c

William GOODMAN Esquire who was appointed to receive Lists of the Taxables and Taxable property in the County Captaincy of Captain Mills LEWIS &c

James GREGORY Esquire who was appointed to receive Lists of the Taxables and Taxable property in the Captaincy of Captn. Isaac HUNTER made report of his proceedings &c

Mills R FIELD Thomas RIDDICK Moses DAVIS William W RIDDICK & James B SUMNER Freeholders & Patrick HEGERTY Surveyor of this County who were appointed to make a Division of the Real Estate of Wright HAYSE decd made report of their proceedings &c

Samuel SMITH former Sheriff of this County who was security for the personal appearance of John POWELL delivered the said POWELL up to this Court, at same time the said John POWELL produced James ---- JONES as his security who acknowledged himself to be special Bail

Deed of Sale of Land John BAKER against to Lawrence BAKER proved by the oath of Seth WILLIAMS &c

Ordered that David HARRELL Exr. of William ELLIS decd sell the perishable part of the Estate of the Decedent so as a Division may be made agreeable to the Will of the decedent

   Then the Court adjourned until tomorrow morning 8 oClock

   Thursday morning the Court met
   Present
   Joseph RIDDICK)
   Jethro BALLARD) Esquires Justices
   Henry GOODMAN)

(249) 137 In the following actions Judgment was entered up by a Justice of the peace out of Court Execution issued and the Constable having returned the same no personal property to be found and levied on Land (to wit)
Patrick HEGERTY against Kedar WIGGINS .. 20/7 & 8/. Costs
John SAUNDERS? against..ditto ... 12/6.. 8/. do.
Levin DUER.... against ditto ... 43/4. 8/.do. Issued
Riddick CROSS against Ann PILAND 20/ 12/.do
John ODOM... against Jos John SUMNER £19..16.7 & 8/ Costs
ordered that Exn. be issd against the Lands & Tenements as above &c

Ordered that the suit William GATLING against Peter MARBLE (which has not been brought forward after the Guarnisment of William WALTERS and Elisha CROSS, and it being suggested that Elisha CROSS one of the Guarnishees had at the time of his Guarnisment a sum of Money in his hands of the said MARBLE) be brought forward as if it never had been brought off the docket

Ordered that a Commission issue to the County of Nansemond Virga. to take the Deposition of Elijah LEWIS in the suit William KATLING agains Peter MARBLE &c

The late Sheriff of this County exhibited into Court an account of Insolvants in this County for the year 1799 ordered that the same be allowed (to wit) The Tax on Edward KELLY Henry CHAMBERS Aaron DOUGLASS Robert LASSITER Ashbery MC KEE Abraham READ William TAYLOR Michael WARD John RUSSEL Jesse MARTIN Lewis SUMNER Wm GATLING except for 150 Acres Land & one black Poll Jesse HIAT of Jesse Helson WILLIAMS

Agreeable to the Petition of David HARRELL for leave to build a Water Grist Mill at the Place where Titus JONES formerly had a mill, it is Ordered that he have leave to build the said Mill &c

   Then the Court adjourned until tomorrow morning 8 oClock
   Friday morning the Court met

Present
Joseph RIDDICK)
James GREGORY) Esquires Justices
David RICE)

(250) 138 Ordered that Jesse SAVAGE who was charged for begeting a Bastard Child on the Body of Joanna HUDGINS, that he pay the said Joanna HUDGINS the sum of Five pounds for the first month and five pounds for each year that shall commence thereafter for Seven years

Additional Inventory which were of the Estate of William ELLIS decd was exhibited into Court by David HARRELL Exr on oath &c

Ordered that Miles ROUNTREE be appointed Guardian to Zacheriah SPIVEY orphan of Jesse SPIVEY and that he give Security in the sum of One thousand pounds at same time Joseph RIDDICK & Simon STALLINGS came into Court and offered themselves as Secys

By Courts order   Law BAKER CC

(251) 139 State of No.. Carolina   November 18 1799
          Gates County)
At a Court of Pleas and Quarter Sessions begun and held for the County of Gates at the Court House on the third Monday in November in the XXIVth year of the Independence of the said State Anno Domini MDCCXCIX.

Present
Wm BAKER   )
Wm GOODMAN) Esquires Justices
David RICE)

Grand Jury impannelled and sworn (to wit) John ODOM Foreman Elisha HARREL of Peter, Seth ROUNTREE, Thomas HOBBS, Hillory WILLEY, Charles POWELL Thomas SMITH John HOFFLER Abraham MORGAN Jesse B BENTON Philip ROGERS Kedar PARKER Asa HARRELL & Wm HINTON son of Kedar

Deed of Sale of Land William KING to Isaac PIPKIN Ackd

Deed of Sale of Land George LASSITER to Aaron LASSITER proved by the oath of Hance LASSITER &c

Deed of Sale of Land Matthias WILLEY to Hillory WILLEY proved by the oath of Henry GRIFFIN &c

Deed of Sale of Land Aaron MANER, Milley MANER Levi MANER, Levina MANER, & Aaron MANER to Charney CURL proved by the oath of William VANN &c

Deed of Sale of Land Richard ODOM Uxor to Isaac LANGSTON proved by the oath of Wm VANN &c

Deed of Sale of Land Micajah RIDDICK Senr & Micajah RIDDICK Junr to Anthony MATTHEWS Senr proved by the oath of James SMALL &c

(252) 140 Bill of Sale John ELLIS to Nathaniel NEWSOM for three Negroes named HANNAH, LIDDEY & AMEY, with a receipt thereon proved by the oath of Willis WOODLEY &c

Bill of Sale with a Receipt thereon John ELLIS to Nathaniel NEWSOM for Goods & Chattels proved by the oath of Willis WOODLEY

Deed of Sale for Land John ELLIS to Nathaniel NEWSOM proved by the oath of Willis WOODLEY &c with a Rect thereon

Deed of Sale of Land John ELLIS to Nathaniel NEWSOM proved, with a receipt thereon by Willis WOODLEY &c

Deed of Sale of Land Thomas TROTMAN to Henry WALTON proved by the oath of Noah HILL &c

The Last Will of Christian BROWN deceased was exhibited into Court by Willis BROWN Executor therein appointed and was proved by the oath of George WILLIAMS one of the subscribing witnesses thereto and on motion was ordered to be Recorded at the same time the said Exor qallified himself for that office &c

Inventory of the Goods & Chattels rights & Credits of Christian BROWN was exhibited into Court by Willis BROWN Exor on oath &c

Last Will and Testament of Nathaniel RIDDICK decd was exhibited into Court by Isaac HUNTER one of the Exors therein appointed and was proved by the oaths of Willis WOODLEY & David HARRELL Witnesses thereto and was ordered to be Recorded at same time the said Exor came into Court and quallified himself for that office &c

Then the Court adjourned until tomorrow morning 10 oClock

(253) 141 Tuesday morning the Court met
Present
William BAKER)
David RICE   ) Esquires Justices
Jethro BALLARD)

Ordered that Easther JONES be Allowed the sum of seventeen pounds ten shillings out of the Estate of Moses HARE decd. for the maintenance of Winson & Moses JONES natural children of the said Moses HARE decd on the body of said Easther JONES &c

Josep GARRETT & Nancy SPEIGHT called out on their Subponas fined Ni Si Issue Scere Facies

Deed of Sale of Land David BULLOCK & Uxr to Timothy WALTON Ackd and private examination of Elizabeth BULLOCK taken by Wm BAKER Esqr.

Deed of Sale of Land Micajah RIDDICK Jur. to Thomas SMITH proved by the oath of Richard SMITH &c

Deed of Sale of Land Amos LASSITER to Thos SMITH proved by the oath of Richard SMITH &c

Ordered that Isaac PIPKIN, Jur. Philip LEWIS Luten LEWIS & William GOODMAN Junr Audite & State the accounts of Richard ARNOLD Admr. of Henry H BENTON decd and that they make a division of the Estate of the decedent &c

Deed of Sale of Land John POLSON to Timothy WALTON Ackd

Deed of Sale for Land Caleb POLSON to John POLSON proved by the oath of Jethro BENTON &c

Nov. 1799

Deed of Sale of Land Amos PARKER to Jethro BENTON proved by the oath of Miles BENTON &c

(254) 142 Inventory of the Goods & Chattels rights & Credits which were of the Estate of Jonathan CULLINS decd was exhibited into Court by Thos CULLINS Admr &c

Deed of Sale of Land Moses LASSITER to Demsey JONES proved by the oath of Frederick LASSITER &c

John HOFFLER came into Court and mooved for Administration on the Estate of Sarah HURDLE decd. Ordered that he give Bond & Security in the sum of Two hundred pounds at the same time I?saiah RIDDICK & Noah FELTON came into Court and offered themselves as security &c

Last Will of John BETHEY was exhibited into Court by Bray SAUNDERS the Exor therein appointed and was proved by the oath of Wm GOODMAN & Henry GOODMAN two of the witnesses thereto which was ordered to be recorded at the same time the said Exor came into Court and qualified himself for that office &c

Inventory of the Goods and chattels Rights and Credits which were of the Estate of John BETHEY decd was exhibited into Court by Bray SAUNDERS Exor on oath &c

Ordered, that John ODOM Benjamin BARNES, Mills EURE & Lewis SPARKMAN or any three of them audite & State the accounts David HARRELL with the Estate of Shadrach ELLIS dec

Then the Court adjourned until tomorrow morning 10 oClock

Wednesday morning the Court met
    Present
        William BAKER   )
        William GOODMAN)
        David RICE   ) Esquires Justices
        Jethro BALLARD   )

(255) 143 Ordered that Kedar HINTON, Thos MARSHALL, David HARRELL, & Jethro MELTEAR or any three of them Audite & State the Accounts of Joseph PARKER Admr of James PARKER & Kedar PARKER with the Estate of the decedents, and that they also make a division of the Estates of the Decedents agreeable to Law.

Ordered that John HOFFLER Admr on the Estate of Sarah HURDLE decd sell so much of the Estate of the decedent as will pay her just debts &c

Ordered that John COWPER, Kedar BALLARD, Isaac HUNTER & James SMALL or any three of them ae make a Division of the Estate of Sarah HUNTER decd agreeable to Law. &c.

Ordered that John COWPER, Kedar BALLARD, Isaac HUNTER & James SMALL or any three of them audite & State the Accounts of James GORDON Admr of the Estate of Mary? ELLIS deed & William ELLIS junr decd with the Estate of the decedent.

In the Action David LEWIS against Jesse TAYLOR & Levi EURE Jury impannelled and sworn (to wit) Wm W RIDDICK Isaiah RIDDICK, John BRINKLEY, Jeremiah SPEIGHT Noah FELTON David CROSS, Richard BOND, James COSTEN Joseph PARKER George WILLIAMS Willis BROWN & Benjamin BAKER say the Defts did not assume

Ordered that John COWPER, Kedar BALLARD, Isaac HUNTER & James SMALL or any three of them audite & State the accounts of James GORDON, Exor on the Estate of Mary ELLIS deceased with the Estate of the decedent

David HARRELL Executor to the Last Will of William ELLIS decd exhibited into Court the Account of Sales of the Estate of the decedent on oath &c

In the action on a Peto. in Equity James BARNES Admr. De Bonis Non of John SUMNER decd against the Administrators of Luke SUMNER decd Judgment of the Court against the pleas of the Defendants from which Judgment the Defendants appealed to the Supr. Court of Law for the District of Edenton and gave for their Securitys Jethro SUMNER & William HARRISS &c

(256) 144 Henry GOODMAN Esquire who apeared after being summoned as Guarnishee to at the instance of Elisha CROSS againt William GATLING Junr. & Jesse SAUNDERS, he sayeth that he tended a Piece of ground in Corn to which the said GATLING was entitled to one fourth part, and that when the corn is grathered the Attachment will of __? affect it &c

Deed of Sale of Land James SUMNER to Thomas RIDDICK with a relinquishment on the back thereon from Jethro SUMNER proved by the oath of Mills R FIELD, &c.

In the Action William GATLING Junr. against Stephen SHEPHERD Jury impannelled and sworn to wit Robert RIDDICK, James BRADY William WILLIAMS, Miles GATLING, James FIGG Henry Eborn SEARS Jesse SAVAGE, James JONES, John PARKER Timothy WALTON Stephen EURE & Samuel SMITH say Plaintiff called Nonsuit

Bill of Sale for a Negro Woman named AMEY Joseph DILDAY to Isaac PIPKIN &c

In the Action James COTTEN & Henry Ebron SEARS against Wm GATLING Junr & Elisha CROSS Conditional Judgment against Jesse SAUNDERS Jury impannelled & Sworn assess the Plaintiffs damage £250 & 6d Costs

Ordered that James GREGORY & David RICE Esquires Samuel HARRELL and Isaac? HUNTER or any three of them make a division of the Real Personal Estate of Thos HUNTER decd &c

Barsheba JOHNSON came into Court and mooved for Administration on the Estate of Reuben MUNS decd Ordered that she give Bond & Security in the sum of One thousand pounds at the same time Timothy WALTON & William WALTERS came into Court and offered themselves as Securitys who were appproved of at the same time the said Administratrix came into Court and qualified herself for that office &c

Bill of Sale for a Negro Man VOLINTINE to Peggy CUNNINGHAM Ackd. &c

Deed of Sale of Land Jesse PARKER to Willis BROWN proved by the oath of Thomas MARSHALL &c

(257) 145 Ordered that Jonathan ROBERTS Admr on the Estate of Susanna FORREST sell the Negroes belonging to the Estate of the decedent to make a Division &c

Ordered that the Sheriff of this County summons Henry LEE, Thomas BARNES, James BRADY, Mills LEWIS, William CRAFFORD, Benjamin BARNES, Elijah HARRELL, David LEWIS Blake EURE, William BROOKS Jonathan PARKER, Michael LAWRENCE, Jonathan ROGERS Elisha CROSS, William DOUGHTIE, Jonathan WILLIAMS Aaron HOBBS Kedar HINTON James FREEMAN, Noah HARRELL Bond MINSHEW Miles WALTON Timothy FREEMAN, David DAVIS Thomas PARKER William ARNOLD David RIDDICK John HAYSE John ARNOLD Hardy EASON personally to be and appear as Jurymen at this Court next Term

    Then the Court adjourned until tomorrow morning 10 oClock

    Thursday morning the Court met
      Present David RICE   )
                  Jethro BALLARD) Esquires Justices
                  Henry GOODMAN   )
                  Simon STALLINGS)

Ordered that Robert PARKER Admr of James BROWN dec'd sell a Negro Man named BEN the property of the decedent agreeable to Law so that a Division be made between the Heirs &c

Ordered that Thos MARSHALL, Samuel SMITH, George WILLIAMS & Moses DAVIS or ~~three~~ any three of them audite and state the accounts of Robert PARKER Admr of Robert PARKER decd with the Estate of the Decedent & that they (End of entry.)

Ordered that John BEST Orphan Child who was bound as an Apprentice to John SHEPHERD be released from his said apprenticeship and that he be bound to Robert TEAR Merchant

(258) 146 Ordered that Robert RIDDICK son of Micajah be appointed Guardian to Jacob POWELL orphan of James POWELL decd and that he give Bond & Security in the sum of One thousand pounds at same time Noah FELTON & James COSTEN came into Court and offered themselves as Secys &c

Timothy WALTON who became Bail for Willis WOODLEY in an action brought by Seth EASON against him the Bail came into open Court and surrendered the Principal to the Sheriff of this County in discharge of himself.

In the Action James BAKER against Daniel SOUTHALL Jury impannelled & Sworn (to wit) William W RIDDICK, James COSTEN, Isaiah RIDDICK John LEWIS, Charles EURE Noah FELTON, David CROSS, Jonathan SMITH William WILLIAMS, Miles BENTON Jesse TAYLOR & Stephen EURE say the Defendant is not Guilty

Bill of Sale Timothy WALTON to Levin DEUR for a Negro Woman SAVORY acknowledged &c

Ordered that Jas H KEYS Esquire Attorney for the State in this County be allowed the sum of Twelve pounds for his services for the year passed &c

Ordered that Willis BROWN Exr. of the Estate of Christian BROWN sell the Esta__ (faded) of Christian BROWN decd agreeable to Law

            By Courts Order
            Test L BAKER CC

END OF VOLUME I

INDEX

As spelling variations are very common, it is highly recommended that any name be checked for all possible spellings.

ALLEN, Edward 220,223,231
  Edwd. 103
  Eliza 103,220
  Elizabeth 220,231
  Sarah 42,51,53
ALPHIN, Joseph 51,122,210
ARNOLD, John 12,16,44,51,
  52,54,71,82,83,85,86,92
  93,100,102,105,125,153,
  159,167,188,216,220,257
  Richard 253
  William 25,51,84,92,106,
    115,124,125,136,159,162,
    212,242,257
  Wm. 124
ASKEW, John 212
BABB, John 215
BAGLEY, Docton 5,195
  H. 100
  Henry 5,53,100,145
  Jacob 5,53,100
  Trotman 5,53,100,145
BAKER, B. B. 5
  Benjamin 4,246,255
  Blake 8,104,138,139
  Bray 4,57,108,187
  James 2,6,11,12,26,30,36,
    59,60,64,67,68,84,103,
    104,106,118,126,138,139,
    149,159,162,191,193,229,
    235,245,258
  Jas.? 58
  Jno. 30
  John 5,6,14,25,32,33,36,
    37,46,67,68,70,71,73,75,
    84,86,90,95,97,105,107,
    108,114,248
  L. 130,258
  Law. 37,61,72,74,107,127,
    137,146,150,161,171,180,
    189,202,211,219,230,240,
    250
  Lawe. 119
  Lawrence 9,13,36,58,78,

BAKER (Cont.)
  Lawrence (Cont.) 84,106,
    108,119,127,150,160,161,
    169,170,179,183,189,193,
    194,198,208,216,222,230,
    248
  Peggy 5,57,142
  Sam 148
  Saml 4,5,8,104,108,148,
    226
  Samuel 4,8,57,120,187,226
  Susanna 5,57,142
  William 5,8,12,14,19,24,
    28,30,31,35,38,42,46,48,
    65,70,73,84,91,95,104,
    107,108,110,116,122,133,
    134,137,158,159,160,161,
    163,164,177,179,181,185,
    195,198,200,201,203,205,
    208,210,214,217,222,226,
    227,229,234,238,239,253,
    254
  William H. 5
  Wm. 17,25,31,47,90,107,
    110,120,150,169,218,242,
    251,253
BALLARD, Jethro 10-12,21,
  25,47,78,81,82,85,89,108,
  111,115,116,124,125,127,
  132-135,137,147,166,179,
  187,198,199,201,205,212,
  214,215,224,225,234,239,
  241,242,244,246,248,253,
  254,257
  Kedar 10,29,31,47,55,66,
    78,80,90,93,96,107,113,
    114,121,127,132,135,137,
    179,185,187,194,195,199,
    201,207,208,212,221-224,
    229,234,241,242,255
  Thomas W. 196
  Thos. W. 215
BARCLIFT, William Barnes
  132,140

BARNES, ___ 21
  Benj. 226
  Benjamin 3,5,12,23-26,
    36,47,54,102,110,114
    115,130,136,145,188,
    191,196,204,212,235,
    241-245,254,257
  Benjn. 20,32,44,81,123,
    208
  Binj. 71
  Demsey 23,26,30,55,84,
    100,126,134,135
  James 10,59,67-69,71,
    93,102,105,132,136,
    138,140,159,168,174,
    176,184,220,245,255
  Richard 7,15,36,40,82,
    83,85,93,96,116,168,
    174,179,200,229,232,
    242
  Richd. 39,41,71,83,98,
    110
  Tho. 157
  Thomas 24-26,36,43,50,
    59,67,74,84,86,116,
    120,136,141,153,166,
    179,181,229,232,242,
    247,257
  Thos. 12,24,157,247
BARROW, John 139
BARROW?, John 138
BEASLEY, Benjamin 4,5
  James 5
BEASLY, Mary 87
BEEMAN, Abrah 114
  Abraham 108,109,115,
    121,123,136,177,239,
    246
  Benjamin 108
  Israel 19,29,39,99,104,
    109,115,149,200,209,
    246
BELL, Bethal 157
BENNETT, Joseph 32

BENNETT (Cont.)
  William 168
BENSON, William 141
BENTON, ___ 168
  Abraham 204,232,233,242
  Christian 232
  David 60,106,159,167,188,
    216,220,235
  Elisha 157,232,233,242
  Henry 227
  Henry H. 253
  Henry K. 227
  Isaac 60,61,102,170
  Jacob 60
  James 204
  Jeremiah 9
  Jesse 10,24,27,40,44,47,
    54,71,82,89,116,125,141,
    142,151,157,159,167,184,
    185,188,193-195,202,208,
    225,236,239-241,247
  Jesse B. 247,251
  Jesser? 200
  Jethro 71,84,92,106,113,
    114,126,134,143,156,201,
    204,216,220,236,239,242,
    253
  John 10,33,47
  Josiah 156
  Miles 10,25,45,61,64,78,
    80,90,92,93,102,106,113,
    114,134-136,143,154,156,
    157,170,179,193,198,201,
    204,207-209,215,223,225,
    227-229,232,233,235,236,
    238,240,242,247,253,258
  Mills 58,71,75,93,102,
    105,170,200
  Robert F. 142
  Robert Foster 141,157,
    247
  Robt. F. 89
  Robt. Foster 141
  Samuel 9
BERRIMAN, William 43,99,105,
  125,152,170
BERRYMAN, Edward 68
  William 7,36,50,71,75,163,
    173,179,194,223,229,232
BEST, John 190,257
  Lewis 190
BETHEY, ___ 35,81
  James 36,144,165,192
  John 19,22,24,25,39,54,
    67,71,144,165,192,254

BETHEY (Cont.)
  Trestram 20
  Tristram 22,39
  Tris?tram 19
BETHRY, John 20
BILLUPS, Thomas 77,152,155
BLAIR, William 133
BLANSHARD, Aaron 82,83,106,
  117,163,165
  Abner 11,93,185,204
  Absalom 168
  Absolam 140
  Absolom 9,52,135,186,224
  Ameriah 96,126,169
  Amerias 71,82,83,85,118,
    168,171
  Barnaby 214
  Demsey 82,83,102,106,117,
    163,165
  Frederick 9,52,109,131,
    140,168,186,224
  Friderick 108
  Keziah 6,122
  Mary 9,52,100,140,168,224
  Micajah 17
  Palatiah 82
  Paletiah 112
  William 52,100,108,135,
    140,186,224
  Wm. 9,100
BLUNT, Jno. 181
  John 181
BOND, Demsey 7,55,77,102,
  113
  Elisha Hance 7,113,147
    184
  Mary 18
  Richard 7,18,26,32-35,
    37,40,50,64,77,87,106,
    113,136,147,149,164,184,
    190,193,209,239,255
  Richard, Jr. 164,196
  Richard, Sr. 178,247
  Richd. 22,48,87
  Selah 7,55,102,113
  Thomas 77
  William 59,87,106,115,
    125,164,190
  Wm. 87,193
BOON, James 14,25
BOOTH, Eliza 223
  James 223
  William 6,104
  Wm. 146
BOUKILL, Thomas 11

BOYCE, Jonathan 7
  Miles 193,196,206
  Moses 9
  Partheny 7
  Sion 9
  W. H. 139
  William 86,193
  William H. 138
  Wm. 84
BRADY, Etheldred 219
  James 13,16,30,36,44,
    45,56,57,59,67,74,81,
    88,96,166,208,217,218,
    224,239,241,244,245,
    247,256,257
  James, Jr. 16
  John 241
  Jos. 215
  Joseph 74,120,159,164,
    191,195
  Luten 241
BRICKELL, Thomas 177,199
BRIDGER, John 140
BRIGG, Josiah 235
BRIGGS, Josiah 77
  Moses 26,30,42,77,140,
    170,208,217,229,233,
    235,240
  Rachel 42
  Richard 19,42,54,100,
    136,147,188,196,203,
    208,212,239
  Richd. 44,66,84,90,106
BRINKLEY, David 84,125
  Elisha 71,75,84,192,
    200,209,213,214
  Elizabeth 213,214
  Henry 203
  John 84,87,98,192,193,
    247,255
  Joseph 155
  Martha 213,214
  Simeon 99,106,125,170,
    173,212
  Simion 188,193,199,208
  Thomas 193
  William 192
BRISCO, Edward 164
BRISTOW, James 127,222
  Mary 222
  Warner 222
BROOKS, Geo. 125
  George 36,43,51,56,57,
    63,84,86,106,118,126,
    178,200,209,239,244,245

BROOKS (Cont.)
  Lodowick 64
  William 54,64,84,86,106,
    115,125,131,149,155,
    156,179,181,200,208,
    216,219,222,230,239,
    257
  Wm. 44
BROTHERS, Eliza 203
  John 29
  Tresey 89
BROWN, Albridgton John 241
  Anthony 242
  Christian 140,144,191,
    252,258
  Hardy 19,29
  James 72,84,86,140,144,
    153,182,191,221,233,
    257
  John 212
  Mary 156,165,168
  Samuel 36,170,214
  Willis 10,13,16,36,45,58,
    71,72,74,75,77,93,96,
    106,115,118,125,126,133,
    135,159,162,188,195,199,
    202,211,216,230,235,252,
    255,256,258
BROWNE, Albridgton 241,242
  Anthoney 241
  Edward 241,242
  James 241,242
  Jesse 241,242
  John 242
  Samuel 241,242
  Willis 111,242
BULLOCK, David 253
  Elizabeth 253
BURGES, Eliza 227
  John 120,173
BURGESS, John 176,205
  Nathaniel 169
  Thomas 169
BUTTERTON, Charles 4
  James 4
CAHOON, John 220
CAMPBELL, John 212
CANNON, James 48
  James A. 64
CARTER, Charles 41,98
  Isaac 21,34,141
  James 10,26,32-35,37,80,
    243
  John 10,52,80
  Moor 11,71,82,83,85,93,

CARTER (Cont.)
  Moor (Cont.) 96,97,116,
    120,128,170,173,183,188,
    229,232
  Moore 99
  William 4,80,145,174,179,
    187,216,229,235,240
  Wm. 99,181
CHAMBERS, Henry 249
CHERRY, James 138
CLEAVES, Mary 194
  Robert 32
  William 36,42,45,51,53,93,
    125,147,152,156,179,181,
    200,216,222
  Wm. 149,155,233
COHOON, John 231
COLE, James 244
COLLINS, Josiah 37,82-84,
    124,161
  Josiah, Jr. 124,246
COOHOON, John 231
COPELAND, David 66
  Henry 3,19,33,51,81,88,96,
    125,162,205
  Hester 169
  Jesse 66
  Sally 3
  Silas 52
  Stephen 162
  Zacherias 19
COSEN, James 109
COSTEN, Benjn. 56
  Demsey 2,56,57,65
  Eliza 43,56
  Isaac 2,12,18,25,26,32,40,
    41,56,76,84,86,99,100,
    103,106,115,118,121,123,
    127,133,134,136,147,156,
    160,163,165,168,170,184,
    188,194,239,243,245
  James 2,12,14,18,35,40,56,
    59,76,77,93,102,105,107,
    108,109,134,149,164,174,
    179,182,196,200,216,224,
    236,245,247,255,258
  Nathaniel 109
  Nathl. 56,109
  Polly 56
  Thomas 2,56
COTTEN, James 244,256
  Jas. 246
  Lemuel 155
COWPER, John 7,124,127,131,
    134,149,185,196,198,207,

COWPER (Cont.)
  John (Cont.) 225,236,
    255
  John, Jr. 124
  William 124,196,236
  Wm. 236
COWPLAND, James 169
CRAFFORD, Hetty 233
  William 32,34,36,45,
    56,57,63,68,69,81,121,
    149,155,156,216,220,
    223,247,257
  Wm. 156
CRAPIER, John 156
CRO__, Cyprian 96
CROSS, Abel 5,8,9,21,36,
    43,59,67,84,85,105,114,
    149,152,170,191,200,208,
    212,229,235,248
  Cypn. 79
  Cyprian 5,7,19,29,36,
    47,58,59,62,67,74,79,
    93,104,121,134,141,
    149,166,170,172,173,
    177,188,191,208,213,
    221,226,243
  David 4,19,26,32-35,
    37,51,71,74,116,130,
    136,147,188,191,199,
    200,216,220,229,247,
    255,258
  Elisha 26,32-34,40,96,
    110,125,135,149,152,
    168,174,178,188,194,
    199,205,216-218,220,
    246,249,256,257
  Hardy 76
  Riddick 247,249
CROWELL, Benjamin 114,
    131
CULLENS, Nathan 68
CULLINS, Jonatha_ 51,
    243,254
  Nathan 51
  Thomas 243
  Thos. 254
CUMMING, William 91,137
  Wm. 46,150
CUNNINGHAM, Jno. 43
  John 43
  Peggy 256
CURL, Abraham 142
  Charney 251
  Milicent 162
  Richard 162

CURLE, James 36
CUSTESS, Robt. 49
DANIEL, Elizabeth 112
  Sarah 72,208
  William 112
DARDEN, John 20,21,43,61
  64,102,184,185,194,198
  Mary 184,195,198
DAUGHTIE, William 59
DAUGHTY, William 12
DAVIS, ___ 23
  David 116,242,257
  James 63,173,174,197
  John 80,104
  Joseph 68,98,141
  Keziah 6,173,174,197
  Moses 12,16,44,54,65,98,
    106,136,140,147,159,162,
    188,192,196,199,206,207,
    237,248,257
DEANS, Matt. 138,139
  Matthias 138
DEUR, Levin 179,185,195,
  198-201,207,209,228,258
DEURE, Levin 66,88,89
DICKINS, Robert 89
DILDAY, Amos 17,153,166,183,
  190,191
  Joseph 256
  William 42
DONALDSON, Saml. 156
DORLON, John 67
DOUGHTIE, William 9,43,63,
  93,96,125,138,151,159,162,
  200,216,239,257
  Wm. 136,209,247
DOUGHTY, William 4,36,209
DOUGLASS, Aaron 249
DOWNING, William 138,139
DRAPER, William 22
DUER, Levin 120,123,125,127,
  135,137,143,144,147,159,
  162,187,238,239,243,246,
  249
DUKE, Daniel 35,76,106,148
  John 4,223
  John, Jr. 242
DUNFORD, Philip 200,209
DUNN, ___ 62,247
  George 25,62,79
  Susanna 79
  Thomas 25
DURE, Leven 68,116
  Levin 30,103,148
DUVAL, William 237

EASO_, Jacob 144
EASON, Alexander 197
  Betsey 20,122
  Frederick 163,233
  George 2,8,20,53,122
  George, Sr. 63
  Hardy 2,116,120,149,152,
    163,208,212,229,235,240,
    257
  Jacob 26,32,36,45,136,138,
    147,178
  Jesse 125,131,144,171,185,
    197,207
  Levi 59,67,84,86,213
  Seth 23,25,34,37,43,57,85,
    91,111,131,132,149,150,
    152,156,167,175,195,207,
    224,244,258
  Solomon 59,67,84,163,206,
    245
  William 163,179
EASTWOOD, Wm. 215
ELLEN, Thomas 147
ELLIS, Charity 191
  Daniel 63
  Edith 191
  Elizabeth 226
  Jno. 102,149
  John 20,35,87,107,108,
    111,149,191,194,252
  Josey 31
  Mary 89,214,225,228,235,
    255
  Mary? 255
  Mary (Warren) 31
  Rebeca 235
  Rebecca 244
ELLIS?, Rebecca 233
ELLIS, Reuben 213
  Ruth 126
  Shadrach 224,233,235,
    236,244,254
  Shadrah 220
  William 23,40,57,60,89,
    90,106,107,111,135,149,
    194,201,213,214,226,228,
    229,235,243,248,250,255
  William, Jr. 255
  Wm. 108
EURE, Benjamin 52,171
  Benjn. 52
  Blake 200,239,244,245,257
  Charles 1,10,12,19,20,23,
    24,26,29,30,44,45,54,71,
    75,116,133,136,138,148,

EURE (Cont.)
  Charles (Cont.) 159,
    162,200,216,220,222,
    225,229,233,247,258
  Charney 124
  Danil 147
  Enos 23,64,113,196
  James 210
  John, Sr. 108
  Levi 36,43,59,67,99,
    108,220,225,229,232,
    255
  Mills 37,52,188,190,
    199,208,212,220,223,
    239,254
  Nancy 23,64,113,196
  Ruth 52
  Saml. 115
  Samuel 23,26,30,64,
    106,113,196
  Sarah 124
  Stephen 13,19,24-26,
    36,43,45,97,106,115,
    122,188,190,200,216,
    229,256,258
  Uriah 30,210
  Whitmel 208
EVINS, Francis 138,139
FELTON, Elisha 155
  Job 30,51,153
  John 210
  Noah 40,51,71,75,82,
    92,139,159,162,188,
    199,220,233,247,254,
    255,258
  Sarah 51,153
FIELD, Mills 141,234,237
  Mills R. 222,231,248,
    256
FIGG, James 49,55,59,62,
  67-69,71,78,136,138,
  144,183,256
  Joseph 49,55,62,83,
    188
  Willis 62,78,83,188
FISHER, Wm. 231
FITT, Thomas 196
FLINN, Owin 160
FORREST, Ann 89
  Anna 107,210
  Henry 22,26,29,30,48,
    49,72,89,92,95,97,
    107,112,178,209,214
  Sally 92,95,97
  Susana 209

FORREST (Cont.)
  Susanna 89,107,214,257
  Thomas 89
FORRIST, Henry 110
FOSTER, Joel 36,43,87,114
  Peter 63
  Richard 197
FRANKLIN, Daniel 29,153
FREEMAN, Amos 131
  Ann 221
  Anna 175,212
  David 175,212,221
  Demsey 14
  Jacob 223
  James 7,12,17,24-26,44,
    50,54,93,96,97,99,129,
    152,159,163,164,167,
    170,178,181,194,198,
    221,242,246,257
  John 175,212,221
  Joseph 134,145,175
  Richard 7,14,50,99,141,
    152,194,216
  Sarah 241
  Solomon 175
  Thomas 164
  Thos. 225
  Timothy 35,124,129,131,
    149,152,188,190,193,
    194,196,222,225,257
  William 9,16,118,140,
    155,164,189,235,241,242
  William, Jr. 145,198,211
  Wm. 154,181
FROST, William 194
FRYER, Isaac 233
  Richard 217
  William 121,216,229
FRYOR, William 169
FULKS, D. 95
FULLINGTON, Thomas 242
GALE, Christopher 193
GARRETT, Jas. 10
  Josep 253
  Joseph 187
  Nancy 10
GARROTT, James 58
  Nancy 58
GATLING, Edward 47,110,115
  Edwd. 11
  George 183
  J___ 216
  James 6,11,15,21,24-26,
    45,50,59,60,69,72,81,84,
    91,107,109,110,114,115,

GATLING (Cont.)
  James (Cont.) 121,123,165,
    166,169,188,197,212,213,
    224,238,247
  John 11,47,110,115
  John Parker 1,93,96,155,156
  Miles 149,152,169,173,177,
    194,204,208,210,216,217,
    219,229,247,256
  William 48,52,64,145,175,
    183,200,221,244,249
  William, Jr. 82,83,153,
    170,180,183,184,188,215,
    217,244,256
  William, Sr. 64,134,153,
    173,184,212,217,221,228,244
  Wm. 83,249
  Wm., Jr. 183,199,256
  Wm., Sr. 172
GAYLE, Christopher 144
GIBSON, ___ 156
GLOVER, Mary 95
  William 22,68,81,109
GLOVER?, William 68
GOODMA , HY 215
  William 77
GOODMAN, Cyprian 96,193
  Henry 5,14,15,22,24-28,31,
    32,38,39,43,44,47,62,70,
    81,91,110,119,127,128,
    134,138,143,145,148,151,
    160-163,165,168,172,174,
    175,178,183,188,190,192,
    198-201,203,205,208,210,
    212,213,215,217,220,221,
    224,226,227,228,231,234,
    235,238,239,241,242,244,
    246,248,254,256,257
  Hy. 102
  James 7,39,50,75,76,88,
    193
  Joel 39,50,75,77,88
  John 88
  Timothy 39,50,76,88
  William 2,3,5,11,14,16,
    22,24,25,30-32,34,38,39,
    43,44,47,48,52,62,67,70-
    73,75-77,81,86-88,90,91,
    94,98,101,110,111,115,
    116,119,120,129,133,134,
    140,145,151,154,155,158,
    159,161-163,165,168-170,
    172,174,176,192,194,197,
    199,200,203,205,208,209
    212,214,216,217,224,227,

GOODMAN (Cont.)
  William (Cont.) 228,
    234,235,237-239,241,
    244,246,248,254
  William, Jr. 193,216,
    253
  Wm. 3,9,15,58,110,
    119,147,188,191,198,
    205,251,254
  Wm., Jr. 179
GORDAN, Jacob 20
GORDON, Benjamin 12,36,
    43,84,125,129,132,134,
    179,236,242,245
  Benjn. 2,15,42,59,86,
    245
  Elizabeth 119
  Jacob 2,12,20,25,131,
    140,159,162,167,195,
    245
  James 119,125,131,134,
    179,185,195,196,200,
    209,213,225-229,232,
    235,236,245,255
  John 2,35,42,43
  William 18,22,25,45,
    118,119,121
GRAGORY, James 24,25
GRAHAM, Ebenezer 193
  Ebinezer 69,72
GRANBERY, ___ 156
  James 133,174,218
  John 218
  Jos. 20
  Josiah 30,33,37,55,
    65,91,124,126,127,
    179,198,204,243,
    244
  Josiah, Jr. 218
  Thos. 212
GREEN, Abraham 44,54,
    170,173,179,229,235,
    240
  Easther 153
  Elee? 99
  Isaac 210
  Saml. 226
  Samuel 159,162,175,
    226
GREGORY, James 1,17,28,
    32,34,41,46,54,57,58,
    64,65,67,70,78,81,84,
    85,87,90,102,105,111,
    116,119,122,124,128,
    143,145,147,155,158,

139

GREGORY (Cont.)
  James (Cont.) 159,161
    167,176,178,179,181,
    198,204,205,207,216,
    217,218,231,232,234,
    237-239,244,248,249,
    256
GRIFFIN, Henry 92,96,
  232,239,251
GRIFFITH, Burwell 134,
  135,191
  H. 96
GWINN, Daniel 132
HAIR, John 118,125
HALL, William 64,130,
  144
  Wm. 136
HAMILTON, Jno. 91,239
  John 91
HARE, Elisha 5,20,52,
  71,75,93,102,105,142,
  194,208,212,213,247
  Henry 156
  Honour 31
  John 103,113,126,147
  Joseph 21,120
  Moses 21,31,58,93,155,
    242,253
  Moses, Jr. 18
  Peggy 195
HARRALL, Noah 102
HARRELL, Aaron 153,192
  Abraham 62,63,167
  Ann 80
  Asa 19,29,93,96,125,
    170,173,192,208,217,
    229,232,243,247,251
  Benjn. 51
  David 12,24-26,35,37,
    42,44,49,54,63,96,
    100,106,111,116,120,
    126,147,149,151,167,
    181,183,195,215,224,
    226,230,233,236,237,
    243-245,248-250,252,
    254,255
  David, Jr. 119,220,224
  David, Sr. 136,178,216,
    220,239
  Demsey 62,112,151
  Elijah 67,93,138,257
  Elish 59
  Elisha 63,84,247,251
  Isaac 44,88,100,126,
    149

HARRELL (Cont.)
  Isaac, Jr. 55,63,75,143,
    186,192,230,239
  Isaac, Sr. 75
  Isau?c, Jr. 140
  Jesse 229,232
  John 192
  Josiah 39,44,51,54,71,
    75,116,120,233
  Judith 233
  Lemuel 97,104,114,123,
    136
  Mary 97
  Noah 35,59,93,103,105,
    109,116,117,152,188,190,
    196,216,227,257
  Peter 226,247,251
  Saml. 88
  Samuel 20,49,66,90,120,
    122,123,126,141-143,163,
    165,179,181,192,198,203,
    215,221,242,256
  Stephen 112,122,153,195
  Theophulis 242
  Thos. 122
HARRESS, William 43,51
HARRIS, Norfleet 157
  William 118,224
HARRISS, ___ 116
  William 19,26,33-35,44,46,
    54,57,69,71,78,80,83,100,
    103,106,122,125,154,158,
    159,176,178,179,193,195,
    200,207,238,239,255
  Wm. 24,43,177,187,190,218
HART, Morgan 197
HASLETT, Jethro 50
HAYS, Hance 136
  Herman 157
  Jacob 55
  William 55,154,155,157
HAYSE, Hance 58
  Henry 157
  Herman 113
  Hosey 157
  Howell 58,136
  Jacob 98,141,157,200
  James 63,101
  John 101,149,152,257
  Mary 157
  William 55,57,63,98,114,
    136,141,176,185,208,222,
    243
  Wm. 56,63
  Wright 55,58,63,105,113,

HAYSE (Cont.)
  Wright (Cont.) 136,
    157,176,185,186,229,
    237,248
HEGARTY, Patrick 9,199
HEGERTY, Pa. 3,79,89
  Patrick 20,29,36,56-
    60,79,82,105,126,
    136,160,175,177,179,
    199,207,216,229,232,
    235,238,246,248,249
HEGIRTY, Patrick 165
HIAT, Jesse 249
HIATT, Jesse 15
  Thomas 67,190,194
  Thos. 191
  Timothy 15
HILL, Abraham 144,154
  Ann 144,154,213
  Christian 175,183,226
  Clement 191
  David 103
  Eliza 50,235
  Guy 13,14,50,59,60,
    64,104,109,147,148,
    163,183,190,199,239
  Henry 20,47,113,117,
    122,130,151,152,222
  Himbrick 47
  Hy. 235
  John 14,60,147,190,
    199
  Kedah 13
  Kedar 5,6,49,53,59,
    84,98,100,104,129,
    142,148,154,163,175,
    183,199,233
  Mary 175
  Miles 5,53,100,145
  Moses 1,6,8,18,32,46,
    52,58,84,105,106,
    113,117,118,122,
    136,144,145,150,
    154,156,158,162,
    173,175,182,183,
    186,226
  Noah 252
  Polly 183,226
  Robert 6,49,98,129,
    142,233
  Robt. 49
  Thamar 154
  Thamor 145
  Thomas 233
  Thos. 109

HILL (Cont.)
  Whitmell 49,98
  Whitmill 6,129,142,233
HILS?, Henry 97
HINES, Moses 69,152
HINTON, Kedar 12,22,24-26,
  44,54,102,112,116,125,
  135,149,152,163,170,173,
  208,215,231,232,239,244,
  245,247,251,255,257
  Leasbrook 232
  Nancy 232,245
  Noah 179
  Seasbrook 232,233,245
  William 6,49,61,98,102,
    132,147,149,179,204,
    215,247
  William, Jr. 188
  Wm. 10,125,251
HOBBS, Aaron 12,16,36,45,
  96,106,113,117,118,121
  136,138,147,172,178,182,
  208,212,229,232,257
  Abigal 177
  Aron 181
  Guy 1,7,53
  Henry 105,118,126
  Jacob 26,32,59,67,117,
    118,121,147,172,176,
    177,179,182,183,188,
    198,199
  Jesse 1,7,53
  John 8,179,188,213
  Moses 1,7,53
  Reubin 139
  Samuel 8,53,179,188
    213
  Solomon 213
  Thomas 71,126,136,138,
    170,247,251
  Thos. 75
  William 7,53
  Wm. 1
HODGES, James 12,63,82,
  89,112,114,116,118,120,
  126,152,153,163,164,177,
  181,183,197,209,222,243
HOFFLAR, John 162
HOFFLER, John 62,71,82,83,
  85,118,136,138,144,151,
  152,175,177,178,181,186,
  188,189,191,199,220,221,
  247,251,254,255
  Thomas 71,75,106,115,
    147,183,229

HOLLAND, Joseph 13
HOWARD, Hardy 17,143
HUDGINS, Humphry 2,14,26,29,
  38,41,46,51,55,57,63,67,72,
  100,118,127,136,143,148,
  152,153,167,168,170,174,
  193,195,196,198,207,220-222,
  232,233,238
  Humphy. 158
  Humpy. 81,158
  Hy. 121
  Joanna 250
  John 100,220
HUDGIS, Humphry 187
HUGHES, ___ 96
HUGHS, Sarah 85,169
HUNTER, ___ 13,122,164
  Elisha 131,187,196,229,
    239
  Isaac 24,26,30,34,35,57,64,
    65,71,76,77,82,85,104,116
    118,120-123,129,132,142
    143,159,163,167,174,176,
    177,179,183,185,200,204,
    215,233,239,242,243,248,
    252,255
  Isaac? 256
  John 51,149,154-156,173,
    245
  Riddick 25,120
  Sarah 185,196,198,236,245,
    255
  Theopholis 51
  Tho. 47
  Thomas 1,11-13,17,24-26,
    41,46,48,51,54,57,58,62,
    65,70-72,82,93,99,116,121,
    122,127,129,131,133,143,
    145,147,155,158,159,183,
    186,187,196,198,229
  Thos. 27,37,58,65,91,127,
    139,187,194,196,198,236,
    256
  William 1,3,26,30,59,67-69,
    71,111,125,149,156,170,
    173,188,208,217,229,235,
    236,240
  Willm. 170
  Wm. 155,199
HURDLE, Abraham 8,12,23,26,
  44,45,47,50,56-58,65,71,82,83
  85,98,116,120,146,149,152,
  154,155,163,170,172,182,183,
  188,198,216,223,233,235

HURDLE (Cont.)
  Eliza 45,46,50,58,65
  Elizabeth 45,47
  Judith? 232
  Mills 154,155
  Sarah 254,255
  Thomas 13,45,72,84,
    106,147,232
  Thos. 154,155
  William 36,45,203,
    208,217
INDIANS
  ROBBINS, John 109
JAMES, William 100
JAMESON, Saml. H. 32,
  37,69,82,83
  Samuel H. 32,84,161
  Samuel Heath 11
JENKINS, Winborn 19,
  162,183
JOHNSON, Barsheba 256
  Charles 24
  Jacob 80
JONES, Benton 211
  Charles 112
  Davd. 179
  David 28,84,106,111,
    115,136,170,181,
    194,225
  Dem. 125
  Demsey 7,12,20,26
    32-35,37,40,44,52,
    55,114,118,125,126,
    152,153,206,254
  Demsey, Jr. 141,222
  Demsey, Sr. 222,231,
    234
  Demsey O. 152
  Demsey (Odom) 35,56,
    57,59,84,102,149,234
  Easther 253
  Evin 32
  Hardy 114,152
  Hezekiah 182
  Jacob Parker 111,186
  James 28,35,36,59,
    67,84,106,111,115,
    136,143,149,152,153,
    166,168,170,174,179,
    181,186,222,225,240,
    245,246,248,256
  Jesse 152,170
  John 42,225
  Joseph 131
  Lewis 106,192

JONES (Cont.)
 Milley 112
 Moses 253
 Priscilla 44
 Sarah 222
 Thomas 225
 Titus 249
 Willie 44
 Winson 253
JORDAN, Jeremiah 130,235
 Sarah 235
KATLING, William 249
KEEN, Lemuel 43,51
KELLY, David 2,56
 Edward 80,211,249
KEY, ___ 40
KEYS, ___ 56
 James H. 137,171
 James Henry 211
 Jas. H. 258
KILLY, David 142
KING, Charles 86
 Charlotte 11,16
 Eliza 15
 Henry 9,15,21,28
 Hugh 223
 Norman 174
 Purnell 223
 Sarah 28
 Solomon 42,91,102,148,
  188
 William 11,16,21,26,28,
  32-35,37,44,54,116,136,
  147,163,179,200,229,
  233,245,251
 Wm. 8,21,192
KITRELL, Eliza 6
KITTRELL, Charity 6,114,
  194
 Eliza 114,194
 Elizabeth 8,114,194
 George 8,114,194
 John 19,78,90
 Moses 8,194
 William 8,114
KNIGHT, Demsey 19,114,175,
  195
 James 12,19,43,44,54,
  71,79,82,83,85,106,113,
  114,116,131,170,173-175,
  204
 John 43
 William 153
LAMB, John 211
LANDIN, James 4

LANDING, Elisha 51,63
 John 142
 Mills 4,37,166,193
LANG, Elizabeth 99
 James 99
 John 24,26,32-34,37,44,
  45,54,64,99,133,199,
  246
 Joshua 199
LANGSTO, Isaac 170
LANGSTON, Demsey 1,21,47,
  71,75,87,93,96,116,170,
  227,228,238,242
LANG?STON, Demsey 224
LANGSTON, Isaac 3,13,16,
  21,36,47,52,58,59,62,67,
  79,84,87,114,123,125,136,
  138,173,216,226-228,242,
  243,251
 John 212
 Luke 29,30
LASSETER, Sarah 77
LASSITER, Aaron 32,78,131,
  210,236,251
 Abner 152,153
 Absilla 149
 Amos 44,54,93,96,179,
  181,215,253
 Frederick 153,254
 George 10,76,112,121,152,
  153,163,165,236,251
 Hance 251
 Henry 134,182,224
 James 52,87,134,182,224
 Jean 78
 Jethro 6,21,221,225,226
 Jonathan 1,114,153,173,
  222
 Josiah 131,235
 Margaret 182,224
 Mary 235
 Michel 6,21
 Moses 76,112,121,163,165,
  177,196,214,243,254
 Peggy 134
 Reuben 116,120,164,200
 Robert 249
 Sarah 40,65,69,76,78,104,
  143,167
 Timothy 12,40,41,60,65,
  69,127,133,134,182,224
 William 10
 Winnefred 152
LASSITOR, Sarah 41
LAWRENCE, Charles 12

LAWRENCE (Cont.)
 John 57
 Michael 136,138,179,
  203,208,217,219,
  239,242,244,245,257
 Michl. 216
LEDSAM, Thomas 20
LEE, Henry 2,36,43,59,
  67-69,71,99,109,116,
  133,169,170,173,187,
  208,217,229,232,257
 Levi 84,86,225
 Willey 225
LENORE, Thomas 83
LEWIS, David 26,32-35,
  37,44,45,56,57,67-69,
  71,74,106,108,114-116,
  123,136,149,152,159,
  165,200,216,232,237,
  239,240,255,257
 Elijah 194,249
 Elizabeth 135
LEWIS?, Henry 120
LEWIS, John 21,36,44,
  54,75,84,93,102,121,
  135,166,200,216,220,
  247,258
 Leah 113,135,138
  139,146,148
 Luten 13,35,84,118,
  120,156,157,160,
  163,175,184,202,
  215,240,253
 Mary 135
 Mills 13,21,26,32-35,
  46,74,93,96,149,155,
  156,173,176,200,205,
  208,212,218,221,224,
  239,240,243,245,247,
  248,257
 Philip 12,14,16,21,22,
  36,39,43,74,79,89,
  134,145,149,155,156,
  165,179,188,192,212,
  221,247,253
 Sarah 135
 William 10,12,20,24-
  26,30,47,68,81,95,
  103,109,113,117,126,
  135,138,146,148,160,
  227,239
 Wm. 109,148
LIGGETS, Edward 24
LITTLEJOHN, Thos. B
  245

MC KEE, Ashberry 249
MANER, Aaron 251
  Levi 251
  Levina 251
  Milley 251
MARBLE, Peter 194,217,
  218,249
MARCH, John 213
  William 213
MARSHALL, Thomas 14,29,
  45,48,60,68,93,103,
  109,133,147,148,150,
  155,161,171,175,178,
  185,199,201,208,209,
  220,233,255,256
  Thos. 103,204,209,221,
    227,245,257
MARTIN, E. 217
  Jesse 249
MASON, Stephen 80
MASSEY, James 10
MATTHEWS, Andrew 21,51
  Anthony 40,92,167,234
  Anthony, Sr. 251
  Clement R. 40
  Easther 76
  James 76
  William 8,241
  Wm. 92
MATTHIAS, William 12,24-
  26,71,82,83,99,106,125,
  157,188,212,223
  Wm. 85,98,208
MELTEAR, Jethro 119,159,
  180,182,200,203,237,
  255
MERONEY, Henry 68,100,140,
  203
MICHELL, Richard 189
MILLEN, Alexander 124,246
MILLER, Fanny 220
  Isaac 20,136,150,153,
    170
  Isaac, Sr. 81,91,127,
    143,175,234
  John 4,28,181
  Reuben 4,28
  Robert 4
  William 28
MILTEAR, Jethro 18,23,
  118,215
MILTIAR, Jethro 68
MINOR, Nicholas 87
MINSHEW, Augustin 76
  Bond 44,54,89,121,125,

MINSHEW (Cont.)
  Bond (Cont.) 136,149,152,
    154,155,171,200,208,209,
    257
MIRONEY, Patty 214
MITCHELL, Menney 80
  Richard 21,71,83,85,106,
    136,138,160,178,181,
    184,239
  Richd. 82,83
MOOR, James 138
MOORE, James 139
MORAN, John 111
MORGAN, Abraham 12,16,36,38,
  39,78,80,92,122,154,247,251
  Charity 232
  John 45,64
  Ruth 38,39,78,92
  Seth 92,100
MORRIS, Charity 103
  Christian 98
  Ephraim 98,110
  Uriah 232
  William 232
MORRISS, Christian 97,110,
  114
  Ephraim 97,114
MULATTOES
  JONES, James 112
  ROBBINS, John 109
MUNS, Reuben 256
MURFREE, Hardy 62,79,124
NAO?TALL, William James 240
NAPPER, Robert 42
NEGROES
  Abb 86
  Abraham 164
  Abram 151,181
  Agatha 216
  Aggy 169,228
  Amey 252,256
  Amy 114
  Baccus 134
  Ben 257
  Benjamin 144
  Bob 240
  Bobb 164,232
  Boson 133
  Burril 168
  Cambridge 73
  Carry 193
  Cary 183
  Cate 131,165,166
  Ceasre? 169
  Cherry 76,164

NEGROES (Cont.)
  Clarissa 78
  Cloak 152
  Cloe 151
  Daniel 140
  Davey 87
  Demsey 19
  Dinah 164-166
  Easter 183
  Fanny 242
  Frank 89
  George 204
  Gilbert 234
  Hannah 165,166,252
  Harry 69,151,193
  Hetty 144
  Isaac 89,114,151
  Jack 76,99,131,164,
    168
  Jacob 33,107,114
  James 77
  Jeremiah 183
  Jim 64
  John 192
  Jucob 107
  Kedar 203,244
  Kitty 247
  Lewsy 216
  Liddey 175,252
  Lidia 21
  Lucy 168,247
  Mary 163
  Mike 73,74
  Miles 51
  Milley 122
  Mingo 171
  Moll 88
  Nancy 63
  Ned 183
  Nelson 168
  Pater 125
  Patt 19,167,191,228
  Paul 177
  Penny 216
  Peter 7
  Phebe 114
  Phil 135
  Phill 131
  Phillis 151,168
  Pleasant 88
  Randell 78
  Reuben 171
  Robin 63
  Rose 20,214
  Rozella 12

NEGROES (Cont.)
  Sam 229
  Saml. 214
  Sarah 12,165,166
  Savory 258
  Sear? 168
  Seney 152
  Silas 222
  Siller 214
  Steel 123
  Sue 62
  Suiah? 193
  Suky 183
  Toby 247
  Tom 20,78,178
  Toney 111,131
  Venus 12
  Violet 99
  Volintine 256
  Winney 12,99
NEWBY, Frederick 78
NEWSOM, Nathaniel 252
NICHOLS, Jonathan 103,147
  Mary 103
NORFLEET, Abraham 7
  Charlotte 151
  Cordel 169
  Elisha 20,33,62,64,68,
    213,214
  Eliza 242
  Elizabeth 134,212
  Jacob 5,22,52,56
  James 7,12,20,64,89,115,
    125,127,134,185
  Kinchen 22,56,115,131,
    213,214
  Mary 134
  Mourning 5,52,142
  Philissia 134
  Polly 151
  Sarah 114,134,186,196
NORRIS, Thos. 4
NUTTALL, William James 140
ODOM, Benjamin 19
  Demsey 13,16,19,20,56
    57,98,105,125,165,174,
    178,183,215,246,248
  Elisha 146,161
  Jacob 146
  Jemima 158
  Jemmima 166
  Jesse 146,160,161,165,
    170
  Jimmima 166
  Jno. 64

ODOM (Cont.)
  John 3,13,16,21,23,32,35
    37,38,40,41,44,51,62,69,
    71,79,80,104,106,114,123,
    125,126,143,157,166,170-
    172,177,188,197,216,220,
    224,226,235,238,239,243,
    244,247,249,251,254
  Mills 135
  Polly 165
  Richard 251
  Uriah 64,101,114,166,171,
    215
  William 40,41,69,158,165,
    166
  Wm. 157,188,197
OMALLEY, Matthew 32
OSTIN, Claiborn 32
OUTLAW, David 133,234
  George 19,99,100,103,118,
    123,187,216,231
  George, Jr. 52,160,184
  Jacob 147
  James 9,44,52,99,100,103,
    105,123,130,133,160,184
  Jas. 234
OWNLY, Edward 174
  Levi 174
PARKER, Abigal 178
  Amos 12,24-26,84,113,114,
    136,204,247,253
  D. 96
  Daniel 96,130
  Danl. 3
  Demsey 96
  Easther 152
  Elisha 3,4,120
  Elizabeth 225,236
  Esther 3,4,120
  Fereby 79
  Francis 79
  Humphry 112
  I. 96
  Isaac 96,116,206
  Isaac, Jr. 239
  James 2,104,135,153,178,
    180,185,203,221,225,226,
    236,237,245,255
  Jas. 225
  Jesse 36,256
  Jesse Benton 170
  Jno. 47
  Jno. (Gatling) 37
  John 21,51,52,56-58,76,
    103,104,107,141,142,152,

PARKER (Cont.)
  John (Cont.) 163,164,
    166,172,177,214,243,
    256
  John (Babtist) 245
  John (Gatling) 149,
    216,220,226,239,244,
    245
  Jonathan 73,166,232,
    257
  Jos. 104,185
  Joseph 112,116,120,
    149,155,156,164,178,
    180,185,203,246,255
  Josiah 2,96,118,147,
    222,229,235,240
  Kedar 5,104,178,180,
    185,203,247,251,255
  Mary 31
  Miles 35,54,167
  Nancy 104
  Peter 59,67-69,71,130
  Polly 31
  Priscilla 17
  Prissey 104
  Robert 29,74,84,93,
    96,105,125,127,133
    136,153,170,171,174,
    178,179,186,196,208,
    219,221,222,229,233,
    239,257
  Robert, Jr. 71,144
  Robert, Sr. 55,171,
    174
  Robt. 169,171,182,216
  Robt., Jr. 36,140
  Thomas 12,16,22,25,
    38,44,54,56,60,86,
    93,106,135,184,185,
    187,194,195,208,214,
    228,229,235,236,240,
    242,257
  Thos. 181,194,212
  William 112,135,204
  William, Jr. 114
  William, Sr. 113,114
  Wm. 114
PARNEL, Peggy 147
PAYNE, Michael 133
PEARCE, William 59
PEIRCE, Abner 236
  Isaac 235
  Jacob 59
PERRY, William 112
PHELPS, Demsey 29,182

PHELPS (Cont.)
  Demsey (Cont.) 186,204
  James 29,51,58,220,233,
    238
  James, Jr. 2
  James, Sr. 2,67
  Jesse 58
  Kinchin 238
  Micajah 4,106,115
  Renthy 40
  Sarah 182,186,204
PHILLIPS, Solomon 19
  Thomas 87
PIERCE, Abner 236
  Isaac 71
  Jacob 67-69,71
  William 1
PIKEN, Isaac, Sr. 183
PILAND, Ann 232,240,249
  Edward 11,64,94,131,132
  Edwd. 93,94
  George 111,114,131,132
  James 5,29,30,45,131,
    148,179,181,186,231
  John 84,86,106,112,138,
    210,231
  Katherine 245
  Peter 94
  Reuben 94
  Stephen 133
  Thomas 5,29,30,45,133,
    148
  Thos. 186
  Willis 112,133,148,153,
    223,231
PIPKIN, I., Jr. 88
  Isaa_, Jr. 76
  Isaac 63,75,77,122,136,
    165,171,174,188,197,
    205,251,256
  Isaac, Jr. 35,79,81,88,
    94,119,161,165,166,172,
    174,183,188,192,193,198,
    212,213,221,228,244,253
  Isaac, Sr. 161,165,172,
    193,212,213,221,228,244
PITMAN, Samuel 114
PLATT, Joseph 171
POLSON, Caleb 253
  John 231,253
  William 231
POWELL, Charles 2,14,78,
  99,159,162,175,208,212,
  246,247,251
  Daniel 12,65,118,126,147,
    222

POWELL (Cont.)
  Elizabeth 204
  Isaac 86,139
  Jacob 12,143,258
  Jacob Sumner 244
  James 12,65,66,90,106,
    187,199,258
  John 12,16,32,44,54,67-69,
    84,87,116,120,127,143,186,
    200,203,221,228,236,248
  John, Jr. 186,207
  John, Sr. 159,167,244
  Kedar 221
  Lemuel 33,203
  Robert 65,66,159,162,187,
    193,200,209,216,220
  Robt. 66,90,199
  William 86,193
  Zelpha 106
PRICE, Benjamin 202
  Jack 247
  Rachel 247
  Robert 202
PRUDEN, Jacob 76
  James 12,24-26,29,76,116,
    159,162,170,175,225,233,
    236
  Lodowick 29
PURNELL, John 11
R_DICK, Micajah, Jr. 16
RANEY, William 197
  Wm. 197
RANSOM, James 2,11,16,192,
  215
RANSONS, Thos. 63
RAWLS, David 174,212
  James 6,104,223
  Pennina 212
  Richard 135,192,219,242
RAYNOR, Amos 245
REA, James 236
  Jas. 236
  William 196,204,223,236
  Wm. 196,223,236
READ, Abraham 249
REED, Katey 223
REID, Benjamin 211
  Benjn. 80
  Catey 231
  Hardy 80
  Katey 103
  Micajah 153
RICE, David 11,12,16,21,22,
  24-26,31,33,34,38,40-43,57,
  65,67,71,75,78,81,82,85,87,

RICE (Cont.)
  David (Cont.) 90,94,
    102,105,108,111,116,
    119,120,124,127-129,
    131,133,140,143,147,
    155,158,159,162,166,
    167,170,179,181,182,
    185,186,190,198,204,
    210,212-214,216,220,
    224,237-239,241,244,
    249,251,253,254,256,
    257
  Davd. 58,67
  Peggy 164
  William 196
RICHARDS, John 63
RICHARDSON, Archibald
  220,231
RIDDICK, Abraham 42,51,
  86,89,101,164,173,191,
  193,203,222,244
  Christo. 57,58,70,71,
    100,130,136,144,155,
    159
  Christoph. 144
  Christopher 11,14,24,
    25,28,31,33,34,38,
    55,57,62,70,72,73,
    86,105,119,120,127,
    129,131,136,138,147,
    151,153,162,172,176,
    178,186,194,198,201,
    204
  Cristo. 116
  Daniel 106,241
  David 20,35,42,131,
    140,143,144,156,165,
    167,195,203,229,243,
    244,245,257
  Edward 97
  Eliza 123,142
  Elizabeth 142
  Isaiah 123,154,155,
    247,255,258
  I?saiah 254
  James 5,17,97,136,
    153,177
  Jo. 11,15,27,47,85,
    110,119,128
  Job 12,118,121,127,
    133,163,177
  John 19,36,61,71,82,
    83,85,102,106,115,
    132,168,170,174,175,
    188,190,220,229,233,
    248

RIDDICK (Cont.)
  John H. 121,142
  John Hunter 233
  Jos. 6,8,14,51,65,147,
    159,162,221
  Joseph 2,11,17,18,20,22,
    24-26,33,34,36,43,46-48,
    54,58,59,64,67,70,72,85,
    103,104,108,109,117,
    119,122,123,126,138,141,
    143,145-147,150,158,160,
    163,164,166,170,172,181-
    187,189,191,195,196,198-
    201,204-206,210,220,227,
    229,233,234,237,238,245,
    246,248-250
  Kedar 127,136,153
  Lassiter 190,220,239
  Leah 123,181
  Micajah 12,54,69,92,93,
    96,115,139,168,187,208,
    223,225,229,231,232,
    234,235,237,238,240,
    258
  Micajah, Jr. 44,71,80,
    82,83,85,116,122,179,
    208,220,221,226,229,
    233,237,251,253
  Micajah, Sr. 116,251
  Mills 42,144,195
  Nathaniel 71,195,203,252
  Nathl. 20,36,42,75,77,
    106,115,125,143,145,165
  Raseter 54
  Reuben 44,45,122,123,164
  Reube?n 143
  Reubin 71,72
  Robert 35,77,93,98,100,
    102,105,125,135,147,
    159,164,170,176,203,
    208,220,229,231,232,
    242,256,258
  Robert, Jr. 208,217
  Robt. 66
  Seth 121,123,142
  Soseph 189
  Thomas 89,183,200,229,
    232,237,239,241,248,
    256
  William 116,131
  William R. 247
  William Right 46
  William W. 34,199,208,
    212,216,222,232,237,
    248,258

RIDDICK (Cont.)
  William W. Wright 105
  William Wright 194,203,
    209,219
  Willis 5,17
  Wm. W. 131,173,186,188,
    204,229,255
  Wm. Wright 170
RITTER, Ann 98
  Tho. 157
  Thomas 101,156,157
  Thos. 157
ROBBINS, Charles 10
  Elisha 80
  James 10,71
  Jethro 192
  John 10,80,109,215
  Mary 192
  Nanny 10
  Samuel 80
  Sarah 10
  Thaney 10
ROBERTS, ___ 85,96
  Benjamin 223
  Jonathan 23,24,34,35,42,
    48,49,68,71,83,89,95,
    102-104,109,110,112,
    117,119,135,148,150,
    152,160,163,178,180,
    182,195,203,209,210,
    214,215,220,227,232,
    239,257
ROBINS, Hardy 80
ROCHELL, John 19
ROGERS, Enos 78
  Hillir?y 59
  Jesse Hiatt 15
  John 6,59,60,107
  Jonathan 26,30,40,78,93,
    96,101,106,108,110,112,
    136,138,166,168,173,174,
    192,200,209,216,239,241,
    257
  Lott 98
  Philip 2,36,43,71,75,136,
    170,208,217,229,235,240,
    247,251
  Priscilla 7
  Robert 110,112,174
  Sarah 77
  Stephen 6,7,59,60,67,77,
    84,86,99,103,105,107,
    153
  William 6,60,107
  Zelpha 112,168

ROGERS (Cont.)
  Zilpha 101,108,110,
    174
ROOKS, Cyprian 152
  Demsey 110
  Edith 46
  Jesse 46
  Joseph 134
  Thomas 152
ROSS, Solomon 49
ROUNTRE, Seth 187
ROUNTREE, Abner 36,239
  Charles 9,17,20,121,
    145,188
  Jno. 145
  John 9,11,16,72,99,
    145,188,189
  Josiah 17
  Mary 8,9,16-18,20,
    64,121,189
  Miles 17,59,67,84,
    86,93,99,102,118,
    126,136,137,163,
    168,188,210,250
  Penay 9
  Peney 55
  Peny 103
  Sarah 36
  Seth 9,35,36,51,52,
    55,96,99,100,103,
    105,123,129,149,
    152,160,184,189,
    247,251
  Solomon 36
  Thom__ 55
  Thomas 9,103
RUSSEL, John 130,146,
  249
  John Armstead 235
  Mary 149
  Sarah 130,146
RUTTER, Thos. 156
SAMESON, Peggy 43
SAUNDERS, Bray 12,72,
  89,170,192,213,239,
  243,245,254
  Bryant 35
  Francis 28,31,40,101,
    114,123,130,132,136,
    143,167,171,172,177,
    215,221
  Jesse 2,21,56,57,89,
    165,195,200,209,212,
    246,256
  John 192

SAUNDERS?, John 249
SAUNDERS, Joseph 222
  Law. 165
  Lawrence 167
  William 64,130,132,145,
    215,221
  Wm. 215
SAVAGE, Abel 141
  Andrew 63
  Caleb 130
  Jesse 130,244,245,247,
    250,256
  William 63
SCOTT, Christian 7,54,
  139,194
  Joseph 7,54
  Sarah 7,54
  William 139,194
SCULL, Elisha 138,139
SEARS, Ebron 49,96,159,
  164,166,247
  Etheldred 219
  H. Ebron 183
  Henry E. 76,167
  Henry Eborn 256
  Henry Ebron 76,170,191,
    209,244-246,256
  Mary 76
SEVILS, William 207
SHEPHERD, John 177,190,
  222,257
  Stephen 256
  William 222
SHERIFFS
  BAKER, John 32
  CHERRY, James 138
  GATLING, James (Dep.) 11,
    15,21,25,45,69,72
  GOODMAN, Henry 70,127,
    128
  PIPKIN, Isaac 171,197
    Isaac, Jr. 119
    Isaac, Jr., (Dep.) 94
  SMITH, Henry (Dep.) 166,
    205
    Samuel 158,164,167,
      176,183,195,198,202,
      206,211,225,240,248
  STALLINGS, Simon 26,80
    118,184
  SUMNER, Jethro 238,247
SIMONS, Ann 172,173,191
  John 51,52,58,86,141,
    154,155,172,173,191
SIM?ONS, John 113

SIMONS, Joshua 138,139
SLADE, W. 224
  William 246
  Wm. 218
SLAVIN, Jethro 152
  Mary 149
  Rachel 149
SMALL, Christian 156
  David 57,156
  James 35,36,40,44,57,107,
    116,120,121,132,135,147,
    148,164,165,185,187,195,
    201,206,228,229,236,242,
    251,255
  John 12,24-26,28,36,43,
    57,60,120,125,136,147,
    159,164,167,188,195,201,
    208,212,239,242
  William 32
SMITH, Ann 227
  Charles 51,87,114,152
  Charles Matthew 87
  Henry 34,36,101,112,150,
    166,171,176,187,201,
    205,216,231,238
  Jonathan 101,159,162,
    208,216,217,258
  Joseph 213,214
  Richard 231,253
  Richd. R. 51
  Saml. 137,158,160,176,
    222,228
  Samuel 101,130,158,164,
    167,176,180,183,185,195,
    198,202,206,211,216,225,
    240,248,256,257
  Thomas 13,24-26,36,43,59,
    67-69,71,91,93,96,125,
    139,149,155,156,158,
    179-181,185,200,209,
    216,231,247,251,253
  Thomas, Jr. 101,167,176
  Thos. 138,156,176,253
  Thos., Jr. 34
SOUTHALL, Danie 177
  Daniel 180,206,258
SPARKMAN, Lewis 23,37,68,
  97,109,115,118,119,134,
  149,152,208,216,217,224,
  226,229,238,247,254
  Willis 68,153
SPARLING, ___ 57
SPEIGHT, ___ 116
  Ann 168,213,221
  Anna 228,244,246

SPEIGHT (Cont.)
  Anna? 228
  Barsheba 168
  Basheba 183
  Bathesha 172
  Bathsha 172
  Bathsheba 172
  Francis 1,9,11,14,22,
    28,35,39,45,47,56,
    57,63,67-69,71,74-76,
    79,81,88,89,93,102,
    105,110,115,149,155,
    156,159,163,165,169,
    172,183,191,202,246
  Frans. 37
  Henry 11,13,16,21,36,
    56,57,79,81,89,125,
    141,159,166,167,175,
    181,188,195,212,213,
    221,246,247
  Jeremiah 24,26,32,33,
    35,37,44,51,54,78,
    93,102,107,109,125,
    149,152,168,174,187,
    196,231,247,255
  Jos. 212
  Joseph 134,145,165,
    221,228,244
  Moses 42,116,120,136,
    138,188
  Nancy 253
  Susanna 163,165
  William 78,107,168,
    170,174,175,190,194,
    223
  William, Sr. 193
SPEIGHT'S, Henry 43
SPIVEY, Abraham 26,30,
  213
  Elijah 1
  Jacob 52,118,126,154,
    155,159,162,163,167,
    177,183,186,199,214
  Jesse 14,169,171,240,
    250
  Mary 9,52
  Moses 72
  Mosess 14
  Priscilla 36
  Sally 4,53,100,146
  Senith 2
  Seth 2,56,142
  Thomas 4,53,146
  Thos. 100
  William 56

SPIVEY (Cont.)
  Zacheriah 250
STALLINGS, Simon 6,8,17,
  18,20,22,25,26,32,39,
  71,72,78,80,85,87,94,
  102,116-119,127,129,130,
  133,140,147,150-152,158,
  159,171,172,175,178,182-
  186,189,190,191,198-200,
  204,213,227,231-234,237-
  239,241,245,248,250,257
STEED, Green 78
STOTT, ___ 231
SUMN__, Jas. B. 1
SUMNER, ___ 165
  Abraha__ 183
  Abraham 8,47,56,98,146
  Barsheba 167
  Barshiba 91
  Bathsheba 96
  Busheba 73
  David Edwin 90
  Demsey 13,19,42
  Edwin 6,57,73,90,91
    96,100
  J. B. 141
  Jacob 8,47,56,98,146,
    183,223
  James 78,85,105,156,
    256
  James B. 24,34,51,59,
    62,64,67-69,71-73,78,
    84,106,113,116,120,
    121,123,126,144,147,
    160,165,171,186,229,
    234,237,245,248
  Jas. B. 156,244
  Jethro 1,6,9,10,16,18,
    19,21,24,25,33-35,42,
    47,57,61,64,71,78,80-
    82,85,90,95,102,106,
    111,113,114,116,122,
    125,129,134,137,141,
    143,151,154,159,162,
    165,167-169,174,177,
    181,183,184,190,193,
    195,200,207,212,215,
    223-225,227,228,231,
    234-239,247,255,256
  John 176,255
  Jos. John 249
  Joseph 222
  Joseph Jno. 65
  Joseph John 22,36,37,
    167,200,205,207,214,

SUMNER (Cont.)
  Joseph John (Cont.) 222,
    223,234,239
  Judith 89,228,236
  Lewis 80,222,249
  Luke 12,16,19,21,29,65,
    69,85,87,89,90,99,124,
    137,153,157,158,192,193,
    195,203,207,208,215,221,
    228,236,255
  Martha 72
  Milicent Hunter 158
  Mourning 132
  Seth 156
  Seth Elisha 207
  William 62,72
TAYLOR, Hillory 184
  Jesse 52,63,108,121,226,
    244,245,255,258
  John 1,93
  Jonas 1,93
  Joseph 1,4,52,53,100,130,
    142,146,159,167,168,186,
    195
  Lemuel 141,142
  Lidia 52
  Nathaniel 44,141,195,231
  Nathl. 168
  Robert 184
  Samuel 108
  William 4,204,211,249
  Winnefred 4
TEABOUT, Nicholas 120
TEAR, Robert 257
THOMAS, Jacob 187
  James 86
THOMAS?, James 84
THOMPSON, ___ 202
  Lewis 132,179,204
TRAVIS, Thomas 195
TROTMAN, Amos 1,6,7,155,
  233,245
  Demsey 1,3,7,54,84,88,
    89,100,105,113,122,
    145,164
  Elisha 247
  Ezakial 100
  Ezekial 88,89,105,194
  Ezekieel 139
  Ezekiel 113,122,125,136,
    139,145,155,164,193,214
  Joseph 11,70,104,146,182,
    234
  Love 11,70,104,146,182,
    234

TROTMAN (Cont.)
  Noah 88,139,222
  Rachel 8,18,32,39
  Riddick 35,144,150,
    156,173,175,181,182,
    199,216,220,226
  Seth 175,222
  Thomas 6,11,60,159,
    182,189,210,239,252
  Thoms. 104
  Thos. 2,104,234
  Willis 11,70,104,146,
    182,234
TUGWELL, James 152,216,
  239
  Jas. 62
TURLEY, Henry 127
TURLINGTON, Miles 107
TURNER, Pasco 26,169
TWINE, Pleasant 85
  Thomas 88
UMFLEET, Asa 103
  David 39,44,47,50,58,
    69,109,115
  William 39,44,103,115
VALENTINE, William 122,
  203
VALINTINE, William 160
VALLENTINE, William 113
VAN, Jesse 79
VANN, ___ 96
  Dorcas 3,29,32,38,44
  Jesse 23,32,35,38,44,
    45,55,62,79,172,177,
    191,196,204,218,221,
    247
  John 23,35,36,57,74,
    100,114,120,134,142,
    205,208,212,223,245
  John, Sr. 227
  Rachel 218
  Thomas 42
  William 30,49,191,
    218,224,251
  Wm. 218,251
VARNELL, John 100
VOLENTINE, Sealah 220
  Selah 203
  William 46,48,100,106,
    126,133,145,154,159,
    177,178,185,220,221
  Wm. 151,155,167
VOLINTIN, William 201
VOLINTINE, Selah 191,
  201,206

VOLINTINE (Cont.)
　William　5,8,18,32,33,
　　35,37,39,52,53,58,65,
　　84,93,191,206
　Wm.　8,86,199
VOLLENTINE, William　26
VOLLINTINE, William　117,
　119
WALERIDGE, Abraham　138,
　139
WALLIS, William　51,55
WALTARS, Lewis　153
WALTERS, Bryan　217
　Bryant　184,209
　Edith　192
　Isaac　19,215
　Isaac, Jr.　183,221
　Isaac, Sr.　221
　Jacob　41
　Lewis　1,80,92,200,248
　Mary　41,192,209,217
　William　4,27,56,57,72,
　　83,100,108,118,120,
　　160,184,185,187,194,
　　195,202,217,240,249,
　　256
　Wm.　9
WALTON, ___　116
　Amelia　142
　Eliza　2
　Emelia　49
　Emilia　221
　Halladay　121
　Henry　136,138,252
　Holladay　20,55
　Holloday　58,63
　James　8,18,19,32,36,39,
　　59,67,72,84,93,99,102,
　　127,149,151,152,159,
　　160,162,175,177,178,
　　181,184,186,189,199,
　　200,216,237
　James B.　162
　Jas.　62,239,248
　Jno. B.　40,86,102,147,
　　186,188,239
　John　49,142,186,221
　John B.　1,13,20,26,30,
　　40,44,48,54,59,72,77,
　　84,89,96,99,104,112
　　148,155,158,163,170-
　　173,178,180,182,183,
　　186,194,196,198,199,
　　203,208-210,216,220,
　　221,227

WALTON (Cont.)
　John Benbury　18
　John Bunbery　175
　Melison　49
　Miles　142,149,155,156,179
　　181,188,200,222,229,232,
　　257
　Milicen　221
　Millisen　142
　Thomas　49,142,186,221,
　　222
　Thos.　142,222
　Timothy　13,17,22,26,30,35,
　　36,84,89,93,96,102,105,
　　108,116,120,133,134,151,
　　152,170,171,173,179,180,
　　203,216,220,227,234,235,
　　239,244,245,253,256,258
　William　49,142,221,222
WARD, Jesse　131,225,226
　Michael　249
　Rebecca　246
WARREN, Bray　32
　Edward　31
　Eliza　31
　Etheldred　31
　John　14,71,76
　Joseph　19,31
　Olive　31
　Patience　31,41
　William　19,21,31,50,76,
　　141,142,163,214,226,243
　William, Jr.　35,76
　Wm., Jr.　1
WATSON, ___　231
　David　40,87,114
　William　19,71
WEATHERLEY, Jno.　5
　John　5,17,23,25,38
　John, Jr.　2
　Joseph　38
WHITE, Thomas　34
WHITEHEAD, John　124
　Mariam　124
WHITLOCK, Charles　207
WIGGINS, Ambroose　174,222,
　242
　Bridget　182
　Bridgit　186
　Jacob　242
　Kedar　242,249
　Pugh　242
　Robert　195,241,242
　Thomas　242
　Willis　80,89,126,242

WILKINSON, John R.　143
　John Randelph　143
　John Randolph　137
　Martha　143
　Mary Reanalds　143
　Patsey　143
　Patty　89
WILLEY, Hillory　15,26,
　30,40,75,76,88,92,93,
　96,99,125,159,188,199,
　218,224,247,251
　Matthias　251
　Sally　96
WILLIAMS, Absolom　5
　Anthony　133,196
　Christian　152
　Demsey　8,36,45,59,66,
　　67,71,90,104,148,
　　149,152,170,200,226,
　　229,232
　Dorothy　152
　Frederick　66
　Geo.　233
　George　6,14,29,36,42,
　　55,83,128,133,148,
　　150,171,188,222,247,
　　252,255,257
　Halan　44,54
　Halen　174,183,247
　Halon　92
　Helson　249
　James　231
　Jethro　34
　Jonathan　1,8,26,30,
　　44,54,66,78,92,104,
　　183,200,218,224,229,
　　235,240,257
　Mills　66
　Moses　91,101,112
　Reuben　164
　Saml.　66
　Seth　248
　William　83,93,152,
　　183,185,204,245,
　　256,258
WILLS, Britain　15
WILSON, Seasbrook　107,
　111,206
WINBORN, Hamilton　190,
　191
　Henry　15
　Philip　15
　Sarah　125
WOODLEY, Willis　164,
　170,181,184,193,203,

WOODLEY (Cont.)
  Willis (Cont.) 207,247,
    252,258
WYNNS, Thomas 196
YOUNG, Thomas 157